T0372496

The Economics of Catalan Separatism

Ferran Brunet

The Economics of Catalan Separatism

palgrave
macmillan

Ferran Brunet
Faculty of Economics
Autonomous University of Barcelona
Bellaterra, Spain

ISBN 978-3-031-14450-9   ISBN 978-3-031-14451-6   (eBook)
https://doi.org/10.1007/978-3-031-14451-6

This Palgrave Macmillan imprint is published by the registered company Springer Nature
Switzerland AG.
The registered company address is: Gewerbestrasse 11, 6330 Cham, Switzerland

FOREWORD

Catalonia is one of the 17 autonomous regions of the Kingdom of Spain. It is located in the northeast of Spain, below the Pyrenees and it borders with France. It has an extension of 32,108 square kilometres, somewhat larger than Belgium, and a population of seven and a half million. Approximately half of the voters are in favour of secession, while the other half are not.

While the separatists and secessionists claim that "Catalonia is not Spain", it is necessary to remember, looking back into history, that the territories of present-day Catalonia formed part of Roman Hispania, with one of its capitals in Tarragona, and later, without there being any problem, it formed part of the Visigothic Kingdom centred around Toledo.

It was only with the rupture of the unity of the peninsula brought about by the *Reconquista* that the Kingdom of Aragon and the county of Barcelona came into being, and these went their own way, in parallel with the other peninsular kingdoms of Castilla, Portugal, Navarre and the kingdom of Granada.

The question of separatist pretensions for Catalonia's independence from the rest of Spain is not new, and it always surfaces in moments of weakness in Spain. This is what happened when, Spain being at war with France, the clergyman Pau Claris proclaimed an ephemeral Catalan republic in 1640 which, after surrendering to the protection of Luis XIII, culminated in French sovereignty over the Catalan territories north of the Pyrenees.

After this episode, the end of the War of the Spanish Succession in 1714 saw how some Catalans erred by supporting the House of Habsburg instead of accepting, as they had done initially, that a grandson of Luis XIV, Felipe V, succeed Carlos II and occupy the Spanish throne.

Felipe V eliminated a large part of the Catalan institutions and unified the 'Peninsular and Overseas Market' by means of the Decree of the New Plan of 1715, approved in a manner resembling France, centralised in Paris.

Despite the criticisms levelled against this Decree by today's separatists, that unification benefitted the Catalan economy by creating an integrated Spanish market, something which put the Catalan economy in an advantageous position within Spain, an advantageous position that was consolidated and extended with the customs protectionism of the nineteenth and twentieth centuries. Such protectionism was very favourable for Catalan industries, which saw how the Spanish market was reserved for them through the application of high import duties, restrictive import quotas and other protectionist measures adopted in Madrid by governments influenced and pressured by Catalan protectionists.

During the Peninsular War, Napoleon Bonaparte turned Catalonia into a French province between January 1812 and May 1814 and, taking advantage of the cantonal confusion of the First Spanish Republic, Baldomer Lostau, the first Catalan member of the Socialist International and member of Barcelona Provincial Council since 1872, proclaimed an ephemeral Catalan state within the federal Spanish Republic in March 1873, which failed when the government of the First Spanish Republic reacted by annulling the independence proclamation two days after it was issued.

In the midst of the romantic nationalist enthusiasms of nineteenth-century Europe, a Catalan proto-constitution, known as the Bases, was drafted in Manresa in 1892. In the twentieth century, Solidaritat Catalana was established. It almost monopolised Catalan representation in the Congress of Deputies between the elections of 1907 and its rupture as a consequence of the events known as the Tragic Week in 1909.

With a pragmatic attitude, which has always been the most advantageous one for Catalonia with regard to its relations with the central government, the leaders of the Lliga Regionalista, Enric Prat de la Riba and Francec Cambó, managed, without aiming for Catalonia's independence, to bring together Catalonia's four provincial councils as a regional government known as the Mancomunitat de Catalunya, or Commonwealth of Catalonia. This carried out an interesting task of administration from 1914 to the coup d'état of General Miguel Primo de Rivera, which was in response to the disturbances during the separatist demonstration of 11 September 1923. The Catalan bourgeoisie supported him since it suppressed social disorder.

Later, with the arrival of the Second Spanish Republic, Colonel Francesc Macià extracted the establishment of the Generalitat de Catalunya from the republican government that had recently been installed after the elections on 14 April 1931. He was its first president, a position he held until his death, upon which he was substituted by Lluis Companys in 1933. With the establishment of the Generalitat, Macià's initial proclamation of a 'Catalan republic as a member state of an Iberian Federation' was annulled.

This republican Generalitat, governed by the Statute of 1932, ceased functioning normally when President Companys attempted to instal Estat Català within the Spanish Republic in October 1934 with a failed uprising. Accused of rebellion against the Spanish Republic, he was imprisoned along with the other members of his government.

Nevertheless, after the elections held in February 1936, which were won by the Frente Popular, Companys and the others who had been imprisoned for rebellion were released and the Generalitat de Cataluña was re-established. During the Spanish Civil War (1936–1939) it functioned precariously because of its conflict with the government of the Republic about the exercise of powers, and also because of the disputes between the parties and unions that supported it, which led to a kind of 'internal civil war' in May 1937, something that strengthened the role of the Communist Party.

Having won the war, Franco suppressed the Generalitat, although it continued to operate in exile under the presidencies of Companys—until his execution in Barcelona in 1940 after a summary trial—Josep Irla (1940–1954), and Josep Tarradellas (1954–1977), the latter being reinstalled as president upon the re-establishment of democracy.

In 1978, during the transition to democracy, the Catalan president in exile, Tarradellas, achieved the re-establishment of the Generalitat de Catalunya and, after the elections of 1980, the leader of Convergència Democràtica de Catalunya (CDC), Jordi Pujol, became president. The press at the time considered him to be the 15th president of the Generalitat, not the 126th, a figure made up in a history book published in 2003 by Enciclopedia Catalana, which drew an equivalence between the presidents of the fiscal and administrative entity created in 1358 and the current

Generalitat, the real antecedent of which is the Generalitat created under the 1932 Statute, the first president of which was Francesc Macià.

On this point, it is curious to note that separatist analyses constantly dwell more on Catalonia's past, which is presented as glorious, than on establishing a governance suitable for creating a country for the future.

Jordi Pujol remained in the presidency of the Generalitat until 2003, and the constitutional autonomous system underwent changes resulting from the constant struggle between supporters of autonomy, aiming to improve the content of the Regional Statute of Autonomy, and separatists, aiming not only to obtain greater funding and wider powers but also to establish an independent Catalan Republic through the so-called secessionist process.

Attempts at secession started during Artur Mas' presidency of the Generalitat and reached their peak with the illegal 'laws of disconnection', approved by the Parliament of Catalonia—without reaching the required majority—on 6 and 7 September 2017, the illegal independence referendum of 1 October 2017, and the Parliament of Catalonia's approval of a proposed law to establish a Catalan republic as an independent and sovereign state on 27 October 2017, based on the erroneous idea that this was legitimate given the result of the tumultuous, uncontrolled and illegal referendum of 1 October in favour of independence. King Felipe VI issued a message in favour of the unity of Spain on 3 October 2017, something that provoked the hostility of the most conspicuous separatist groups, to the point where the city of Girona declared the King of Spain persona non grata, so that the 'Princess of Girona' prize awards ceremony had to be held in Barcelona instead of Girona.

The Constitutional Court, unsurprisingly, annulled all these separatist texts that contravened the legality upon which the unity of Spain is founded, as established by the Constitution. For its part, in a long court case that was broadcast on television, the Supreme Court of Spain sentenced the separatist leaders on 14 October 2019 to serve prison sentences for terms of between 9 and 13 years, as well as to pay fines and be disqualified from holding public office.

These sentences were handed down to the members of the government of the Generalitat who had declared the frustrated attempt at independence, as well as some separatist leaders who had contributed to it. The need, however, of the Spanish prime minister, Pedro Sanchez, to secure the votes of secessionists in parliament led the PSOE-Podemos coalition government to pardon the prisoners in June 2021, something that was highly controversial given that the prisoners repeated time and again that they would again promote the independence of Catalonia from the rest of Spain.

The former president of the Generalitat (2016–2017), Carles Puigdemont, and other separatist leaders, escaped Spanish justice by fleeing abroad and, due to problems caused by a lack of coordination between Spanish and European justice, Puigdemont was able to become a Member of the European Parliament, something that has enabled him to move freely around other European countries creating publicity for internal and external campaigns with the slogan, "Catalonia is not Spain", in which the meaning of words has been twisted to make the separatist message coincide with broad sections of the formerly Carlist population of inland Catalonia that is highly influenced and indoctrinated by messages on Catalan television, certain social media, and by media outlets subsidised illicitly from the Generalitat de Catalunya's own budget.

Pere Aragonès has been the president of the Generalitat de Catalunya since 2021. He has accepted entering into discussion with the Spanish prime minister, Pedro Sánchez, in order to try and solve the dispute between autonomy and separatism.

This has had the effect of impeding the excesses of the secessionists, excesses that have even included street disturbances, but it has not stopped the president of the Parliament of Catalonia, or the president of the Generalitat himself, from continuously repeating that their aim is to continue fighting for the independence of Catalonia from Spain.

At the same time, the Generalitat is carrying out actions at the international level to the same end and, in all forums, separatists insistently repeat that "we will do it again", in reference to the unilateral actions taken by the Generalitat to achieve independence.

The government of the Generalitat has continued to open embassies abroad and has mobilised foreign professionals and leading influencers of opinion, always with the aim of discrediting Spain and attempting to convince the world that Catalonia has the right to become independent from Spain on account of its history (often falsified or reinterpreted), and of a supposed right to self-determination, something that is only contemplated by the United Nations for colonial territories and the like. This is certainly not the case with Catalonia, the population of which enjoys all the rights recognised by the Spanish Constitution and are the same to those enjoyed by all other Spaniards and similar to those enjoyed in the democratic states in Europe and the western world.

It is curious how separatists have created a peculiar semantics by changing the meaning of words in an attempt to convince people of the virtue of their message.

Thus, instead of talking about respect for the law, they talk about the mechanisms of oppression or political harassment, instead of justice they speak of repression. The application of legality is reinterpreted as anti-democratic harassment and many proclaimed human rights are simply separatists' wishes that put their ideology before reality.

Furthermore, the word 'Catalonia' is used by media sympathetic to the secessionist cause to refer only to the half of the population that is separatist.

The prison sentences handed down to those who did not respect the law, the judicial sentences and decisions, are called attacks on the freedom of expression, or simply expressions of fascism and the lack of respect for human rights.

The government of Spain is simply regarded as a state oppressor, not to mention that, for separatists, Spain does not exist, and that the Crown is only ever mentioned as the enemy to be beaten because of King Felipe VI's message on 3 October 2017, calling for respect for the Constitution after the illegal separatist vote of 1 October. This has led to the King being considered persona non grata in some Catalan towns, accompanied in many cases by the burning of his photographs and offensive remarks proffered by separatists.

On the other hand, for separatists, the only democrats are those who think the same as them, and anyone who disagrees is dismissed contemptuously as a unionist, a fascist, a reactionary and even a Francoist. And those who do disagree are denied access to the media sympathetic to the separatist cause or controlled by the Generalitat de Catalonia.

At the international level, the Catalan government, and separatist organisations such as the Assemblea Nacional Catalana (ANC), Omnium Cultural, FemCat, Associació de Municipis per a la Independència (AMI) and the Consell de la República—managed by the former president Puigdemont from his refuge in Waterloo—and others, have mobilised many public and private media to disseminate to the world an image of a declining, authoritarian Spain that is simply a continuation of the Franco dictatorship. This was, to some extent, assisted by the failure of the central government to rebuff this propaganda, disseminated by separatists in universities, NGOs, the media and social media with the idea that a lie told many times can, as Joseph Goebbels observed, become a truth for those who let themselves be convinced.

The central government has not devoted the necessary resources to countering the secessionists' campaigns abroad. This only changed when, in October 2018, the 'Global Spain' secretariat was created within the Ministry of Foreign Affairs, European Union and Cooperation. Amongst other things, its task is to counter the deceptions disseminated by the separatists, improve the image of Spain abroad and vouch for its good reputation. In this it is also assisted by the Spanish Chamber of Commerce.

Separatism has reached 2022 without convincing the governments of the world that Catalonia has a supposed right to decide, which is nothing more than a euphemism for the desire to achieve independence from the rest of Spain. The fugitive former president of the Generalitat, Carlos Puigdemont, does everything possible in his attempt to internationalise the separatist narrative from his Casa de la República in Waterloo and from his controversial seat in the European Parliament.

He has even organised separatist events in Perpignan, with the justification that Perpignan is in north Catalonia, albeit in French territory as a consequence of the oddly revered Pau Claris enabling the separation of Catalan territory when he put Catalonia under the sovereignty of the King of France after proclaiming the 'Catalan Republic' in 1640, a separation that was confirmed by the Treaty of the Pyrenees in 1659.

In spite of having failed to convince the governments of the world, separatism continues to mobilise a mass of people willing to demonstrate on the streets, impede access to Barcelona airport and block roads, streets, squares and railway lines, something which, as the author of this book explains, generates hesitation when it comes to foreign investment in Catalonia, as well as legal insecurity, and this damages the reputation Barcelona had earned for itself with the 1992 Olympic Games, which Juan Antonio Samaranch (president of the International Olympic Committee from 1980 to 2001) managed to promote for Barcelona.

The 1992 Olympic and Paralympic Games would not have been possible without the spur of investment from the government of Spain, but the Olympic Games are not the only important international event to have been held in, and given lustre to, a 'Barcelona within Spain'.

We should remember, in this regard, that Barcelona has hosted, as a Spanish city, a series of events that have helped shape the city and give it the attraction it has today. It was 500 years ago, in March 1519, that Barcelona hosted the chapter of the Order of the Golden Fleece, called by

Emperor Charles I, it being the only one to be held outside of Flanders. Let us also remember the Universal Exposition held from 8 April to 9 December 1888; the Society of Nations General Conference on Freedom of Communications and Transit, with the signing of the Statute on 20 April 1921; the International Exposition of 20 May 1929 to 15 January 1930; the International Eucharistic Congress of 27 May to 1 June 1952; the Mediterranean Games held from 16 to 25 July 1955, the 1992 Barcelona Olympic Games held from 25 July to 9 August; the Paralympic Games held from 4 to 15 September 1992; the European Council on 15 and 16 March 2002, which brought all the European heads of state and heads of government together in Barcelona; and the Universal Forum of Cultures, held from 9 May to 26 September 2004. All these events have shaped modern-day Barcelona: the Parc de la Ciutadella, the hill of Montjuïc, the Olympic Port and Village, the opening of Diagonal to the Mediterranean, the creation of the Forum district and port, and the construction of the ring road, to name just some examples.

A part of Barcelona's urban attractiveness today is the Eixample district with its grid system and chamfered corners. It corresponds to Ildefonso Cerdá's plan for the renovation and expansion of the city of Barcelona that the government in Madrid imposed over the slipshod Urban Plan which Barcelona City Council wished to implement, with streets which, even in that far off 1860, were ridiculous in comparison to the town planning standards of the day, a plan that only reflected the narrow vision of the owners of the affected plots of land.

Thanks to the success of the Euro-Mediterranean Conference held in Barcelona on 27 and 28 November 1995, promoted by the then Spanish Minister for Foreign Affairs, Javier Solana, the city, together with the Spanish government, was able to tender to host the headquarters of the Union for the Mediterranean, established in 2008, the secretariat of which is housed in the Palace of Pedralbes in Barcelona. It is also thanks to the Spanish government that Catalonia was chosen for the ALBA synchrotron and Barcelona chosen for the Mare Nostrum5 supercomputer and the secretariat of the European ITER Consortium.

But that is not all. Catalonia is part of the European Union and is in the eurozone. It participates in the work of the United Nations and all the international organisations, not on its own account, but because it forms part of the Kingdom of Spain, and it is the Kingdom of Spain that has been accepted as a member of the EU and the international organisations, which is to say that if Catalonia were to separate from Spain, it would no longer participate in the EU or those international organisations.

And it would not be easy to join them except by acquiring the label of 'state' for which it would have to receive the endorsement of the members, with the right of veto, of the Security Council of the United Nations, something that does not seem easy given the separatist threats also faced by some of the five members of the Council with the right of veto. The same could be said of a potentially independent Catalonia's problematic rejoining of the EU, given that this would require unanimous acceptance of the candidature presented by the state aiming to become a member of the European Club.

The other side of the coin to all these positive aspects of the 'Spanishness of Catalonia' is the insecurity generated by the separatist altercations of October 2017, which prevented Barcelona from having the option to host the European Medicines Agency, which was seeking new premises after being obliged to move from London on account of Brexit, a candidature that was strengthened by the smooth operation on the Barcelona Forum waterfront of the European Consortium for the establishment of an experimental thermonuclear reactor for the development of fusion energy (ITER).

These examples of Barcelona's international standing thanks to the actions of the Spanish government show that Catalonia forming part of Spain should not be appraised only in terms of fiscal balances between Catalonia and the rest of Spain, as the separatists did at the start of the *process*, but also in terms of many other parameters, which are analysed with precision in this book by professor Ferran Brunet.

I think I should add that this foreword is due, not only to my affinity with the author, but also to a desire to draw attention to a period in the history of Catalonia, one that opened up with the transition to democracy after the death of Franco, in which many of us Catalans contributed with our professional experience to creating the incipient Administration of the Generalitat de Catalunya.

A great deal of work was done from the autonomous Administration of Catalonia to highlight Catalonia, its culture, its language, its industry, its art, its exporting and tourist potential, its trade, and not just its trade within Spain but also abroad. This was done with great verve and determination with the help of the entities and institutions of all kinds that Catalonia has, as well as through fairs and exhibitions, and in the spirit of constitutional loyalty which then existed, and which separatism has squandered.

With such efforts Catalonia was considered to be one of the Four Motors for Europe and the then president, Jordi Pujol, was considered Spaniard of the year and was one of the promoters of Europe of the Regions, just as democratic Spain was able to join the European Communities in 1986.

Whoever was not working then, whoever did not live through the resurgence of an autonomous Catalonia deeply committed to the recognition of a Spain that had recently left Franco's dictatorship behind, cannot be conscious of the huge amount of work done by Catalan institutions during the process of adhesion to European integration, which occurred in 1986.

I write these lines for the foreword to the book by professor, and founder of Societat Civil Catalana, Ferran Brunet, thinking about how much I worked to disseminate a dynamic image of autonomous Catalonia within Spain, working in Jordi Pujol's first government, always supporting Catalonia as part of Spain, and not the assumptions of separatists that have divided Catalan society and which, as professor Brunet shows in this book, are negative for Catalonia and, above all, negative for its capital, Barcelona.

It is surprising that a part of the Catalan bourgeoisie that had done so well during the Franco regime, and during the constitutional and statutory period for Catalonia that emerged after the transition to democracy, should support Catalan separatism without seeing that, were independence to be achieved, they would lose, as this book demonstrates, many of the elements that have stimulated the Catalan economy. Such elements would be difficult to recover given the brain drain and flight of companies that is undermining Catalonia's capacity to lead Spain, as was the case in the past.

Today's great challenge is to achieve a kind of incorporation of Catalonia in Spain that corresponds to what King Felipe VI invited people to agree to in his speech to open the 14th Cortes Generales (Spanish Parliament) on 3 February 2020 when he said, "Spain cannot be some against the others, it must be everyone's and for everyone".

If such an understanding is not achieved, we will continue to be immersed in what Brunet unambiguously asserts is a "*process* that robs us of peace, understanding, employment, activity, investment and it robs us of the future", and I would add, it robs us of our ability to get along with

each other as friends, like before when we had a shared feeling of a
united people.

It's worth turning the page, abandoning separatism and following the
path once again of the Catalonia that, until recently, had contributed to
Spain's progress and reputation, and was considered a motor of the EU
and of the activities of its regions and cities.

Faculty of Economics,   Francesc Granell Trias
University of Barcelona,
Barcelona, Spain

CONTENTS

LIST OF FIGURES

LIST OF TABLES

CHAPTER 1

Introduction

Two main questions are analysed in this book:

- The economic consequences of the Catalan separatists' challenge to democracy, the democratic State of Spain, the rule of law and the territorial integrity of this country over recent decades.
- The economic consequences of a hypothetical secession of Catalonia from Spain.

The argument is presented in three parts.

- Part I. On what should not have happened: the challenge to democracy, a coup promoted and carried out by a regional government against the rule of law and Spain. The destruction of democracy in Catalonia.
- This section includes a consideration of: separatism; nationalism; regionalism; populism; democracy; the rule of law; Barcelona; Catalonia; Spain; Europe; the global world; bilingualism; academic failure; voters; rebels … It's what shouldn't have happened.
- Part II. On what has happened. The economic consequences of the separatist *process*, the destruction of Catalonia and its decline.

© The Author(s), under exclusive license to Springer Nature Switzerland AG 2022
F. Brunet, *The Economics of Catalan Separatism*,
https://doi.org/10.1007/978-3-031-14451-6_1

- This section includes a consideration of: details concerning the social fragmentation of Catalonia, economic destruction, and gradual decline. This is what has happened—lamentably! It is the cost of the challenge there has been in Catalonia to the rule of law.
- Part III. On what will not happen. An examination of the changes a hypothetical secession would generate in the shape of falling trade, employment, and GDP. Separatist fantasies, fallacies and lies are dismissed.
- This section includes a consideration of how separatism would lead Catalonia to ruin and totalitarianism. It is what will not happen, fortunately! It would be the price of independence.

Thus, readers whose primary interest is political can start with Part I of the book (on the separatist attack on the rule of law in Spain). Readers whose primary interest is economic may start reading or consulting Part II of the book (the economic consequences of the separatist challenge). Readers interested in the utopias of independence can start with Part III (the economic consequences of independence).

This is a book I would have preferred not to have written, not to have had to write, not to have yielded to writing. This is a book about the demolition of Catalonia. In all modesty, it is a book about the destruction of Catalonia over recent decades and its inescapable decline. The consolidation and continuance of the Catalan separatist movement is leading to the erosion of Spanish democracy and to the disintegration of Spain.

It's hard to swallow. It is not at all pleasant to reconstruct the truth about the real fragmentation of your country and to refute the lies about the supposed benefits of the separatist challenge and of a utopian secession of Catalonia from the rest of Spain and the European Union.

For quite some time now, and most acutely so over the last decade, the separatist confrontation has been destroying Catalonia in the face of inaction by the central government, and the bewilderment and dismay of ordinary Catalans who have been left deserted, abandoned, indignant, powerless, and persecuted. The situation in Catalonia continues to evolve, slowly. How could it not be otherwise? Indeed, the false separatist slogan, *Espanya ens roba* ('Spain robs us'), has been substituted for the truth, *El procès ens roba!* (The *process* robs us!).[1] Of course, it does! The *process* has

---

[1] Throughout the book the word *process* is used to refer to the challenges made to the democracy in Spain by the separatist Catalan parties and the regional government of Catalonia.

robbed us of understanding and our ability to get along well with each other, and it has robbed us of money, work, freedom and the future.

A version of this book has been published in Spanish.[2] The book can be read from cover to cover, or chapter by chapter, consecutively or not, in almost any order.

---

[2] Ferran Brunet (2022), *Economía del separatismo catalán,* Barcelona, Ediciones Deusto.

PART I

Defying the Rule of Law and Democracy

CHAPTER 2

Contemporary Spain: Democratic and Decentralised

MODERN DEMOCRATIC SPAIN

Spain is a democratic and decentralised country. This configuration stems from the Spanish Constitution, approved on 6 December 1978 by 85.6% of Spanish voters, 90.5% in Catalonia. This Constitution sealed the transition to democracy after Franco's authoritarian dictatorship (1939–1975), which succeeded the Spanish Civil War (1936–1939) and replaced the Second Spanish Republic (1931–1936).[1]

Since then, Spain has lived in democracy and has developed the institutions of a social and democratic state under the rule of law. It joined the European Union and NATO. The economy was industrialised and has now shifted to the service sector. Production grew and the quality of life

---

[1] There are extraordinary works on the dynamics of Spain. Here I would draw attention to:

- Synthesis: Stanley Payne (2011), *Spain: a unique history*, Madison, WI, University of Wisconsin Press; William Chislett (2013), *Spain. What everyone needs to know*, Oxford, OUP; and Nigel Townson (ed.) (2015*), Is Spain Different? A Comparative Look at the 19th & 20th Centuries*, Eastbourne, Sussex Academic Press.
- On the modern era: John H. Elliott (2009*), Spain, Europe and the Wider World, 1500–1800*, New Haven, CT, Yale UP; and John H. Elliot (2020), *Scots and Catalans: Union and Disunion*, New Haven, CT, Yale UP.
- On more contemporary aspects: Paul Preston (1986), The Triumph of Spanish Democracy, London, Routledge; and Paul Preston (2020), *A People Betrayed: A History of Corruption, Political Incompetence and Social Division in Modern Spain, 1874–2018*, London, William Collins.

F. Brunet, *The Economics of Catalan Separatism*, https://doi.org/10.1007/978-3-031-14451-6_2

improved in an extraordinary manner, and Spain excels in international rankings on the quality of life.

Spain's transition to democracy was a model for the processes of political change in other countries, especially in Latin America and in Central and Eastern Europe. Spain's political transition was exemplary because of the large obstacles it overcame, its sense of civic responsibility and the absence of violence with which change was achieved, as well as the quality of the institutions it established. Under the form of a parliamentary monarchy, Spain is a full democracy. Amongst the countries of the world, it usually occupies a position between 10 and 25.[2]

The quality of the transition and of Spanish democratic institutions was accompanied by another important development, a widely admired one, and one that has inspired similar tendencies in Western Europe and many other countries: decentralisation. As we shall see in this book, in Chap. 6, for example, Spain is the most decentralised country in Europe. Public expenditure by the Autonomous Communities, the political and juridical form adopted by the regions, is close to 50% of all public expenditure. Except for the collection of taxes, pensions, the armed forces, diplomacy and police, the Autonomous Communities exercise all the public powers. Sovereignty, however, naturally rests in Spain as a whole, together with the essential aspects of legislative power on rights and liberties, taxation and employment.

Over these four decades of Spain's history, there have been governments of different hues and even a multi-party coalition. The Spanish parliament, the Cortes Generales, is bicameral. The Congress of Deputies represents national sovereignty and chooses the government of Spain. The Senate represents the 50 provinces, 17 Autonomous Communities and two Autonomous Cities into which Spain is organised.[3]

The two dominant parties that alternate in forming the Spanish government are, on the left and centre-left, the Partido Socialista Obrero Español—PSOE (Spanish Socialist Workers' Party) and on the right and centre-right, the Partido Popular—PP (People's Party). Each forms part of their respective European political party grouping. Two new parties, Vox and Podemos, appeared in 2013 and 2014, respectively. Vox is to the

[2] The Economist Intelligence Unit (n.d.), *Democracy Index* <https://www.eiu.com/n/democracy-index-2021-less-than-half-the-world-lives-in-a-democracy/>. See Chap. 15.
[3] Government of Spain (2022), *Institutions of Spain* <https://www.lamoncloa.gob.es/lang/en/espana/spanishinstitutions/Paginas/index.aspx>.

right of the PP and collects leaders and votes from the PP, centrism and regionalism. Podemos, also called Unidas Podemos, and branded differently in various Autonomous Communities, is to the left of PSOE. It is a synthesis of the Communist Party—which was of significance during the last phases of the dictatorship—and various other leftist groupings.

DEVELOPMENT OF SPANISH DEMOCRACY

Elections to the Cortes Generales (Congress and Senate) are held regularly every four years. Between 1979 and 2022 there were 14 legislatures. Autonomous Community elections have their own calendar and often do not coincide with other elections. Elections to the 8131 town councils in Spain also have their own calendar and are held simultaneously in all municipalities. Elections are usually held on Sundays.

The dominant parties in the Autonomous Communities and municipal councils have usually been the PSOE and the PP. The exceptions have been in the Autonomous Community of the Basque Country and the Autonomous Community of Catalonia, where the Partido Nacionalista Vasco—PNV (Basque Nationalist Party) and Convergència i Unió—CiU (Convergence and Union) party, respectively, were the dominant parties. Since 1978, these parties, whose orientation has successively been autonomist, regionalist, nationalist, sovereigntist and finally secessionist, always governed in these Autonomous Communities, except for one term of office in each of them. PNV and CiU also usually won most of the mayoralties in the Basque Country and Catalonia.

In Catalonia, the political forces have positioned themselves with respect to the challenge of their successive regional governments to democracy and the rule of law in Spain, a dynamic of confrontation, the economic consequences of which are the subject of this book. Moreover, in addition to the economic impact of political instability, we shall see how this effervescence has led Catalan politics into chaos. CiU has disintegrated and the separatist regional government of Catalonia rests, in its 2022 version, on the majority of seats held by the pro-independence groups of Esquerra Republicana de Catalunya (ERC), Junts per Catalunya (whose far-off starting point was CiU) and Candidatura d'Unitat Popular (CUP, a kind of anarcho-communist grouping).[4]

---

[4] See Chap. 19.

Spanish democracy has been consolidated through a series of events:

- Approval of the Spanish Constitution on 6 December 1978.
- Failed coup d'état of 23 February launched by military figures on the extreme right.
- Implementation of the Autonomous Community System through the establishment of 17 such entities and the transfer of powers and resources, especially in the 1980s and 1990s. The more extensive powers of the communities with a particular historical background (Navarre, the Basque Country, Catalonia and Galicia) were extended to the rest of the regions.
- Development of the rule of law. (For the quality of Spanish democracy, see later in this book.)
- Joining of NATO (1982) and the European Community (1986), later to become the European Union.
- Terrorism, especially that of the Basque separatist group, ETA. There were more than 850 assassinations between 1968 and 2010. Seventy-two such crimes were committed during Franco's dictatorship; the others were committed under the democratic system.
- 11 March 2004 terrorist attack, perhaps jihadist, on rush-hour trains in Madrid causing 193 deaths and 2057 injuries. The crime was committed three days before the general elections, which were won by the PSOE.
- Succession to the throne of King Felipe VI in 2014, after the abdication of King Juan Carlos I.
- A kind of political guerrilla warfare carried out for decades by the regional government of Catalonia, culminating in a coup d'état in autumn 2017. The constitutional order was restabilised by applying Article 155 of the Spanish Constitution, a coercive measure contemplated in most countries' constitutions.

All things considered, Spain is a full and consolidated democracy with a high level of decentralisation, as we will see in the coming chapters. Spain is one of the best countries to live in, the best of all according to one analysis. But it is marred by Catalan secessionism that presents a challenge to the whole country.

SUMMARY

- Contemporary Spain is a full democracy and a very decentralised country.
- Democratic Spain has overcome many challenges, the main one being that from the regional Catalan separatist government.

CHAPTER 3

The *Process* Robs Us, Not Madrid

NATURE OF THE SEPARATIST CHALLENGE

The separatist challenge has consisted of:

- A mass movement created by the political parties Convergència i Unió (CiU), Esquerra Republicana de Catalonia (ERC) and Candidatures d'Unitat Popular (CUP); two broad-based opinion-forming organisations, Omnium Cultural and Assemblea Nacional Catalana; and a myriad of small groups campaigning in a number of fields and subjects.
- A public administration, the Generalitat de Catalunya, or government of Catalonia, that has all the powers of a developed state—in education, health, police, etc.—except social security, defence and foreign affairs, which are used to provide complete coverage for separatist aims and actions.
- Comprehensive media coverage through publicly funded media (TV3...) and subsidised private media.
- Entryism of civil organisations, trade unions, employers' organisations, professional colleges.
- An external enemy: Spain, blamed for all ills and a dark past, present and future.
- Populism and opportunism: taking advantage of representative democracy when it suits. For example, separatists, with fewer votes

© The Author(s), under exclusive license to Springer Nature Switzerland AG 2022
F. Brunet, *The Economics of Catalan Separatism*,
https://doi.org/10.1007/978-3-031-14451-6_3

than constitutionalist Catalans, obtain more seats and in sufficient number to prolong their power.

- Rule of law: the sidestepping of legality whenever it suits the separatists.
- Catalan as the only language.
- Decoupling from Spain, the creation of parallel state structures with which to substitute those of the Spanish state, which has vanished.
- Control of the territory, overwhelming visibility of separatist flags and slogans to demonstrate who is in charge.
- Internationalisation of the separatist challenge, presenting it as a supposedly insoluble ethnic conflict.

THE PROCESS ROBS US!

Espanya ens roba ('Spain robs us') was the slogan that marked the turning point from conservative autonomy to revolutionary independence and the destabilisation of Catalonia brought about by the *process* over the last decade. Having accomplished the separatist coup d'état in the autumn of 2017, the dominant refrain you are now most likely to hear is no longer 'Spain robs us', but 'The *process* robs us'.

Today it is clear that the ills of Catalonia do not derive from 'perfidious Spain' but from the *process* itself. It can be summed up as *'the process robs us'*[1]:

- The current GDP of Catalonia is 4.6% lower than it would be without the separatist campaign. That is the equivalent of a loss of €1384 per year, per capita, that is, €4 a day.
- The accumulated growth of Catalonia's GDP since 2005 is 11.2% less than that of the Autonomous Community of Madrid.
- Catalonia's proportion of total Spanish GDP has held at 18.5%, while that of Madrid has climbed to 19.1%.
- In 1981, the per capita income of a Catalan was 21% higher than the Spanish average. Today it stands at 19% higher. That of a person in Madrid was 19% higher and is today 35% higher.
- Catalonia's competitiveness has plummeted: amongst the regions of Europe in 2010, it was in position 103. In 2019, it had fallen to position 161. Madrid is in position 98.

[1] What follows is a summary of the main issues discussed in Part II of this book.

- Madrid is Catalonia's main competitor and the main beneficiary of the separatists' excesses.
- Catalonia occupies sixth position in terms of doing business amongst the Spanish Autonomous Communities. Madrid occupies second position, and La Rioja is in first position.
- Every year the Generalitat de Catalunya publishes 104,042 pages of official gazette. It is followed in terms of regulatory intensity by Madrid, which publishes 88,000 pages. Other Autonomous Communities, such as La Rioja, get by with 18,000.
- Autonomous-separatist Catalonia is a fiscal hell: it occupies the last place amongst the Autonomous Communities because it levies the highest rates in terms of the bands of state taxes levied by the Autonomous Communities, such as the autonomous band of personal income tax (IRPF) and special taxes, as well as levying 15 of its own taxes (the region with the next highest number of its own taxes has but six).
- The separatist *process* expels companies, activities and people. Every year Madrid has a net increase of 42,000 inhabitants from all over Spain, and now from Catalonia as well.
- The housing and office market in Barcelona and its metropolitan area represents only half the volume of Madrid, even though Catalonia has a larger population. There are no urban projects.
- Catalonia owes its historical and current strength to its specialisation in selling to the whole Spanish market. Over the last decade, exports to the rest of Spain have been falling, even in absolute terms. The balance between exports and imports to the rest of Spain is shrinking. This decreasing interior balance with the rest of Spain is compromising Catalonia's trade deficit with the rest of the world.
- Catalonia sells more to Aragon than to the whole of France! More to Madrid than to the United Kingdom, more to Castilla la Mancha than to China... So, we can see just how important it is to be Spanish or not.
- Catalonia's fiscal balances with the rest of Spain are like ground zero in the separatist argument. Interpreting them to their whim they assert that now Spain is robbing from us, a lot, and that with that money, when Catalonia is independent, it will be possible to pay for... Regardless of the discussion about the real level of the fiscal balances, if Catalonia were independent, these fiscal balances would disappear due to the collapse in trade between an independent Catalonia and the rest of Spain!

- Madrid is the Autonomous Community that makes the largest net contribution to the Spanish public purse: put simply, Madrid contributes double the amount Catalonia does. 'Spain robs Madrid'!
- The level of solidarity, or territorial redistribution, in Spain is considerably lower than federal countries such as the United States or Germany.
- Is the Catalan independence movement the result of fiscal egotism or of its elite?
- Companies and persons resident in the province of Barcelona finance those in Girona, Lleida and Tarragona. Catalonia's internal fiscal balances reproduce those of Catalonia with the rest of Spain in a very pronounced way. The most separatist districts are by far the ones that receive the most subsidies.
- The Barcelona, Catalonia and Spain brands have suffered great reputational damage. Political and social instability, the separatist insurrection of autumn 2017, the separatists' international campaigns against Spain and the violence, guerrilla tactics and burning of Barcelona in the autumn of 2019, have discouraged tourism from home and abroad.
- Barcelona's attractiveness as a European city in which to invest and live has fallen from 4th place in 2010 to 11th in 2019.
- The Spanish social security system has a yearly deficit in Catalonia for pension payments of €3000 million. An independent Catalonia would not receive this amount from Spain.
- The relocation of companies outside Catalonia was aggravated by the stampede of autumn 2017, and it continues. Social confrontation, political chaos, economic instability, apprehension about the payment of invoices, the boycott of Catalan products, services and companies, corruption, the fiscal hell and juridical insecurity are all prejudicial to economic activity and they increase risk. The Catalan banks fled simply to avoid the bankruptcy that would ensue after a run on the banks in Catalonia, and the flight of deposits beyond its borders.
- Foreign investment in Catalonia collapsed. Foreign investment received by Madrid between 2010 and 2019 was four times greater than that received by Catalonia, its traditional destination. After the separatist coup of 2017 Catalonia now receives 15 times less foreign investment than Madrid!

- Generalitat budgets, always very expansive, went up 3.5 times between 2000 and 2020, to reach €46,057 million euros, or 18.2% of Catalan GDP. The budgets apply basically to health, education, police and expenses caused by the *process*.
- The debt accumulated by the Generalitat, for the most part through the Autonomous Liquidity Fund, by means of which it was bailed out by the Ministry of Finance, stands at €79,243 million, more than double the debt of the Community of Madrid. Given the unsustainability of the separatist Generalitat's finances, it has a junk bond rating and does not have access to the capital markets.
- Catalonia's current decline will have profound consequences in the medium and long term, all the more so the longer it takes to put an end to the Catalan independence movement's venture and the bad government of the Generalitat.
- In this Catalonia dominated by the separatists there is a lot of friction, as there is between Catalonia and the rest of Spain, and this will lead to the erosion of Catalonia and Spain. Unfortunately, this is the chronicle of a decline foretold.

Fortunately, however, a paradigm shift has been developing very slowly, and it is becoming dominant. Today it is clear that it is not Spain that is robbing from us, but the *process*, the persistent separatist defiance. The *process* robs us. It is therefore time to say "That's enough of the *process*, common sense, understanding, reconciliation and harmony. It is time to come to our senses!"

SUMMARY

- Reversing the Catalan separatist challenge and its deep impact will be a long task, and exceedingly costly.

CHAPTER 4

The Rebellion and the Separatist Coup

2017 SEPARATIST COUP D'ÉTAT

Of course, there are many antecedents for the Catalan independence movement's challenge to Spain. One could highlight, in modern history, the War of the Spanish Succession 1701–1713, (called the war of succession by the separatists), in contemporary history, the Second Republic, the Spanish Civil War and the Franco regime, and in the immediate past, corruption, economic crisis, cuts in social spending, the powers of the CiU and ERC political parties, the ruling of the Constitutional Court with regard to the new Statute of Autonomy of 2006 and so forth. Or one could emphasise the present ('Spain robs us') and the future (independent, as a consequence of which Spain will stop robbing us and ... we will be rich, rich rich!).

The fact is that the separatist rebellion is very recent, particularly with regard to the so-called Tinell Pact between the PSC, ERC and Iniciativa per Catalunya (14 December 2003) and their tripartite government (between 20 December 2003 and 26 December 2010), which led to the reform of the Statute of Autonomy.

L'hem feta ben grossa! (We've really done it this time!), as we say in Catalan. Indeed, the rebellion of autumn 2017, in which all the energies generated for years by a regional government against a vanished Spanish state were concentrated and unleashed, led to a terrible fracture in Catalan society. Perhaps it was a postmodern coup d'état on account of the

© The Author(s), under exclusive license to Springer Nature Switzerland AG 2022
F. Brunet, *The Economics of Catalan Separatism*,
https://doi.org/10.1007/978-3-031-14451-6_4

techniques used (massive propaganda, television as an organiser, Internet, social networks) and of the mix of mass performances and juridical and physical violence.

Along with the wide-ranging analysis and extensive bibliography which the separatist *process* has already produced—to which this book will often refer—and the many investigations that will be held in the future, we can, for the purposes of exposition, chronology and the linking of the chain of events, refer to: (1) the bill of indictment of the main leaders of the *process;* and (2) the court ruling on the *process*.[1]

CONSEQUENCES OF THE 2017 COUP D'ÉTAT

The consequences of the autumn putsch of 2017 have been far reaching:

- Political effects.
- Political, institutional and partisan chaos in Catalonia.
- The government of Spain had to awake from its long sleep, at least for a moment.
- Social effects.
- Acute social fracture.

[1] Tribunal Supremo. Sala de lo Penal (2018), *Causa especial núm.: 20907/2017. Auto de procesamiento* <http://www.poderjudicial.es/stfls/tribunal% 20supremo/documentos% 20de% 20inter% c3% 89 s/auto% 20procesamiento.pdf>; y Tribunal Supremo. Sala de lo Penal (2019), *Sentencia núm. 459/2019 de la causa especial núm. 3/20907/2017, seguida por los delitos de rebelión, sedición, malversación, desobediencia y pertenencia a organización criminal* <http://www.poderjudicial.es/cgpj/es/poder-judicial/noticias-judiciales/el-tribunal-supremo-condena-a-nueve-de-los-procesados-en-la-causa-especial-20907-2017-por-delito--de-sedicion>. The Supreme Court perceived delusion amongst the accused and, in its sentencing, reduced the severity of the coup plotters' crime by a degree, from rebellion to sedition.

On the antecedents and implementation of the coup, as well as the bill of indictment and sentence, see Enric Millo (2020), *El derecho a saber la verdad. El testimonio del Delegado del Gobierno en la Cataluña del 155*, Barcelona, Península. A list of analyses of the attempted coup d'état can be found in *El Cronista del Estado Social y Democrático de Derecho*, No. 71–72, monográfico *¿Cataluña independiente?* <https://dialnet.unirioja.es/ejemplar/470557>. A chronology can be found in Anon. (2020), "Una cronologia del Procés. 40 anys d'impunitat de l'elit catalana", <https://resd9.blogspot.com/2014/11/una-cronologia-dels-fets-35-anys.html>; and also in Andrés Boix Palop (2017), "El conflicto catalán y la crisis constitucional española: una cronología", *El Cronista del Estado Social and Democrático de Derecho*, No. 71–72, pp. 172–181.

- Lamentations of the separatists due to the loss of this key battle and an attempt to maintain their position by claiming the victimisation of the imprisoned coup-plotting politicians.
- Economic effects
- An increase in the risk premium of Spanish debt and of the Catalan bond and a run on the stock exchange.
- A fall in retail trade, the registration of new vehicles, demand for electric energy and bank deposits throughout Catalonia.
- A drop in Catalan GDP in 2017 of between -0.3 and -1.5%; an accumulated drop until the end of 2019 of -2.5%; and a drop in Spanish GDP of between -0.4% and -1.2%.[2]

After the autumn of 2017, the application of Article 155 of the Spanish Constitution, that is to say, the administration of the Generalitat by the central government, pacified Catalonia. That was when the mourning of the separatists could begin, although this was soon interrupted by the liturgical rites of many people wearing a yellow ribbon on their lapels, as well as the ubiquitous sale of yellow *churros* or sugary fritters and the appearance of yellow crosses in the squares and on the beaches. Countering the extremely strong investment made by the independence movement promises to be a long and difficult process. In this regard, 2018 was a relatively quiet year with the central government administering the Generalitat in application of Article 155 of the Constitution from 27 October 2017 until 2 June 2018, when a new separatist government was formed.

After the Coup

The court's judgement, delivered on 14 October 2019, stirred a hornets' nest. In the absence of any action whatsoever by the Mossos d'Esquadra (Catalan police force), Barcelona's local police force, the Guardia Urbana and the fire brigade, the Comités de Defensa de la República [sic] (Committees for the Defence of the Republic—CDR) competed with Tsunami Democràtic [sic] in the burning of Barcelona, in a manner reminiscent of the anarchist Semana Trágica, or Tragic Week of 1909. There

---

[2] See Part II of this book. A first summary of the results of our research can be read at Ferran Brunet (2021), "Consecuencias económicas del separatismo catalán", *Revista de Libros*, 10 November <https://www.revistadelibros.com/consecuencias-economicas-del-separatismo-catalan/>.

was evidence during these acts of an extraordinary and very strict level of organisation[3] and of violence. New aims were aired, such as *Ofec econòmic de l'Estat* (choke the state) along with new slogans such as *Independència o barbàrie* (independence or barbarism).

During the week of 20 to 27 October 2019, with the pretext of the court's judgment on the *process*, and thanks to the collaboration of the Mossos d'Esquadra and the absolute impunity of the vandals, there was chaos in various areas of Barcelona. The disturbances left 600 injured, 194 were arrested (154 by the Mossos d'Esquadra, 32 by the Policía Nacional and 8 by Barcelona's Guardia Urbana), 28 were sent to prison and the resultant destruction cost an estimated €2.5 million.[4]

For their part, Catalan constitutionalists responded with an important demonstration on 27 October 2019 during which the most frequently heard slogan was *Barcelona no es crema!* (Barcelona is not for burning!). Once again, the brazenness tolerated by the state and the rule of law was notable.[5]

An example of the point to which the rule of law is applied in Catalonia concerns the return of funds taken from the public purse that the leaders of the government of the Generalitat used in the coup d'état of autumn 2017.

[3] Enrique Luján (2019), «Una élite clandestina está a punto de lograr el control efectivo de todo un territorio, operando desde la oscuridad», 17 October <http://despiertaalfuturo. blogspot.com/2019/10/una-elite-clandestina-esta-punto-de.html>.

[4] EFE (2019), "Casi 600 heridos, 200 detenciones, daños... Las cifras de una semana de disturbios", *La Vanguardia*, 20 October <https://www.lavanguardia.com/politica/20191020/471095242135/cataluna-disturbios-detenidos-policia-heridos-barcelona.html>.

[5] With regard to the rule of law, the perspicacity of the philosopher from Vic, Jaime Balmes, is astonishing. In 1845, at the age of 35, with no knowledge of the genocidal barbarity of Communism and Nazism, or the consolidation of the rule of law during the second half of the twentieth century, and in the midst of the Catalan Carlist conflict, he wrote, "Liberty does not consist either of turmoil in the streets nor of the dictatorship of the sabre, but in the rule of law. [...] From the moment the law starts to be infringed, alleging necessity or urgency, or public convenience, one is immediately in the realm of arbitrariness and with arbitrariness all imaginable revolutions and reactions are possible. [...] In both cases it is not the law that governs, it is the will of man. Society is in both cases at the mercy of a discretional, arbitrary power, despotism in different forms, but always despotism. [...] The breaking of the law when committed by the government is a much greater scandal than when committed by the mob. [...] Governments never fail to give the law its due respect on account of the very serious ills caused to the public good otherwise, and for the great danger failure to do so poses for their own conservation". Jaime Balmes (1845), *El criterio* <http://www.ataun.eus/bibliotecagratuita/Cl% C3% A1sicos% 20en% 20Espa% C3% B1ol/vJaume% 20 Balmes/El% 20criterio.pdf>.

In June 2021, the Council of Ministers, presided by Pedro Sánchez, pardoned the nine who were convicted for the coup d'état on the grounds of 'public interest' and to open up a 'new moment for dialogue'.[6] The manner in which the beneficiaries of this act of grace by the government of Spain responded is notorious: "*Ho tornarem a fer*" (We will do again!).

As we will see in this book, the separatist challenge has two peculiarities and two consequences:

1. It is the fruit of actions by a regional government in the face of …
2. …the ineffectiveness of the Spanish government resulting from a mixture of incredulity and passivity.
3. The political, social and economic cost of the independence confrontation was multiplied due to the negligence of the central government, and
4. This all leads to the fragmentation and decline of Catalonia and a constitutional crisis for Spain.

SUMMARY

- The coup of autumn 2017 marked the peak of the challenge posed by the independence movement.
- The impunity of the rebels and of those given to violence is the worst enemy of the rule of law and democracy.

---

[6] Ministerio de Justicia (2021), *Reales Decretos* 456/2021 a 464/2021, *Boletín Oficial del Estado*, 23 June <https://www.boe.es/boe/dias/2021/06/23/>.

CHAPTER 5

Geographical Dimension and Historical Perspective of Catalonia

Extent of Catalonia

From a physical point of view, Catalonia is a mosaic of coastal and mountainous areas with some inland plains. From the climatic point of view, Catalan territory can be divided into zones: coastal; pre-coastal; continental Mediterranean (central), pre-Pyrenean Mediterranean and Mediterranean Pyrenean (north) and oceanic (Arán). Some social and economic indicators for Catalonia include:

- Population: 7.6 million inhabitants, equivalent to 16.3% of the total population of Spain.
- Extension: covering 32,000 square kilometres, Catalonia is one of the largest Spanish regions and a medium-sized one with respect to others in Europe.
- Urbanization: 90.4% in comparison with 97.2% for the Community of Madrid and 76% for Spain as a whole.
- GDP: €236,814 million, exceeded by the GDP of Madrid in 2018.
- Per capita income: 107 of the Spanish average.
- Public finance: large Generalitat deficit, a much more indebted entity than Spain as a whole, as confirmed by the total and per capita debt. Catalonia's ratings are therefore not very favourable.

© The Author(s), under exclusive license to Springer Nature Switzerland AG 2022
F. Brunet, *The Economics of Catalan Separatism*,
https://doi.org/10.1007/978-3-031-14451-6_5

- Exterior trade: its industry has a strong export specialisation in goods and services, up to 32% of GDP, as well as imports of 38% of GDP.
- Social indicators: unemployment 11%, low rate of marriage, very low birth rate.

INDUSTRIALISATION AND THE SPANISH MARKET

With economic development the population and economic activity of Catalonia became concentrated on the coastal strip, firstly on the plain of Barcelona and then in adjacent districts. A comparison of the population pyramids for Catalonia in 2000 and 2015 shows an ageing population (a reduction in the birth rate) and an increase in the population born abroad. Catalonia's industrial specialisation relative to the Community of Madrid, Spain as a whole and the EU continues to hold. Between 2000 and 2019 there was a high level of de-industrialisation in Catalonia.[1]

Manufacturing industry fell from representing 22.6% of Catalan GDP to 14.6%. This is an 8% reduction of GDP in two decades. In 2019, the manufacturing sector accounted for 17.1% of employment in Catalonia and 14.6% of GDP, the corresponding proportions for employment in manufacturing industry in Madrid, Spain and the EU being 7.3%, 12.5% and 15.4%, respectively.

Some historical events are relevant for understanding the current situation in Catalonia where the re-writing of history is a frequent exercise. The Kingdom of Aragon, and places within it such as the County of Barcelona and others in Catalonia and the rest of the Kingdom, such as Valencia and the Balearic Islands, are a constituent part of Spain. They formed Hispania centuries before the Catholic monarchs. Spain is one of the first European nations to be integrated with stable borders.[2]

Being part of Spain is as normal for Catalonia as it is for the other regions of modern Spain, none of which were ever colonised by Spain. Being part of Spain represents a great advantage for modern Catalonia, as will be seen by analysing the economic impact of the current separatist confrontation and that of a hypothetical secession (Table 5.1).

[1] Salvador Marín and Raúl Mínguez (dirs.), *45 años de evolución económica, social y empresarial de las Comunidades Autónomas en España, 1975–2020. Una visión por Comunidades*, Madrid, Consejo General de Cámaras de España <https://www.camara.es/sites/default/files/publicaciones/45-caa1502_1.pdf>.

[2] Henry Kamen (2015), *España y Cataluña. Historia de una pasión*, Madrid, La Esfera.

Table 5.1 Catalonia, Madrid, Spain and Europe: some economic indicators

	Community of Catalonia	Community of Madrid	Spain	European Union 27
Population, inhabitants	7,565,099	6,640,705	46,934,632	440,660,421
Urbanisation, as % of total population	90.4	97.2	76.0	75.0
Area, km^2	32,113	8,028	505,940	4,233,478
GDP, M euros / year	236,814	240,130	1,202,193	14,015,406
GDP per capita, € / year	31,119	35,913	26,430	28,060
Income per capita, UE = 100	107	124	91	100
Public debt, M euros	78,743	33,448	1,173,348	10,823,517
Public debt, as % GDP	34.40	14.50	97.60	77.2
Rating S&P	B+	A-	A	AA
Rating Fitch	BB	BBB	A-	AAA
Maximum income tax rate	48.0	43.5	43.5	, ,
Activity rate, as % population 16-64 y	61.6	63.4	58.7	73.2
Unemployed, persons	507,000	459,000	3,723,000	14,316,000
Unemployment rate, as % active p.	13.2	13.3	14.4	6.7
Exports, M euros	70,829	30,510	293,459	, ,
Exports, as % GDP	31.99	13.78	24.41	, ,
Imports, M euros	84,322	60,884	330,636	, ,
Imports, as % GDP	38.08	27.50	27.50	, ,
Trade balance, M euros	-12,198	-29,056	-37,177	+342,017
Trade balance, as % GDP	-5.97	-14.32	-3.09	+2.63
Birth rate, as ‰	8.13	8.32	7.94	10.57
Mortality rate as ‰	8.86	7.07	9.10	10.50
Life expectancy, in years	83.41	84.78	83.00	81.06
Crude marriage rate, as ‰	3.69	3.76	3.54	4.54
Crude divorce rate, as ‰	2.45	2.06	2.10	1.82

Data preferably for fourth quarter 2019 (before Covid-19 pandemic), or closest year

Database <https://ec.europa.eu/eurostat/web/main/data/database>; Institut d'Estadística de Catalunya (2022), *Població* <https://www.idescat.cat/tema/xifpo>; and Instituto Nacional de Estadística (2022), *Datos por temas* <https://www.ine.es/>

Source: Author's calculations based on Eurostat data (2022)

In the past, being part of Spain was also a great advantage, especially as trade developed. This occurred particularly after the promulgation of the Nueva Planta Decrees, or Decrees of the New Plan, by Felipe V between 1707 and 1716. As a consequence of these decrees some economic conditions were made uniform throughout Spain.[3] From then onwards, Catalonia became the main focus of Spanish industrialisation along with other ports and enclaves such as Bilbao, Asturias and Malaga.[4]

The three main focal points of the Spanish empire, Europe, Spain and America, constitute the settings for the Spanish Black Legend of Spain's enemies. The houses of Austria, Habsburg and Bourbon, emperors and kings of Spain, played a key role in European events. With the War of the Spanish Succession, Spain's position in Europe changed, as did the accounts of foreign propaganda and historiography with regard to Spain, which then centred on its development in America and its internal development (Fig. 5.1).

The characteristic features of Spain's task in America can be gleaned from an analysis of American colonisation.[5] Spain oversaw the protection of the Indians, the Laws of the Indies and mixed marriage, but was not capable of affirming the reality of its task in America. Then, in the nineteenth century, Spain's development was complicated by the wars of independence and the disintegration of the empire, along with, on the Iberian

---

[3] Gabriel Tortella, José Luis García Ruiz, Clara Eugenia Núñez and Gloria Quiroga (2016), *Cataluña en España. Historia y mito*, Madrid, Gadir; Jesús Laínz (2017), *El privilegio catalán. 300 años de negocio de la burguesía catalana*, Madrid, Encuentro; Idem (2010), *Negocio y traición: La burguesía catalana de Felipe V a Felipe VI*, Madrid, Encuentro; Juan Velarde Fuertes (2019), "Promotores del suicidio económico catalán", *El Economista*, 4 noviembre; e Idem (2019), "Raíces del disparatado separatismo catalán", *El Economista*, 10 diciembre.

[4] Jordi Nadal (1984), *El fracaso de la revolución industrial en España, 1814–1913*, Barcelona, Ariel.

[5] John H. Elliott (2006), *Imperios del mundo atlántico: España y Gran Bretaña en América (1492–1830)*, Madrid, Taurus.

The fall of Catalonia.
Contribution to total GDP, in p. 100

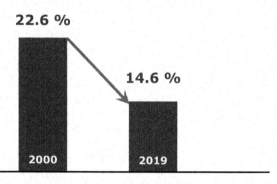

Fig. 5.1 Deindustrialization of Catalonia. (Source: Author's calculations based on data from Institut d'Estadística de Catalunya (2022), *Anuari estadístic de Catalunya* <https://www.idescat.cat/pub/?id=aec&n=198&lang=es>)

Peninsula, the Carlist wars, civil wars, which were also quite common in other European nations.[6] A shadow was cast over the story of Spain.[7]

As a sequel, to bring the Black Legend up-to-date, the Spanish anomaly happened after 1898[8] with the establishment of Primo de Rivera's

---

[6] Jaume Vicens Vives (1965), *Historia económica de España*, Barcelona, Editorial Vicens-Vives, 1987.

[7] On Catalanism and its relationship with tradition, modernity, and Spain, see Francisco Canals Vidal (2006), *Catalanismo and Tradición catalana*, Barcelona, Scire; Enric Ucelay-Da Cal (2003), *El imperialismo catalán. Prat de la Riba, Cambó, D'Ors and la conquista moral de España*, Barcelona, Edhasa; Javier Barraycoa (2013), *Cataluña hispana*, Barcelona, Libros Libres; and Josep Ramon Bosch (2020), *Cataluña, la ruta falsa: El problema catalán: cómo solucionarlo and no sólo conllevarlo*, Barcelona, Deusto.

[8] According to the contemporary Francisco Jaume ((1907), *El separatismo en Cataluña. Sociología aplicada. Crítica del catalanismo según el análisis de los hechos*, Barcelona, Imprenta de Francisco Altés y Alabart), Catalonia accounted for 50% of the Spanish economy at the end of the nineteenth century and identified itself as completely Spanish. Cuba practically belonged to the Catalans. With the loss of Cuba in 1898, the wealthy classes in Catalonia recoiled from the Spanish government and separatism appeared.

dictatorship,[9] the failure of the Second Republic,[10] the Spanish Civil War and Franco's dictatorship. Later the achievement of a democratic and decentralised Spain would eclipse the Black Legend and Spain would be admired on account of its history, the social and political course it had embarked upon and its current development. Perhaps the first cracks appeared after the terrorist attacks of 11 March 2004.

The separatist challenge grew during this period of Spain's relative weakness, and it increased during the crisis of 2007–2010. In their account, separatists will make abundant use of the Black Legend against Spain, against democracy, against the rule of law, against the integrity of the nation, both within Catalonia itself as well as on the international front.

DYNAMICS OF THE POPULATION AND GDP

With regard to Catalonia's relative position within Spain as a whole we shall consider three key aspects from a long perspective: the population, the GDP and the per capita GDP. From the early Spanish census conducted by the Conde de Floridablanca (1787) until today, Catalonia's proportion of population has grown from 7.8% to 16.3%. In the second half of the nineteenth century, the Catalan population stood at around 11% and, from 1950, it grew until 1980, and did so again in the 2000s with foreign immigration. In 2020, the resident population of Catalonia represented 16.3% of the population of Spain.[11]

A breakdown of the population data for Catalonia between the province of Barcelona and the rest of the Catalan provinces shows that these

---

[9] Miguel Primo de Rivera, to be precise, at that time captain general of Catalonia, launched his coup d'état on 13 September 1923 and remained as prime minister until his resignation on 28 January 1930.

[10] Agustí Calvet a. *Gaziel* (n.d.), *Tot s'ha perdut. El catalanisme polític entre 1922 i 1934*, Barcelona, RBA, 2013. In spite of the social and historical differences that make it difficult to assert that history repeats itself, the lack of will by the governments of Spain in the face of the separatist challenge can be seen now, and could be seen during the Second republic. The short-lived republican governments also ignored the seriousness of what was happening in Barcelona. (Alejandro Nieto (2014), *La rebelión militar de la Generalidad de Cataluña contra la República. Los sucesos de octubre de 1934 en Barcelona*, Madrid, Marcial, Pons.) The extremism of the current separatist Generalitat is reminiscent of the extremism of the republican Generalitat.

[11] Instituto Nacional de Estadística (2022), *Cifras de población* y *Censos demográficos* <https://www.ine.es/dyngs/INEbase/es/categoria.htm?c=Estadistica_P&cid=1254735572981>; and Roser Nicolau (2005), "Población, salud y actividad", in Albert Carreras and Xavier Tafunell (coords.) (2005), *Estadísticas históricas de España*, Vol. I, 2ª ed., Bilbao, Fundación BBVA, p. 153.

other provinces go from accounting for 4.4% of the Spanish population (56.4% of the Catalan population) to 4.3% of the Spanish population (and to 26.4% of the Catalan population). Consequently, the relative increase in the population of Catalonia is due to the province of Barcelona. Let us observe the dynamics of the province and Community of Madrid. It goes from 2.8% in 1787 to 14.1% in 2020 in a sustained manner. The growth profiles of the provinces of Barcelona and of Madrid are parallel, except since the last decades of the twentieth century, when Madrid's population takes off and that of Barcelona levels out.

Let us consider the dynamics of Catalonia's GDP since the beginning of the nineteenth century as a proportion of the Spanish total. If in 1802 Catalonia's GDP was 8.3% of Spanish GDP, in 1849 it was 14.7% and would reach 21.4% by 1930. Then it fell to 18.3% and approached 20% by the end of the 1970s and stood at 19% in 2020.[12]

The historical profile of the Community of Madrid's GDP is slightly different. If in 1802 Madrid's GDP accounted for 2.7% of the Spanish total, by 1849 it reached 11.6% and fell to 7% in 1930. In 1955 it stood at 14.7%. This proportion underwent sustained growth and reached 19.3% in 2020. In 2018, Madrid's contribution to Spain's GDP exceeded that of Catalonia. This is the so-called *sorpasso* or 'overtaking'.[13]

With regard to the standard of living, the per capita GDP (Spain Index = 100) illustrates the process of convergence of the rest of Spain relative to the traditionally more prosperous areas. Thus, Catalonia's per capita GDP, which in 1930 was 1.6 times the Spanish average, fell to 113 in 1980 (industrial crisis), reached 124 in 2000 and stood at 118 in 2019. For its part, Madrid too forms part of the same tendency for convergence between areas of Spain such that its per capita GDP, 203 in 1930, falls relatively to 124 in 1980, stood at 137 in 2015 (Fig. 5.2).[14]

[12] Albert Carreras, Leandro Prados de la Escosura and Joan R. Rosés (2005), "Renta y riqueza", in Albert Carreras and Xavier Tafunell (coords.) (2005), *Estadísticas históricas de España. Vol. III*, Bilbao, Fundación BBVA, 2ª ed., pp. 1365–1367; e Instituto Nacional de Estadística (2020), *GDP y GDP per cápita. Serie 2000–2019* <https://www.ine.es/dyngsINEbase/esoperacion.htm?c=Estadistica_C&cid=1254736167628&menu=resultados&idp=1254735576581#!tabs-1254736158133>.

[13] Ramón Tamames (2022), *¿A dónde vas, Cataluña? Cómo salir del laberinto independentista*, Barcelona, Ediciones Península, 5th ed.

[14] Julio Alcaide Inchausti (2003), *Evolución económica de las regiones y provincias españolas en el siglo XX*, Bilbao, Fundación BBVA; e (2020), *GDP y GDP per cápita. Serie 2000–2019* <https://www.ine.es/dyngs/INEbase/es/operacion.htm?c=Estadistica_C&cid=1254736167628&menu=resultados&idp=1254735576581#!tabs-1254736158133>

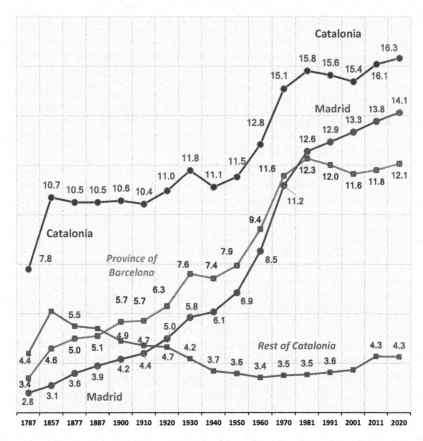

Fig. 5.2 Catalonia and Madrid population dynamics, 1787–2020. (Source: Author's calculations based on data from the Instituto Nacional de Estadística (2022), *Cifras de Población y Censos demográficos* <https://www.ine.es/dyngs/INEbase/es/categoria.htm?c=Estadistica_P&cid=1254735572981>; and Roser Nicolau (2005), "Población, salud y actividad", in Albert Carreras and Xavier Tafunell (coords.) (2005), *Estadísticas históricas de España*, Vol. I, 2nd ed., Bilbao, Fundación BBVA, p. 153.)

Catalonia's period of boom, when the population and GDP went from accounting for 7–9% of the total to accounting for 17–20% occurred from the second half of the nineteenth century until 1959 with the Stabilisation Plan and the opening of Spain to foreign investment. This phase came to a final end between 1970, when the Preferential Trade Agreement was signed with the European Economic Community, and 1986, when Spain joined the European Community.

For a century and a half, therefore, Spain was shielded from foreign competition by protectionist tariffs. The whole of Spain was for Spanish products, produced in Catalonia in large part. And all of Catalonia, like the other regions, was for Spanish producers. Catalonia's advancement and its Spanish and international reputation were moulded during this period.

Since 1959 Spain as a whole industrialised and it then developed its service sector. The economic weight of Catalonia diminished relatively. The 1975–1985 crisis and that of 2007–2013 were deep ones for Catalonia and the economic restructuring was notable. For this reason, it has been said that the 2007–2013 crisis and the emergence of Catalan separatism are related. In 2019, Catalonia's per capita GDP was below the European Union average, standing at 99.9%. Thus ends a long decline in the Catalan economy, under the assault of separatist defiance.[15]

SUMMARY

- The Black Legend of Spain's enemies feeds into the Catalan separatists' account of things.
- The period of greatest splendour for Catalonia and its economy came after the promulgation of the Nueva Planta Decrees, which opened the market of the whole of Spain to Catalan manufacturers. That market would be maintained, shielded from foreign competition by prohibitions and protectionist tariffs until 1959.
- In terms of demography and GDP, the nineteenth century was a boom period for Catalonia, and this was consolidated and improved upon in the second half of the twentieth century.
- Today Catalonia accounts for 6% of the Spanish population and 22% of all Spanish industry.
- The concentration of the population and economic activity on the coastal strip is a physical and economic characteristic of Catalonia.
- The aging of the Catalan population has been compensated by immigration from third countries.
- Catalonia's industrial specialisation persists but has been significantly reduced over the last decades.

[15] Instituto Nacional de Estadística (2020), "Contabilidad Regional de España", *Notas de Prensa*, 17 December <https://www.ine.es/prensa/cre_2019_2.pdf>.

CHAPTER 6

Degree of Decentralisation in Spain and Powers of the Autonomous Communities

HIGH LEVEL OF DECENTRALISATION

Because of the quality of the powers and the quantity of resources, the political, state and administrative structure of Spain is amongst the most decentralised of the advanced states. Thus, for example, the OECD classifies Spain as a regional country in its statistics "on account of its highly decentralised political structure" and is the only country described in this manner. Spain is included in the group of countries which are federations or semi-federations. With regard to the powers, Spain is the second most decentralised country in the world, only behind Germany, and it has more self-government than Belgium, the United States of America and Switzerland.[1]

With regard to the resources administered, expenditure by the Autonomous Communities represents 49.2% of total Spanish expenditure. Here too decentralisation is greater than in the USA (48.4%), Germany

---

[1] European Commission. Directorate-General for Regional and Urban Policy (2022), *Annual Regional Database* ARDECO <https://knowledge4policy.ec.europa.eu/territorial/ardeco-database_en>; and European Commission. Directorate-General for Regional and Urban Policy (2018), *Final report on updating the Regional Authority Index (RAI) for forty-five countries (2010–2016)* <https://op.europa.eu/en/publication-detail/-/publication/5562196f-3d3a-11e8-b5fe-01aa75ed71a1>

© The Author(s), under exclusive license to Springer Nature Switzerland AG 2022
F. Brunet, *The Economics of Catalan Separatism*,
https://doi.org/10.1007/978-3-031-14451-6_6

(48.1%) or Australia (46.3%).[2] With regard to revenue, the Autonomous Communities' own revenues reach 14.7% of the total, a proportion not far from the USA (19.4%), Germany (23.6%) or Australia (16.9%). The Autonomous Communities employ 55% of Spanish civil servants, town councils and local administrations 24%, and the central administration 21%. [3]

The principle of indivisibility, or of the territorial integrity of states, is included in almost all constitutions.[4] Article 2 of the Spanish Constitution states, "The Constitution is based on the indissoluble unity of the Spanish nation, the common and indivisible country of all Spaniards; it recognises and guarantees the right to autonomy of the nationalities and regions of which it is composed, and the solidarity amongst them all".

Article 4.2 of the Treaty on European Union states that one of the essential functions of the state is to guarantee its territorial integrity. Countries are often established as indivisible (Spain, Norway, Estonia, Brazil, Peru) and even indestructible (USA).

In federal and decentralised states, the powers of the regions are conferred and supervised by constituent and sovereign nation states. To make the supervision of the state over its regions effective, constitutions, especially those of composite and federal states, often include the so-called state, constitutional or federal compulsion or coercion clause. This clause stems from the unity of the state. In the case of Spain, it is Article 155 of the Constitution.[5] It is like similar articles in the constitutions of many other countries.

[2] OECD (2020), *Subnational Governments in OECD Countries: Key Data 2020 edition* <http://www.oecd.org/regional/regional-policy/Subnational-governments-in-OECD-Countries-Key-Data-2020.pdf>
[3] Spain has some of the highest values for the indicators in the Regional Authority Index, which evaluates the power of the regions within states (Gary Marks (2021), *Regional Authority Index* <https://garymarks.web.unc.edu/>).
[4] Constitute Project (2022), *The World's Constitutions* <https://www.constituteproject.org/>
[5] "Article 155. 1. If an Autonomous Community does not fulfil the obligations imposed upon it by the Constitution or other laws, or acts in a way seriously prejudicing the general interests of Spain, the Government, after lodging a complaint with the President of the Autonomous Community and failing to receive satisfaction therefore, may, following approval granted by an absolute majority of the Senate, take the measures necessary in order to compel the latter forcibly to meet said obligations, or in order to protect the above-mentioned general interests. 2. With a view to implementing the measures provided in the foregoing clause, the Government may issue instructions to all the authorities of the Autonomous Communities." <https://app.congreso.es/consti/constitucion/indice/sinopsis/sinopsis.jsp?art=155&tipo=2>

Comparison with Germany

With regard to the powers of the regions and decentralisation, a case in point is the Federal Republic of Germany, given its high level of decentralisation and its similarity to Spain. We shall refer to four aspects with regard to Germany.

A. Constitutional or federal coercion clause. If the relevant article in the Spanish Constitution is Article 155, in Germany's Fundamental Law it is Article 37. [6]

B. Constitutional Court. Like the Spanish Court, that of Germany establishes that the regions do not have the right to secession, self-determination or to organise plebiscites on the issue.[7] In Italy, the Constitutional Court's ruling number 118 of 29 April 2015 established that the region of Veneto could not organise a consultative referendum on the independence of its territory, and neither could it organise a consultation on the expansion of its fiscal autonomy. The Court reiterated that Italy, as stated in Article 5 of its Constitution, is "one and indivisible", such a fundamental characteristic of its Magna Carta that it cannot be subjected to reform.

---

[6] The Basic Law [Constitution] of the German federal republic establishes: "Article 37. Federal execution. (1) If a *Land* fails to comply with its obligations under this Basic Law or other federal laws, the Federal Government, with the consent of the Bundesrat, may take the necessary steps to compel the Land to comply with its duties. (2) For the purpose of implementing such coercive measures, the Federal Government or its representative shall have the right to issue instructions to all *Länder* and their authorities." (Federal Republic of Germany (2022), *Basic Law for the Federal Republic of Germany* <https://www.gesetze-im-internet.de/englisch_gg/englisch_gg.html#p0184>).

Article 126 of the *Constitution* of the Italian Republic establishes, "The Regional Council may be dissolved, and the President of the Executive may be removed with a reasoned decree of the President of the Republic in the case of acts in contrast with the Constitution or grave violations of the law." (Italian Republic (2022), *The Constitution of the Italian Republic* <http://www.prefettura.it/FILES/AllegatiPag/1187/Costituzione_ENG.pdf>).

Articles 100 of the Austrian Constitution, 234 of the Portuguese Constitution, 75 of the Argentinian Constitution, for example, are similar. The United Kingdom, which does not have a written constitution, has suspended the autonomy of Northern Ireland on four occasions.

[7] German Federal Constitutional Court (2016) <https://www.bundesverfassungsgericht.de/SharedDocs/Entscheidungen/DE/2016/12/rk20161216_2bvr034916.html>.

C. Parties. Germany's Basic Law declares parties that endanger the existence of the Federal Republic of Germany, such as the separatists', to be unconstitutional.[8]

D. Financing of the regions: With regard to the revenues of the Länder, the German system is highly levelling, more so than Spain, and since 2005, it has not maintained the ordinality principle which guarantees that the regions that contribute most will not receive less than those regions that receive.[9]

The exercise of federal coercion is not frequent. Here we will mention two examples, the case of the Canary Islands[10] and the case of Ulster.[11]

---

[8] The Basic Law [Constitution] of the German Federal Republic establishes: "Article 21. Political parties [...] Parties that, by reason of their aims or the behaviour of their adherents, seek to undermine or abolish the free democratic basic order or to endanger the existence of the Federal Republic of Germany shall be unconstitutional. The Federal Constitutional Court shall rule on the question of unconstitutionality." (Federal Republic of Germany (2022), *Basic Law for the Federal Republic of Germany* <https://www.gesetze-im-internet.de/englisch_gg/englisch_gg.html#p0184>).

For its part, the Spanish Constitution establishes: "Article 6. Political parties are the expression of political pluralism; they contribute to the formation and expression of the will of the people and are a fundamental instrument for political participation. Their creation and the exercise of their activities are free in so far as they respect the Constitution and the law. Their internal structure and operation must be democratic." <https://www.boe.es/legislacion/documentos/ConstitucionINGLES.pdf>

[9] The Federal Constitutional Court declared as unconstitutional: (1) that the reception of levelling resources be guaranteed without regard to the efforts of every Länd to improve revenue and administration; and (2) that the order of per capita income between the Länder be changed before and after levelling; the principle of ordinality must not be violated. (Angel de la Fuente, Michael Thöne and Christian Kastrop (2016), "Regional Financing in Germany and Spain: Comparative Reform Perspectives", *Fedea Policy Papers*, No. 2016/05.)

[10] In February 1989, the government of the Autonomous Community of the Canary Islands refused to apply a 15% reduction in tariffs on goods from the rest of the European Community which Spain had joined in 1986. The president of the Canary Islands Autonomous Community was willing to ignore community law and maintain the Islands' protectionism unless the Spanish government, led by the prime minister Felipe González, compensated the Canary Islands with 11,000 million pesetas. The Secretary of State for Finance, Josep Borrell Fontelles, warned that if the Canary Islands did not approve the reduction in tariffs, then Article 155 of the Spanish Constitution should be applied. Given the lack of a response from the Canary Islands government, the Council of Ministers issued a prior requirement to its president, urging him to obey the law in order to avoid an intervention of the islands' Autonomy.

[11] Direct Rule which, given that the United Kingdom has no written constitution, is similar to Article 155 of the Spanish Constitution, has been applied in Northern Ireland on four occasions: (1) 11 February to 30 May 2000; (2) 20 August 2001; (3) 22 September 2001; and (4) 14 October 2002 to 7 May 2007. Between 1972 and 2020 the autonomy of Northern Ireland was suspended either partially or totally for 29 years.

DYNAMICS OF THE AUTONOMOUS COMMUNITIES

The process of decentralisation to the regions coincides with the process of European integration and globalisation. This results in a double transfer (of the exercise) of the powers of nation states to the regions (downwards, decentralisation) and of the nation states to the European Union (upwards, integration). Traditional states have therefore undergone a hollowing out.

Citizens do not have a very positive view of the Autonomous Community system and their views have evolved very negatively. In the European Union, the average degree of confidence in regional powers is of the order of 65%. In Spain, 18% of citizens have confidence in the autonomous governments. It is the lowest level of all the European countries. Since 2008, distrust of the autonomous authorities has grown by 32%! That is three times as much as distrust has grown in other European states. It is as if there has been a stampede of confidence from the Autonomous Communities and a dash towards the extremes, be that towards the independence movement or towards the suppression of the Autonomous Communities.[12]

Although it is often suspected that small countries have big governments, and although there is no known formula for determining the optimum size of a country, state decentralisation can lead to efficiency by having measures that 'fit the territory', having better information and through fiscal and regulatory competition between governments. On the other hand, decentralisation can introduce inefficiencies by not taking advantage of economies of scale and through duplication of functions between different levels of the administration.

Decentralisation is expressed through the regions' budgets, powers and employees. Legislators must choose between asymmetry between regions and diversity of powers and symmetry and the uniformity of powers between regions. The Spanish 'model' started with the asymmetry of the regions as put forward by a Statute of Autonomy during the Second Spanish Republic and finished by being the same for everyone, a policy known as 'coffee for everyone', which, in reality was cocaine for everyone such that the main difference now between Navarre, the Basque Country and Catalonia and all the other Autonomous Communities is having their

---

[12] Replies to the question QA12: "Please tell me if you tend to have confidence or not in public regional or local authorities." (European Commission (2014), *Eurobarometer*, No. 709.2.)

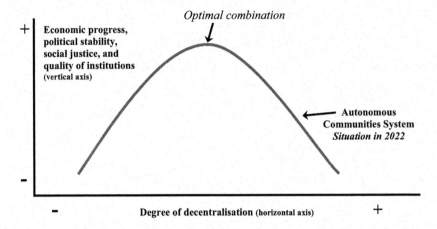

Fig. 6.1 The decentralisation curve: Optimal level of regional autonomy. *Brunet Curve*. (Source: Author's conception)

own police force, and, in the case of the first two regions mentioned, having their own economic agreement.

Thus, for the purposes of analysis, we can plot a decentralisation curve, Laffer style (see Fig. 6.1). There will be an optimum point of decentralisation and autonomy where social progress, economic growth and political stability are maximised. Decentralisation often starts off being virtuous and ends up being catastrophic, as the decentralisation curve suggests. This curve of decentralisation and of the powers within Spain's current Autonomous Communities system is above the optimum point. When the rule of law languishes, centrifugal forces come to the fore, as has been happening in Spain since 2004.[13]

---

[13] The task of decentralising Spain as an autonomous regime ran aground during the Second Republic and precipitated the civil war. That was then, of course, now it is through the Constitution of 1978, and it is a key question for the administration of the state and Spain's being as a country. After the coup of autumn 1934, Agustí Calvet (a. Gaziel, *Tot s'ha perdut*, op. cit., p. 276), remarked lucidly, "Either the introduction of an autonomous regime in Spain was a folly, a ridiculous enterprise, with neither rhyme nor reason, or it was something serious, new, and consequently arduous, difficult".

VALIDITY OF THE RULE OF LAW

The neglect of the rule of law in Spain, at times, in various ways and in important parts of the territory, feeds the longing for a state 'that works' in each Autonomous Community, while also feeding the longing for a state without Autonomous Communities. From an economic point of view, the wastefulness of a system with 17 Autonomous Communities is crystal clear: fragmentation of the market and the multiplication of mini-states. From the political point of view the constitutional disloyalty, the separatist rebellion and institutional chaos in some regions are obvious. From the social point of view, some historical differential rights have come to safeguard the diversity of rights amongst Spaniards and to favour a serious, real disparity between the regions.

It is a widespread belief that centrifugal forces are inseparable from Spain, perhaps because these forces clouded Spain in the nineteenth and part of the twentieth centuries. Are the Autonomous Communities the new taifas that will ruin Spain in the twenty-first century? How are 17 mini parallel states going to manage within Spain? The virtuous and exemplary combination achieved by the Spanish Constitution of 1978 is clearly tottering. The challenge of Catalan separatism—perpetrated for decades *by a regional government*—has been based on unbridled decentralisation and on the debility of Spanish rule of law. After the high political, social and economic cost for the Catalans and for all other Spaniards, in the end, lamentably, this constitutional crisis will brim over into the future of Spain.

SUMMARY

- Like the Spanish Constitution, all constitutions affirm the unity of the state and its territorial integrity, as well as the means of maintaining that integrity.
- Spain, as a state with Autonomous Communities, has, in comparison with federal countries, a very high level of decentralisation in terms of powers, fiscal revenue and public expenditure.
- The ceding of powers from the central government to the Autonomous Communities brings it close to being an empty state.
- Spaniards' confidence in regional and local authorities is the second lowest in the entire European Union: 18%, when the average is 65%.
- In most regions, Spaniards want a less decentralised Autonomous Community system.
- Given the dysfunction caused by centrifugal forces, the Autonomous Community system does not seem to be the optimum one, and it could be incompatible with democracy in Spain.

CHAPTER 7

Urban and Rural Catalonia

THE DISTRICTS

How many Catalonias are there? With the question posed like that, there are at least two:

- Coastal, urban Catalonia, more Spanish speaking, that votes mainly for constitutional parties, and occupying a reduced, high density, part of the territory, with a per capita income higher than the Spanish average and which subsidises Catalonia.
- Rural Catalonia, inland, more Catalan speaking, that votes mainly for separatist parties, and occupying an extensive, low density, part of the territory with a per capita income lower than the Spanish average and which is subsidised by urban Catalonia.

Demographic details are the most indicative of the tendencies of a society. During the period 2000–2019, the increase in the population of Catalonia can be explained by an increase of 1,413,219 Spanish nationals and an increase of 977,837 foreign nationals. Of a total of 42 Catalan districts, 14 have a declining population, including El Barcelonès (-197,794 inhabitants).

If the resident population is considered according to nationality, we can see that the foreign population has compensated for the decrease of the autochthonous population in 14 districts and is accountable for more than

F. Brunet, *The Economics of Catalan Separatism*, https://doi.org/10.1007/978-3-031-14451-6_7

half of the growth of the population in all the other districts of Catalonia. Between 2000 and 2019 there was a very low rate of growth, or negative growth, of the autochthonous population in the districts but there was an increase in the foreign population.[1]

The population of foreign nationals legally resident in Catalonia in 2019 was 15.1% of legal residents. In Spain, it was 10.7%, in Germany 12.8%, in the United Kingdom 9.1%, in Italy 8.5%, in France 7.1% and in the European Union as a whole it was 4.4%.[2] In 2000 the foreign population represented 2.9% of residents in Catalonia, by 2019 the proportion of foreigners had multiplied by 5.

To complete the district demographic perspective, we need to look at the dynamics of per capita income (gross family disposable per capita income) between 2000 and 2017. The balance is catastrophic: in all the districts of Catalonia per capita income has grown less than the Spanish average, and in 33 districts it has grown less than the Catalan average.[3]

TABARNIA

Humour (the little humour some Catalan constitutionalists have left!) dubbed coastal Catalonia as 'Tabarnia' (a word derived from Tarragona and Barcelona) and the interior, seen as an agricultural backwater, as 'Tractoria'. With 5.6 million Catalans, Tabarnia, which comprises Barcelona and Tarragona's coastal strip, accounts for 75% of the Catalan population and creates 81% of Catalan GDP. This coastal strip has a fiscal deficit with respect to inland Catalonia of -13.8% of GDP. (See later in this book.) Catalans resident on the coastal strip, and particularly in the province of Barcelona, might be tempted to say that "Catalonia robs us!" and exclaim, "*The Generalitat robs us!*"

As with other regions, the dualism of Catalonia is not just a present phenomenon, it is also a historical one. Remember the hold Carlism had

[1] Institut d'Estadística de Catalunya (2021), *Anuari estadístic de Catalunya* <https://www.idescat.cat/pub/?id=aec&n=246&lang=es>; and Institut d'Estadística de Catalunya (2022), *Población extranjera por comarcas* <https://www.idescat.cat/poblacioestrangera/?b=4&lang=es>.

[2] Eurostat (2022), *Estadísticas de migración y población migrante* <https://ec.europa.eu/eurostat/statistics-explained/index.php?title=Migration_and_migrant_population_statistics/es>

[3] Institut d'Estadística de Catalunya (2022), *GDP i GDP per habitant* <https://www.idescat.cat/pub/?id=aec&n=358&lang=es>.

on Catalonia.[4] Today's Catalonia, where independence voters constitute a majority, resembles the map of Carlist Catalonia. Catalonia's dualism is socially and economically founded on the activities within the territory. The GDP of the predominantly constitutionalist districts of Catalonia amounts to 195 billion euros. The GDP of the predominantly separatist districts of Catalonia amounts to 45 billion. An industrial and service economy aimed towards the Spanish and global market predominates in this, more open, Catalonia. Inland Catalonia, called 'deep Catalonia' and considered a backwater, has an industrial and agricultural economy predominantly serving the district and Catalan markets.

The unfortunate division of Catalan society, which separatism has provoked, also has a territorial dimension. Those most affected by this confrontation are the Catalans who live inland, whose tendency it is to vote for independence parties, rather than the Catalans who live on the coast.

Inland Catalonia is both the most remote area in Catalonia and where traditional and independence voting tendencies have been strongest and most sustained. Inland Catalonia is also entrenched from the point of view of municipal organisation. Resistance to change during Jordi Pujol's period as president of the Generalitat and those of his successors means that there are still 974 municipalities, of which 603 have a population of less than 2000, and 337 with a population of less than 500, which stands in stark contradiction to all criteria of efficacy and efficiency, but which provides a wide base for 'control of the territory'.[5]

SUMMARY

- Economic activity and three quarters of Catalonia's population are concentrated on the coastal strip.
- Although it has a territorial and economic basis, the current political and social confrontation in Catalonia was tragically exacerbated by separatist propaganda and is the result of their spadework over decades.
- From a being a supposed model of social coexistence, Catalonia has become a place of confrontation, chaos and discomfort.

[4] Jordi Canal (2015), *Historia mínima de Cataluña*, Madrid, Turner.
[5] Lluis Casassas and Joaquim Clusa (1981), *L'organització territorial de Catalunya*, Barcelona, Fundació Jaume Bofill.

CHAPTER 8

Catalonia, Spain, Europe and the World: The Multilevel Governance System

The Place in the Regions of Europe

The European Communities and the European Union (EU) were established to foster peace, understanding between the states, nations and peoples, as well as the freedom and the progress of citizens. European integration has lightened the impact of borders, suppressed interior barriers and facilitated the free movement of citizens, goods, services and capital in accordance with the principle of non-discrimination on account of nationality.

Territorial organisation is an internal question for each state to decide. The borders are somewhat arbitrary. They are frequently established on territories, linguistic communities and formerly integrated families that might be delimited in a somewhat arbitrary way. The regions therefore sit more comfortably in this new Europe without internal borders.

EU integration is a gradual process and there are different rhythms to it. European integration coincides with a historical tendency towards an increase in the division of labour and also in the size of the market. Also, and especially since the end of the division of Europe and the world into two blocks after the collapse of socialism and the Soviet Union in the 1990s, European integration has also coincided with a tendency for the globalisation of economic, social, personal and

© The Author(s), under exclusive license to Springer Nature   47
Switzerland AG 2022
F. Brunet, *The Economics of Catalan Separatism*,
https://doi.org/10.1007/978-3-031-14451-6_8

political relations. That is why, in a single digital world, direct interest in continental or subcontinental integration, such as that of the EU, is different and weaker than in previous periods. Brexit is evidence of this. For different reasons, the United Kingdom's interest in the EU waned after it joined in 1973.

GLOBALISATION, INTEGRATION AND REGIONALISATION

Furthermore, the process of European integration has coincided with the process of decentralisation in many states. Hence the transfer of powers from the member states to the EU and of state powers to their regions. The best example of this transfer of powers to higher and lower levels is Spain. But to varying degrees, it was also the case with Italy and France, as well as Germany and the United Kingdom, and even in the case of other new member states in central and eastern EU.[1]

The processes of integration upwards to a higher entity and decentralisation downwards to a lower one occurs whilst maintaining state sovereignty. For this reason, strictly speaking, state powers are not ceded either to the EU, or to the regions. What is ceded is the exercise of those powers, and conditions apply to that cession of the exercise of powers.

Even for those powers called, or considered to be, exclusive EU powers, or territorial powers, power is maintained by the sovereign state. In the case of the EU, exclusive powers are exercised by community institutions in which power resides, that is, precisely, in the states' governments. In the case of the regions, exclusive powers are exercised by the regional authorities in accordance with national laws and their regional statutes, as ceded by the states and under their supervision.

The triple process of globalisation, EU integration and decentralisation to the regions can give rise to states that are relatively empty. States are the custodians of sovereignty and exercise legislative and decision-making functions. But the implementation of policies is ever more subject to European law, which has primacy over state law, and is increasingly exercised by the regions. This is the case with two pillars of the welfare state, education and health, and sometimes too, the

---

[1] Ferran Brunet (2010), *Curso de Integración Europea*, Madrid, Alianza Editorial, 2ª ed.

police and infrastructure investment. Taken as a whole, these powers frequently account for up to 80% of public expenditure and 40% of GDP. In the new Europe, therefore, the regions are decidedly well positioned.

THE EUROPEAN UNION AND SEPARATISM

The integration of states within a higher community such as the EU tends to lead to a certain disintegration of the states. The tendencies of globalisation and regionalisation,[2] the processes of supranational integration and decentralisation give rise to a multilevel system of governance, in which each tier of the public administration exercises the powers corresponding to it.

In this context, Catalonia's place in Spain, in Europe and the world derives, formally, from being a Spanish Autonomous Community and, materially, from its size and other characteristics. From the point of view of the EU, Catalonia is a region of a member state. In EU statistical terminology, it is a NUTS2, like 280 other regions.

It is often said, and it is true, that the EU is the Europe of the regions, of the *terroir*, of customs, of the small, of the different. But on the other hand, the regional policy of the EU is important for the EU and is very important for the regions. Indeed, the cohesion policy devotes a third of the budget to co-financing investment in infrastructures chosen amongst highly selected EU territories. The EU budget being 1% of the EU GDP, 0.3% of GDP is applied to the regional cohesion policy. This amount corresponds to a tenth of the investments made in infrastructure by the member states.

The EU is opposed to nationalism. Integration is obviously the opposite of separation (disintegration). Given Europe's tragic history—nationalist hatred, national and world wars, genocide—the modification of borders is totally excluded. Numerous member states prohibit separatist, nationalist and xenophobic parties. The EU is a community under the rule of law. Thus, for example, any violation of the law in the form of rebellion or unilateral declaration of independence would, of course, be null and void.

---

[2] A process also known as decentralisation and devolution, amongst other terms.

When an EU institution or representative has been inclined to express an opinion about some nationalist event, or has been specifically asked about the challenge of the Catalan separatists, their position has been absolutely clear:

- It is an internal Spanish affair.
- Absolute confidence in the validity of the Spanish Constitution.
- Reference to Article 4 of the Treaty of Maastricht, "The Union [...] shall respect [the member states'] essential State functions, including ensuring the territorial integrity of the State, maintaining law and order, and safeguarding national security".
- In the event of a hypothetical secession being consumed, it being the Kingdom of Spain that is signatory to the Treaties and the eventual successor state, an eventual Catalan state would automatically find itself outside the EU.
- The right to self-determination is afforded to colonies and territories where there was a violation of human rights,[3] something which is obviously not the case with Catalonia or any other region or part of the EU.

Identical sentiments are to be found in the multiple oral and written declarations of the presidents of the Council of the European Union, the European Commission and the European Parliament as well as other representatives of the EU.[4]

Economic Analysis of Disintegration

In the economic analysis, we can distinguish between the economy of separatism and the economy of separation. The former concerns the motives and economic arguments of the independence movements and the latter concerns the fact of secession and its economic consequences.

---

[3] On the ambiguity of the use of the term 'self-determination' in separatist propaganda see Elena Llorca-Asensi, Alexander Sánchez Díaz, Maria-Elena Fabregat-Cabrera and Raúl Ruiz-Callado (2021), "'Why Can't We?' Disinformation and Right to Self-Determination. The Catalan Conflict on Twitter", *Social Sciences*, No. 10: 383. <https://doi.org/10.3390/socsci10100383>.

[4] El Confidencial Digital (2018), "Las 22 veces que Europa ha dicho 'no' a la independencia de Cataluña", 1st March marzo <https://www.elconfidencialdigital.com/articulo/politica/veces-Europa-dicho-independencia-Cataluna/20180228190710088609.html>.

The economic analysis of secession (separation, independence, exci-sion, fragmentation, split, break up, disintegration) is the negative oppo-site of the economic analysis of integration. Integration implies gains, disintegration implies losses. There are four key aspects to the analysis of (dis)integration:

- The effects of the political, linguistic, cultural, regulatory, fiscal, monetary and commercial borders.
- Trade between areas that integrate/disintegrate. Borders have an effect on trade: the existence of borders, the suppression of borders and the imposition of new borders. To what extent do national bor-ders affect trade?[5] Integration encourages and increases trade, disin-tegration limits and reduces it.[6]
- The resulting size of the market and also of the states: what might be the ideal size for nations, countries and states, of the political econ-omy, of regulation, of monetary areas? What is the match between the characteristics of the economy and the preferences of the leaders or voters and the territorial scope of the state and its powers?[7]
- The quality of the institutions of the resulting states and their relations.[8]

An abstract and empirical analysis of integration gives globalisation the first best position, a world economy without borders and with one, sole smart regulation; thus, sub-continental integration (such as the EU) occu-pies second best position. The economic analysis of integration/

[5] J. F. Helliwell (1998), *How Much do National Borders Matter?* Washington, D.C., Brookings.

[6] Jan Fidrmuc and Jarko Fidrmuc (2000), "Disintegration and Trade", *Review of International Economics*, Vol.11, n.5, pp. 811–829.

[7] The economic analysis of the formation and fragmentation of countries, as well as their number and size, follows the model of Alesina and Spolaore (Alberto Alesina and Enrico Spolaore (1997), "On the Number and Size of Nations", *The Quarterly Journal of Economics*, Vol. 112, No. 4, pp. 1027–1056; Alberto Alesina, Enrico Spolaore and Romain Wacziarg (2000), "Economic Integration and Political Disintegration", *American Economic Review*, Vol. 90, No. 5, pp. 1276–1296; and Alberto Alesina and Enrico Spolaore (2003), *The size of nations*, Cambridge, MA, MIT University Press (v. cat.: *La mida de les nacions*, Barcelona, Lid Editorial, 2008).

[8] Daron Acemoglu and James A. Robinson (2012), *Why Nations Fail: The Origins of Power, Prosperity, and Poverty*, London, Profile Books.

disintegration postulates a cost/benefit for integration/disintegration and quantifies its various economic impacts. It is a question of balancing the benefits of being part of a big country, with the costs of greater heterogeneity.[9]

THE SECESSION OF STATES

Numerous attempts at secession have precipitated a civil war, the most well-known case being that of the USA. [10] Hence another aspect considered in the literature about secession is the ethical basis for secession.[11] Is there, or can there be, a right to secession for regions of advanced, democratic countries similar to the right to self-determination of colonies and oppressed peoples?[12] Could secession, if not an original right, be an obtained right and the remedy for a conflict? A remedial or emancipatory secession comes close to the separatists' grandiloquent prose on conquered sovereignty.

The fragmentation of the state and the subsequent secession of one or more of its parts would be a way of confronting statism. From fragmentation would come fiscal competition, which would be positive for reducing the tendency of states towards giantism. This hypothesis has been shown historically. Instead of Asia, the continent that emerged in modern history was Europe, with its revolutions in knowledge and industrialisation. This difference is due to the fragmentation of Europe and the centralisation of

[9] Thierry Madiès, Grégoire Rota-Grasiozi, Jean-Pierre Tranchant and Cyril Trépier (2018), "The economics of secession: A review of legal, theoretical, and empirical aspects", *Swiss Journal of Economics and Statistics*, Vol. 154, n.1, pp. 142–154 <https://doi.org/10.1186/s41937-017-0015-6>; and Michele Ruta (2005), "Economic theories of political (dis)integration", *Journal of Economic Surveys*, Vol. 19, No. 1, pp. 1–21.

[10] For all the analyses of the American War of Secession, see the summary of the [US] Council for Economic Education (2020), *The South's Decision to Secede: A Violation of Self Interest?* <https://www.econedlink.org/resources/the-souths-decision-to-secede-a-violation-of-self-interest/>

[11] Carlos Closa (2020), "A Critique of the theory of democratic secession", in C. Closa, C. Margiotta and G. Martinico (eds), *Between democracy and law. The amorality of secession*, London, Routledge.

[12] Allen Buchanan (1997), "Theories of Secession", *Philosophy and Public Affairs*, Vol. 26, No. 1, pp. 31–61; and James M. Buchanan and Roger L. Faith (1987), "Secession and the limits of taxation. Toward a theory of internal exit", *American Economic Review*, Vol. 77, No. 5, pp. 1023–1031.

Asia. It has also be seen in contemporary history that small states tend to have big state structures.

The hypothesis concerning the advantages of fragmentation is well illustrated in the case of California.[13] If it were independent, it would not be able to apply the fiscal licenses it currently permits itself. Without the backing it has by forming part of the USA, California would have to behave in a more restrained fiscal manner.

Other consequences of secession, also fiscal ones and of the first order, should be considered to conclude this argument about the advantages of secession for fiscal responsibility. In point of fact, the secession of California would lead to a decline in trade with the rest of the USA,[14] a consequent reduction in its GDP and level of employment, as well as a reduction in the tax revenues derived from them.

A HYPOTHETICAL SECESSION OF CATALONIA FROM THE EU

Applying this argument to the case of an 'independent' Catalonia, the new state would have to stop playing the fool, as it does at the moment, being bailed out by the Spanish Finance Ministry. But together with this qualitative 'benefit' of secession which would assist in applying orthodox policies comes the curse of secession: the cost of secession would be a reduction in trade, of the GDP, in employment and the disappearance of the fiscal deficit (that is to say, what was supposed to be a 'fiscal benefit' of the separation).

- Finally, let us consider secession from the EU. There is complete juridical clarity about it and about the concept.
- In the event of a supposed secession of a part of a member state of the EU, the successor state is the one that signed the treaties.
- The treaties are not applicable to the new state.

[13] Daniel J. Mitchell (2016), "Secession, Federalism, and National Comity", *International Liberty*, 17 November <https://danieljmitchell.wordpress.com/2016/11/17/secession-federalism-and-national-comity-plus-more-intentional-and-unintentional-election--related-humor/>
[14] If there were a fiscal deficit, which in turn would be a fiscal benefit of the hypothetical secession, then, with less trade, this would be reduced until it disappeared. After secession there would be less trade, less GDP, less employment, less fiscal revenue and the benefits of belonging to a larger fiscal union would disappear.

- The new state is automatically out of the EU and of all its structures, policies and measures and, of course, the customs union and the monetary union.
- In the new state neither the law of the successor state, nor primary law, nor law derived from the EU would be valid.

In contrast with this complete juridical clarity and clarity of concept, separatists fantasise about an 'internal expansion', a hypothetical expansion of the EU with new states resulting from secession from member states. Such a supposed expansion would not follow the procedures established in the Treaties for a state to join, something that requires the unanimous approval of all the member states in accepting the new state.[15]

In this kind of discussion there is often a kind of synthesis solution. For example: the independence of a region being neither viable nor convenient, but given that secessionist spirits are very high, regional autonomy might be a solution, either in a manner closely resembling a federation or as an asymmetric, or selective, federalism for certain regions of a state. The autonomy of the regions brings tendencies together and this is an arrangement that might produce efficient decentralisation. But of course, this politically correct solution raises a question: would the autonomy of the regions calm the independence movement or propel it? The way the Catalan case has evolved has made the autonomous solution less attractive.

Summary

- The triple process of globalisation (with world relations and international cooperation), integration (with the exercise of state powers by the EU) and decentralisation (with the exercise of state powers by the regions) tends to lead to a multilevel system of governance.
- Territorial and regional questions are an internal affair for the member states of the EU, which exercise full sovereignty to maintain territorial integrity, guarantee the application of national and European law and ensure non-discrimination and equal treatment for their citizens.

---

[15] Roland Vaubel (2013), "Secession in the European Union", *Economic Affairs*, Vol. 33, No. 3 <https://doi.org/0.1111/ecaf.12028>

- In a manner opposite to the economy of integration, the economy of secession analyses the consequences on trade, and the other remaining aspects within the sequence of consequences, resulting from the fragmentation of a country and its smaller size. Decentralisation, with autonomy and federalisation, is a way of accommodating disparate tendencies such as globalisation and universality and territorialisation and proximity.

CHAPTER 9

Integration and Disintegration: Secession of the European Regions?

THE EUROPEAN MOSAIC

In the new Europe, tendencies and movements have appeared that accentuate particularities and which make diversity a question of difference. Transferring the material and cultural diversity of the different places throughout the geography and history of Europe to contemporary politics is something that introduces considerable instability to a political system based on the intangibility of borders, European integration and globalisation.

From this point of view, Europe is made up of a mosaic of territories and languages.[1] Between six and seven thousand languages are spoken in the world today, although six of them are the native tongue of half of the world's population. In Europe there are 255 languages.[2] If a language is a nation and that nation requires a state… well, if that were ever to become true, the number of languages would multiply quickly, and Europe would have many 'nations' without statehood!

In the Europe of languages and with an 'excess' of history, there are places where separatism is more active. In a context in which politics is

---

[1] TD (2022), *Independence Day* <http://td-architects.eu/projects/show/independence-day/img-2577>.

[2] UNESCO (2022). *Atlas of the World's Languages in Danger* <http://www.unesco.org/languages-atlas/index.php>

more attuned to identity[3] than to economic or ideological questions, the currents of anti-globalisation take root in centrifugal movements of a separatist nature that fragment Europe.[4]

Regions with Separatist Movements

Amongst the regions where the fires, or hot embers, of secessionism are burning, or smouldering, the most outstanding are Catalonia, Scotland, Flanders, Veneto and South Tirol, as well as other provinces in the Po Valley and the north of Italy grouped together under the neologism Padania.[5] Flanders and Padania are like Catalonia insofar as their per capita income is greater than that of the rest of the country of which they form part.[6] Scottish secessionism has the following unique characteristics: (a) it was an independent state until 1707 when, with the Act of Union it unified with England to form the United Kingdom; (b) the independence referendum legally convened by the government in London, in which the 'no' vote won;[7] and (c) the referendum on the withdrawal of the United Kingdom from the EU in which Scotland voted to remain, which would have meant that, if the rest of the United Kingdom had voted likewise, Scotland would still be in the EU (Table 9.1).

[3] Francis Fukuyama (2018), *Identity: Contemporary Identity Politics and the Struggle for Recognition*, London, Profile Books.

[4] Marlene Wind (2020), *The Tribalization of Europe: A Defence of our Liberal Values*, London, Polity Press. There are three aspects to the fragmentation of Europe: separatism, Brexit and the tussle with the rule of law of various governments of eastern members of the EU. What they have in common is populism.

[5] Deutsche Bank Research (2015), "Better off on their own? Economic aspects of regional autonomy and independence movements in Europe", *EU Monitor. European Integration*, 6 February <https://www.dbresearch.com/prod/rps_en-prod/prod0000000000441775/better_off_on_their_own%3f_economic_aspects_of_regio.pdf>.

[6] Anon. (2014), "Separatism in Europe (1)—Characteristics of separatist movements", *[Library of the Council of the European Union] Library Note*, 12 February.

[7] See the series of studies by the UK government with reference to the Scottish referendum campaign. UK Government. The Secretary of State for Scotland (n.d.), *Collection Scotland Analysis* <https://assets.publishing.service.gov.uk/government/uploads/system/uploads/attachment_data/file/321369/2902216_ScotlandAnalysis_Summary_acc2.pdf>.

Table 9.1 Some European regions with secessionist movements: some indicators

State		Spain		Italy		Belgium	United Kingdom
Region		Catalonia	Basque Country	Bolzano	Veneto	Flanders	Scotland
Population, M		7.6	2.2	0.5	4.9	6.6	5.4
Population, in % of that of its State		16.2	4.7	0.8	8.1	57.6	8.1
GDP, M €		236,814	68,817	25,736	155,515	259,786	183,749
GDP, in % of that of its State		18.8	5.9	1.3	9.0	59.2	7.9
GDP per capita, €/year		32,000	35,300	43,400	32,300	35,900	29,300
GDP per capita, EU = 100		110	121	149	111	123	98
Unemployment, in % of active population		10.9	10.0	3.8	6.4	3.5	3.6
Region's public expenditure, in % of that of its State		49.2		28.9		49.8	24.2

Source: Author's calculations based on data from Eurostat (2022), *Database* <https://ec.europa.eu/eurostat/data/database>; and Statista (2022), *Database* <https://www.statista.com/markets/>.

There are also significant similarities between the cases of Barcelona and Catalonia and that of Montréal and Québec. Both cities were economic motors of the states to which they belong and both regions have a differential linguistic element with respect to the rest of the country, Catalan and French, respectively. Both cities also hosted the Olympic Games,[8] the greatest sporting and media event in the world, and in both cases, there has been a long confrontation and a severe economic, social, political and cultural decline. Let us remind ourselves now of some of the historical conclusions drawn from Québec's long experiment with secessionism: [9]

---

[8] Although in very dissimilar circumstances and with opposite results (a huge flop in Montreal 1970 and a huge success in Barcelona 1992). See Ferran Brunet (1994), *Economics of Barcelona 1992 Olympic Games*, Lausanne, International Olympic Committee.

[9] Robert A. Young (1994), "The political economy of secession: The case of Quebec", *Constitutional Political Economy*, Vol. 5, No. 2, pp. 221–245; and Stéphane Dion (n.d.), *Straight Talk: Speeches and Writings on Canadian Unity*, Montreal, Quebec, McGill-Queen's University Press, 2000.

- There is no right to self-determination there either.
- Given the case, separation must be discussed with the government of Canada and the other Canadian provinces.
- The residents of Québec opposed to separation have the right to remain in Canada.

Similar conclusions could obviously be made in a hypothetical secession of Catalonia. Although those European societies in which separatism is brewing are open societies in which, within the law, constitutional changes of importance are possible, secession in the European regions (frequently associated with secession movements arising in large, but not capital cities) goes against the historical tendency towards stability, understanding, respect, progress and equality of treatment.

Summary

- Fragmentation is a historical problem in Europe. It is responsible for many of the most serious events in its contemporary history, precisely those which the EU overcame and which, it is intended, it will continue to overcome.
- A Europe of 281 NUTS2 (or 50 or 100) that were sovereign states with the power of veto in the EU would make little sense and has scant chance of happening.

CHAPTER 10

Challenge, Labyrinth, Mirage, Enigma, Ghost, Fantasy, Illusion, Utopia, Nonsense, Madness, Stagnation, Malaise, Fever, Cancer, Lawsuit, Accident, Slip, Catastrophe, Crisis, Bonfire, Soufflé, Misfortune, Tragedy, Drama, Comedy, Farce, Trap, Twenty-first Century or Postmodern or Liquid Coup d'état, Revolt, Rebellion, Adventure, Problem, Question, Syndrome… (Separatist) Coup

ANALYSIS OF THE CATALAN QUESTION

The banality of the destruction of Catalonia, the stupidity of the demolition of Spain is extremely surprising, worrying, intriguing and deeply painful. Hence the million-euro question: what is Catalan separatism? Why did this secessionist phenomenon come about? How could it grow so quickly? What are the consequences of it and what will the future consequences be? In this book we consider some of these pressing questions, especially with regard to the economy. The title of this chapter brings together some of the terms used to describe the Catalan separatist syndrome.

© The Author(s), under exclusive license to Springer Nature Switzerland AG 2022
F. Brunet, *The Economics of Catalan Separatism*,
https://doi.org/10.1007/978-3-031-14451-6_10

It is from this perspective that some analyses by foreign commentators should be seen.

Thomas Piketty is the author of the celebrated, *Capital in the 21st century* (2013). On 14 November 2017, in the midst of the separatist coup d'état, he published an article in Le Monde about the Catalan syndrome. The article then became a chapter of his book *Capital and Ideology*.[1] The Catalan syndrome is founded on the elite's fiscal egotism. In a world where liberalism has unleashed ferocious competition, the territories compete for fiscal advantages. This could be what lies behind the Catalan syndrome, despite—I would say—the fiscal hell installed by the Generalitat. (See later in this book.)

In the words of the Pulitzer Prize winner, Georges F. Will "The Catalan secessionists ladle a soup of fiction and paranoia [...] Under the elegant surface of this brilliant Mediterranean metropolis boil the passions generated by the Spanish version of identity politics. Demagogues who hope to destroy a nation arouse these passions. Agitation in Catalonia [...] is the price paid for the lies used to invent complaints".[2] And as the Nobel laureate for Economics, Eric Maskin, has commented "There are more benefits in planning secession than achieving it."[3]

THE NATURE OF CATALAN SEPARATISM

Is the Catalan independence movement twenty-first-century nationalist populism?[4] It would seem to be a combination of late nationalism, fiscal egotism, foreign enemy, ethnic hatred, xenophobia, supremacism,

---

[1] Thomas Piketty (2017), "Le syndrome catalan", *Le Monde*, 14 November <https://www.lemonde.fr/blog/piketty/2017/11/14/le-syndrome-catalan/>. This article became a chapter in Thomas Piketty's book (2020), *Capital and Ideology*, Cambridge, MA, Harvard UP.

[2] George F. Will (2020), "Catalan secessionists ladle a soup of fiction and paranoia", *The Washington Post*, 24 January <https://www.washingtonpost.com/opinions/catalan-secessionists-ladle-a-soup-of-fiction-and-paranoia/2020/01/23/b5e62280-3e0a-11ea-baca-eb7ace0a3455_story.html>.

[3] Eric Maskin (2015), "Plantear una secesión da más beneficios que conseguirla", in "La Contra", *La Vanguardia*, 19 February.

[4] Nationalism is an ideology of identity creation. The new Catalan nationalism is a populist movement, it is a populism of separation, it does not share the liberal definition of democracy, it has a limited concept of the Catalan people and has divided society and degraded the institutions. (See Ángel Rivero (2020), "The new Catalan nationalism", *Przegląd Narodowościowy/ Review of Nationalities*, No. 10/2020, special on "A new wave of separatism in the world", <http://reviewofnationalities.com/index.php/RON/article/view/189/207>.)

classism, extractive elites… What motivates the independence rebellion? Do its roots lie in Catalonia's discrimination by the rest of Spain, in its exploitation as a colony, in contempt for the Catalan language and customs or supposed Catalan character? It really does not seem so, on the contrary, it's exactly the opposite.

There is a high level of political energy in contemporary societies, and politics looms large in people's consciousness. As well the traditional role of the press as critic and advocate of good government since the mid-twentieth century, the mass media, and, for the last decade, the Internet and social networks without doubt encourage transparency and participation, but they accentuate the debates and differences and exaggerate the capacity of politics. The new politics takes the form of a spectacle and is based more on identity and confrontation than on moral values, political orientation or economic positions and interests. Populism launches the people against democracy.

Contemporary populism is strengthened by the breadth, scope and immediacy of the Internet and its loud hailer, the social networks. Online radicalisation is a fact and it is a growing problem. Being story based, politics becomes the invention of better worlds so that people's expectations are raised, which are then dashed because they are, of course, impossible to achieve. That is why one of the skills of today's citizens, and not an insignificant one, is the ability, in this period of (dis)information, to distinguish travesty from reality.

In this context, Catalan separatism has had all the elements it needs to come to fruition as a serious social confrontation and a profound challenge to the state and rule of law and democracy. It has brought together all the fragmentary elements and it has been able to count on all the media. For decades, a regional government and the Catalan independence movement have been entirely free and have gone unpunished in the face of the law, by central government and the courts. And now it is time to harvest this long separatist challenge, and the harvest is as evil as the seed that was sown.

Who was it that stoked the Catalan independence movement? The government of the Generalitat and a large part of Barcelona's intellectual and business elite were the instigators of separatism from which was unyoked a broad separatist, proselytising clergy to officiate at the altar of separatism. The time is long gone when it was said that Catalonia did not have a state, but it had a civil society. That was engulfed by Generalitat subsidies, and it either fled along with its companies or succumbed. Bien-pensant society was in communion with three separatist constructs: 'political conflict', the new 'fiscal framework' and the 'right to decide'. Piketty's analysis, mentioned in the previous chapter, forms part of this perspective. Like Piketty, many people maintain that the reason for the independence movement is the fiscal interest of the bourgeoisie.[5]

Coinciding with these analyses are those of the extractive elite. [6] The Catalan elite has been undone, its exponents' credit is nil and it will be a long and difficult process to reconstitute its social role.[7] Without doubt, in many countries, and Spain amongst them, there is a considerable problem regarding the choice of leaders.[8]

---

[5] "In rich regions the independence movements are nothing more than the bourgeoisie's mask of secession as they attempt to leave the national frameworks (in which they have to exercise solidarity). [...] The Catalan example illustrates the fever of a bourgeoisie willing to do anything in order to abandon the common good." (Christophe Guilluy (2018), *No society. La fin de la classe moyenne occidentale*, París, Flammarion. The same judgement is in Laurent Davezies (2015), *Le nouvel égoisme territorial. Le gran malaise des nations*, Paris, Seuil.)

[6] Benito Arruñada and Victor Lapuente Giné (2015), "Las peligrosas ilusiones de Cataluña", *Project Syndicate*, 23 septiembre <https://www.project-syndicate.org/commentary/Cataluña-independence-election-by-benito-arrunada-and-victor-lapuente-gine-2015-09/spanish?barrier=accesspaylog>

See Acemoglu (2017), "La Contra. Entrevista con Lluís Amiguet", *La Vanguardia*, 26 June <https://www.lavanguardia.com/lacontra/20170626/423699679648/la-corrupcion-es-la-ultima-herencia-del-franquismo.html>. More broadly, on the quality of the institutions, see Daron Acemoglu and James A. Robinson (2012), *Why Nations Fail: The Origins of Power, Prosperity, and Poverty*, London, Profile Books; and Daron Acemoglu and James A. Robinson (2019), *The Narrow Corridor: States, Societies, and the Fate of Liberty*, London Penguin.

[7] José Luis Oller (2019), "Cataluña hace tiempo que no tiene clase dirigente", *Crónica Global*, 15 December <https://cronicaglobal.elespanol.com/pensamiento/conversaciones-sobre-cataluna/oller-arino-cataluna-no-clase-dirigente_300833_102.html>; Manuel Pérez (2022), *La burguesía catalana. Retrato de la élite que perdió la partida*, Barcelona, Ediciones Península; and Miquel Macià and Pep Martí (2022), *Els que manen: Vida i miracles de les 50 famílies que mouen els fils de Catalunya*, Barcelona, Edicions Saldonar.

[8] Highly relevant in this regard are the analyses of María Elvira Roca Barea (2019), *Fracasología: España y sus élites: de los afrancesados a nuestros días. Premio Espasa 2019*, Madrid, Espasa.)

SOCIAL ENGINEERING AND PSYCHOSOCIOLOGY

Is what has happened Catalonia over the last decades the result of a task in social engineering?[9] One carried out by a regional government, almost unopposed and with the forbearance of the governments of Spain that should ensure the rights of Catalans in accordance with the Spanish Constitution?

There is an initial document that constitutes a benchmark in this process, *La estrategia de recatalanización* (the strategy of re-'Catalanisation').[10] Basically, for Convergència i Unió, the question was to infiltrate every corner of Catalan civil society and remake it. Mission accomplished. Totally accomplished. With the results we know: social confrontation, political chaos,[11] economic decline, the fragmentation of Catalonia and a separatist caste forevermore at the expense of the public purse.

There are many astonishing aspects to the pro-independence *process*. Some of them leave you baffled. The speed with which the separatist fire spread is astonishing. It is amazing how conservative-voting rural areas became areas voting for revolutionary independence. It is astonishing that Barcelona's business and intellectual elite should let themselves be carried away by all this. Having seen that secession is impossible, the fact that most supporters of separatism are so slow in recognising reality is exasperating. They have their heads in the clouds, they will not come down to earth. It also seems peculiar that, more than coming up with a narrative adapted to the new, post-coup situation, the main aspect of political dialectics is the confrontation between Junts per Catalunya and ERC, basically about who occupies which position. Their business is obviously not in independence, but in the *process*.

Those in favour of independence seem to be completely impermeable to common sense and to narratives different from their own. They probably have no interest or stimulus—other than their own mental health—in mourning and burying their false expectations. The actions of more

---

[9] On linguistic engineering, toponymy and onomastics vid. Jesús Laínz (2011), *Desde Santurce a Bizancio: El poder nacionalizador de las palabras*, Madrid, Encuentro.

[10] Anon. (1990), "La estrategia de la recatalanización ['Programa 2000']", *El Periódico de Cataluña*, 28 October <http://www.tolerancia.org/updocs/ElPeriodico_Programa2000_CiU_1990.pdf>. <http://archivo.elperiodico.com/ed/19901028/pag_026.html>.

[11] Josep Maria Oller and Albert Satorra (2017), "Toward an Index of Political Toxicity", *Boletín de Estadística e Investigación Operativa*, No. 33, pp. 163–182 <http://www.seio.es/bbeio/beiovol33num2/index.html#86>.

outlandish personages are less surprising. Indeed, with regard to this, the Assemblea Nacional Catalana provides "a psychological health service for those affected by the repression. Freephone: 93 347 17 14 extension 1036".[12]

SEPARATIST REGIME AND *PENSÉE UNIQUE*

Do separatists suffer from an illness? Or are they impassioned and besotted? This requires analysis. The psychosociological diagnosis of the group behaviour of Catalan separatists would seem to be collective delirium. Collective paranoia and obsessive, compulsive mass delirium are characterised by fixed, obsessive and absurd ideas based on fantasised or unfounded facts. Paranoia affects a well-preserved individual without the loss of consciousness and without hallucinations. This syndrome is activated by forming part of a group. Like blind obstinacy, these symptoms are those of totalitarianism.

There is also a bandwagon effect, being dragged along, fashion, jumping on the winning bandwagon, joining a long queue without really knowing what for. People do and believe certain things based on what other people do and believe, and that gives them strength and legitimacy in the face of any act considered awful or reprehensible. It is also identified with gregarious behaviour when people tend to follow the crowd, letting themselves be influenced by an idea floating around without examining its merits, known as cognitive dissonance.[13] We can say, with regard to the magnitude of cognitive dissonance, that 6.1% of Catalans assert that the 'independence process' has benefitted Catalonia and that 12.5% say it has improved Catalonia's image.

To overcome the cognitive division between separatists and constitutionalists and thereby close the cognitive breach between some and others, a shared reality must appear based on empirical facts. This would require (a bit of) information and (a lot) of persuasion. It is said that communication should be meticulous, not menacing, and that it should be focussed on people with the aim, not of saying that they are wrong but of influencing the way they see the problem.

---

[12] <https://twitter.com/assemblea/status/1186297179490734081>

[13] Ricard Cayuela (2019), «L'únic objectiu dels instigadors del procés era escripturar la finca», El Triangle, 7 December <https://www.eltriangle.eu/ca/entrevistes/lunic-objectiu-instigadors-proces-escripturar-finca_104387_102.html>.

After the coup of autumn 2017, the failure of the independence movement has not led to any catharsis or mourning that would help recognise reality. Separatist faith resembles that of some religions, and the faith displayed in sects even more so. These sectarian elements permeate the *pensée unique* which prevails in the official, independence-minded Catalonia. Hence the intense violence of autumn 2019 and during the winter of 2021 in false flag disturbances intended to make any progress in reconciliation impossible.

The loss of 641,000 separatist votes between the 2017 and 2021 Catalan elections represents an important element of the independence movement's process of facing reality and coming down to earth. 641,000 Catalans more stopped believing in the *process*.

With its spokespeople, its media, its large public finances and all kinds of subsidies for its supporters, there is a separatist regional political regime that functions like a tyrannical mini-state.

Summary

- The Catalan question is intriguing. It has led to important analyses on account of the depth of confrontation and the combination of elements.
- The risk to Europe of contagion by the Catalan separatist virus is limited on account of the effectiveness of the governments of most European countries.
- Catalan separatism has combined all kinds of elements and arguments that has resulted in a very potent concoction.
- In the separatist potpourri, fiscal egotism is no minor element. To be effective, it has to cover itself with contempt, hatred and, finally, violence.
- A task of social engineering carried out by a regional government has given rise to a totalitarian separatist regime in which *pensée unique* prevails and dissidents oppressed.
- Remaking Catalonia, rebuilding Catalan civil society after this destruction, will be a long task.

CHAPTER 11

The Separatist Regime: Propaganda, Neo-Language, Post-Truth, Alternative Facts, Fake News, Disinformation, Social Networks, Populism and Falsification of the Past, Present and Future

> *You can fool some of the people all of the time,*
> *and all of the people some of the time,*
> *but you cannot fool all of the people all of the time.*
> —Abraham Lincoln

Regime and Propaganda

In this digital age, truth is considered to be relative, changing and malleable. In the end, the truth, and the correspondence of words with the facts is of very little importance in contemporary politics, which is based on mass media, videos, Internet, and social media, which determine both citizens' opinions and their vote. What is important is belief.

In contemporary politics, like in novels and cinema, what is important is not the truth but verisimilitude, the appearance of being possible and consistent. The recreation of the discourse or narrative is essential for forming a political community and for its mobilisation. [1]

---

[1] George Orwell (1938), *Homage to Catalonia*, London, Penguin, 2000; and George Orwell (1949), *1984*, London, Collins, 2021.

Propaganda has been the basis of politics since universal suffrage and the advent of mass media. In order to establish a new regime, it is essential to create a narrative and a specific neo-language or jargon. It is the narrative and the neo-language that give form to the ideas and create followers and devotees. This is what happened with communism, fascism and Nazism.[2] And this is what happens in contemporary tyrannies and autocracies.

In tyrannical regimes, words and language are manipulated and perverted to justify ignominy, in criminal regimes to cover up horror. In dictatorships and autocracies, and even in some electoral democracies, there is great manipulation of language. The mass media, even independent and quality media, and much more so the social media, participate in the fluidity in the use of terminology.[3]

Every political regime based on difference and confrontation, on the creation of an exterior enemy and an enemy within, generates its own narrative and neo-language. Lies and fear are the primordial instruments of all totalitarian governments.[4] Politically correct language is the current expression of the way words, and the mass media, are manipulated with a totalitarian intent.[5]

In the case of Catalan separatism, the evolution of political emotions has been gradual,[6] although it went at a very accelerated rate to the coup of 2017. For fifteen years, the merry-go-round of propaganda and slogans has been spectacular, each one more striking than the last. And it does not stop!

---

[2] Victor Klemperer (1947), *Language of the Third Reich: LTI: Lingua Tertii Imperii*, London, Bloomsbury, 2013.

[3] In this respect the reader will appreciate the effort made in these pages to use words suitably. This we must do with terms such as Catalonia, Spain (Catalonia included) and the rest of Spain. We must also be careful to use nationalist terms precisely: sovereigntist, secessionist, separatist, and the ambiguous adjective, Catalanist. We also need to be watchful with various combinations of words such as secessionist challenge, separatist confrontation, attempted secessionist coup d'état, central administration or government of the state.

[4] Hannah Arendt (1951), *The Origins of Totalitarianism*, London, Penguin, 2017.

[5] Josep Maria Bricall (2022), "Una mirada llarga sobre el 'procés'", *Política & prosa*, No. 42 <https://politicaprosa.com/el-tipus-dinteres-compost/>.

[6] Darío Villanueva (2021), *Morderse la lengua: Corrección política y posverdad*, Madrid, Espasa.

The classical dictum being true that the first victim of war is truth, and all wars are based on deception, in the war generated by the separatists against Spanish democracy, and against the majority of Catalans, the creation of lies has been an exuberant industry. An industry fuelled by all kinds of subsidy and protected by the intimidation of those who persist in the truth, and even of those who maintain a critical distance, as would be consistent with journalism. In this regard, the blatant use of public media, the vassalage of the private media and the persecution of all those who do not glorify the separatists cries out to heaven.

As well as what *Le Monde's* correspondent in Spain, Sandrine Morel, has to say,[7] let us look at what Reporters Without Borders (RWB) say in their report *Respect for media in Catalonia*, "The report describes the constant pressure of the separatist Catalan government on local and foreign media, the harassment of critical journalists by the separatist movement's hooligans on social media, the attempts by crowds of demonstrators to intimidate TV reporters and the generally poisonous climate for the freedom of the press. The report includes some of the many interviews RWB had with Catalan, Spanish and foreign journalists who had been victims of harassment on social media by sympathisers of the Catalan government. The pressure applied to the media opposed to independence and the hostility they encounter on social media is striking".[8]

The separatist leaders set out their case with their own economic jargon. All of which shows the ideological use of the economy. Then they believed their own lies and could not, did not know how, did not want or did not need to stop maintaining them. The aim of separatist lies is to trivialise the real damage already done by the separatist challenge and the damage a hypothetical excision of Catalonia from the rest of Spain would

[7] Sandrine Morel (2018), *En el huracán catalán. Una mirada privilegiada al laberinto del procés,* Barcelona, Planeta.
[8] Reporters Without Borders (2017), *Respect for media in Catalonia* <https://rsf.org/en/news/rsf-publishes-report-respect-media-catalonia>.

cause.[9] They are masters of confusion. That is why they muddy the troubled waters with twisted language, such are the separatists' gains and those of revolutionary professionals. Inversely, clarity and truth reduce those gains.[10] They disappear like demons blinded by the light.[11]

Rather than looking for information, what people are often looking for with their Internet searches and on social media is confirmation of their own opinions. The interest in the truth has consequently become a secondary concern. The Generalitat de Catalunya has not deprived itself of anything in its separatist defiance. An infinite amount of propaganda in the traditional media and in the new ones such as the social networks, Instagram, Facebook, Twitter, Google, bots, fake news and alternative

---

[9] For a refutation of secessionist post-truth see: Anon. (n.d.), *Mitos y falsedades del separatismo catalán* <http://statics.ccma.cat/multimedia/pdf/6/2/1508933378226.pdf>; and Xavier Vidal-Folch and José Ignacio Torreblanca (2017), "Mitos y falsedades del independentismo", *El País*, 24 September <https://elpais.com/politica/2017/09/24/actualidad/1506244170_596874.html>.

For his part, Fernando Savater, says "[…] Separatism is not a political opinion or a romantic dream, such as nationalism might be, but a deliberate, calculated and coordinated aggression against democratically valid institutions and against the citizens who feel them as their own. It is not a delirium of greater or lesser intensity, but an all-out attack on the most important part of our assurance of citizenship, the rule of law. With some patience and a sense of humour it is possible to get along, for better or worse, with nationalists, but with separatists there is no remedy possible other than to oblige them to renounce their goals. There is something especially evil about separatism, even from a mythical and religious perspective. The Devil is, etymologically the separator, *diabolus*, who separates and breaks the established ties. The diabolical undertaking is the quintessential anti-humanist wrongdoing, separating those who live together and obliging them to detest each other, to move away, sowing discord, breaking hearts. It is so unfortunate that so many separatisms, large and small, find fertile ground in Spain, to the point where any regional symbol, if possible, an excluding one, is seen as something liberating and progressive by the dim-witted left and their like: it proves that we have a country with all kinds of demons". (Fernando Savater (2017), *Contra el separatismo*, Barcelona, Ariel.)

[10] As shown in the case of Quebec and Canada: Stéphane Dion (n.d.), *Straight Talk: Speeches and Writings on Canadian Unity*, Montreal, Quebec, McGill-Queen's University Press, 2000.

[11] On the use of Catalan expressions and clichés in independence slogans, see Ignacio Vidal-Folch (2015), "Cómo escribir un artículo", *El País*, 18 July. On the corruption of language as a consequence of moral corruption, see Salvador Oliva (2017), "Corrupció del llenguatge", *El País*, 8 December <https://cat.elpais.com/cat/2017/12/08/cultura/1512735074_256284.html>.

facts.[12] Perhaps these are the weapons of contemporary warfare, hybrid, or liquid. Whatever the case, they manage to stir people up against democracy. A good example of how separatist defiance of the rule of law operates is what they call Catalangate. It concerns the legally-authorised cell phone tapping of separatist leaders by the Centro Nacional de Inteligencia (CNI), Spain's official intelligence agency, with the use of Pegasus software. The separatists' international propaganda campaign had been in preparation for a number of years and was triggered on 18 April 2022 when a report by Citizen Lab,[13] taken up by The New Yorker,[14] was made public. It seems normal for an intelligence agency to legally spy on coup-plotting activists.[15] The scope of this campaign was international and it served the separatists insofar as the prime minister, Pedro Sánchez, who governs thanks to the votes of separatists and communists, allowed both groups to participate in the Parliamentary Official Secrets Commission, whose responsibility it is to control the CNI.[16]

---

[12] "'An independent Catalonia would recognise Crimea as Russian'. This was the first fake news about Catalonia to emerge from the Kremlin's great interference machine. It is an outstanding example of disinformation: the source responsible for uttering the phrase was not an official and was merely expressing an opinion, but Russian state media and their allies turned it into a dramatic headline with enormous implications for political life on the continent of Europe and its allies. And, above all, in a narrative in line with Moscow's interests: more independence movements in Europe, and greater legitimacy for the annexation of territories by Russia." (David Alandete (2019), Fake news: la nueva arma de destrucción masiva. Cómo se utilizan las noticias falsas y los hechos alternativos para desestabilizar la democracia, Barcelona, Planeta; e Idem (2017), "La maquinaria de injerencias rusa penetra la crisis catalana. La red global que actuó con Trump y el Brexit se dedica ahora a España", El País, 25 September.)
With regard to the mutual recognition of Crimea by an eventually independent Catalonia and of an independent Catalonia by Russia, see Marc Marginedas (2020): "Rússia, Catalunya i el 'procés', una història que es repeteix", Política i Prosa, 10 March <https://www.politicaprosa.com/russia-catalunya-i-el-proces-una-historia-que-es-repeteix/>.

[13] John Scott-Railton, Elies Campo, Bill Marczak, Bahr Abdul Razzak, Siena Anstis, Gözde Böcü, Salvatore Solimano, and Ron Deibert (2022), "CatalanGate. Extensive Mercenary Spyware Operation against Catalans Using Pegasus and Candiru", CitizenLab Report, 18 April <https://citizenlab.ca/2022/04/catalangate-extensive-mercenary-spyware-operation--against-catalans-using-pegasus-candiru/>. Elies Campo is a well-known secessionist activist.

[14] Ronan Farrow (2022), "How Democracies Spy on their Citizens", The New Yorker, Issue April 25 and May 2 <https://www.newyorker.com/magazine/2022/04/25/how-democracies-spy-on-their-citizens>

[15] José Javier Olivas Osuna (2022), "'CatalanGate': escándalo útil, investigación teledirigida", El Mundo, 29 April <https://www.almendron.com/tribuna/catalangate-escandalo-util-investigacion-teledirigida/>.

[16] Editorial (2022), "'Catalangate', un montaje propagandístico preparado hasta el mínimo detalle desde hace meses", El Triangle, 22 April <https://www.eltriangle.eu/es/2022/04/22/catalangate-un-montaje-propagandistico-preparado-hasta-el-minimo-detalle-desde-hace-meses/>

The relationship between the Catalan separatists and the government of Russia was and is real. To start off with, it was propaganda, then it was flirtatious, later on, it turned into specific relations that included wild promises. The relationship was clear long before, during and after the coup d'état of autumn 2017 and consists of:

- Hybrid warfare, diplomatic support, the work of hackers and in social media by Russia.[17]
- Meetings with pro-Russian political parties and parliamentarians from various European countries.
- A meeting between the president of the Generalitat, in his official office, with envoys of President Vladimir Putin.
- Visits by envoys of the president of the Generalitat to the Russian government and visits by envoys of the government of Russia to Catalonia.[18]
- In the event of independence, the sending of 10,000 Russian troops to Catalonia along with $500,000 million (!).[19]

THE INDEPENDENCE MOVEMENT'S NARRATIVE

The post-truth of the separatist *process* has been produced by a large intellectual (sic) apparatus and disseminated through a large propaganda apparatus, as we shall now see:

A. Producing apparatus

- Generalitat Department of Economy and Finance.
- National Transition Advisory Council.

[17] European Parliament (2022), *Report on foreign interference in all democratic processes in the European Union, including disinformation* (2020/2268(INI)) <https://www.europarl.europa.eu/doceo/document/A-9-2022-0022_EN.html>; and European Parliament (2022), *Debates on the Council and Commission statements. 18. The relations of the Russian government and diplomatic network with parties of extremist, populist, anti-European and certain other European political parties in the context of the war* <https://www.europarl.europa.eu/doceo/document/CRE-9-2022-07-06_EN.html#creitem30>.

[18] Laura Fàbregas and Alberto Sierra (2022), "Junqueras y otros líderes de ERC se reunieron con una 'agente rusa' tras recibir los indultos", *The Objective*, 23 March <https://theobjective.com/espana/2022-03-23/junqueras-erc-agente-rusa-eurocamara/>.

[19] Antonio Baquero, Kevin G. Hall, Alina Tsogoeva, Jesús G. Albalat, Christo Grozev, Lorenzo Bagnoli, IStories and Stefano Vergine (2022), "Fueling Secession, Promising Bitcoins: How a Russian Operator Urged Catalonian Leaders to Break With Madrid", Organized Crime and Corruption Reporting Project <https://www.occrp.org/en/investigations/fueling-secession-promising-bitcoins-how-a-russian-operator-urged-catalonian-leaders-to-break-with-madrid>.

- College of Economists of Catalonia, captured by separatists.
- Col.lectiu Wilson (Pol Antràs, Carles Boix, Jordi Galí, Gerard Padró i Miquel, Xavier Sala i Martin and Jaume Ventura).[20]
- Assemblea Nacional Catalana (ANC).[21]
- Omnium Cultural.[22]
- Separatist business associations: FemCat, Secot and, finally, the Chamber of Commerce, Industry and Navigation of Barcelona.
- A hundred offshoots of the previously mentioned such as Economists for Independence, Catalan Business Centre, etc.

B. Disseminating apparatus[23]

- TV3 and other subsidised public service media, representing 85% of the output in Catalonia. In terms of time to have their say in the political 'debate' organised by these media, the separatist organisations receive this proportion of time: TV3, 92% of total time; Catalunya Ràdio, 94%; TVE Catalunya, 72%; RAC1, 87%. The remaining time, that is to say between 6 and 28%, is the time given to constitutional entities (which represent 52.6 of Catalan voters).[24]

[20] See the 12,234 people "subscribed " to the Col.lectiu Wilson ((2022), *Llista d'adherits* <http://www.wilson.cat/ca/component/chronoforms?chronoform=list_data>.)

[21] Assemblea Nacional Catalana. Sectorial d'Economia (2015), *Impacte de la independència en l'empresa. La visió de l' ANC* <http://economistes.assemblea.cat/wp/wp-content/uploads/2015/05/5.1-doem.-complet-v1.00-dossier-impacte-de-la-independencia-en-lempresa-11052015.pdf>.

[22] On the decline of Catalan culture, particularly written culture, particularly in Catalan, see Jordi Amat (2018), *Largo proceso, amargo sueño. Cultura y política en la Cataluña contemporánea*, Barcelona, Tusquets.

[23] "[…] The use of marketing techniques applied to political philosophy has given rise to an identity populism that is difficult to counter. A tactical plan that has enabled a moderate nationalism become a new ethno-populism, or identity populism, with an uncompromising final aim: the independence of Catalonia." (David Álvaro García (2019), *Cataluña, la construcción de un relato: ¿Cómo se ha servido el independentismo del populismo identitario para convencer a la mitad de la población catalana de las virtudes de la independencia?* Barcelona, Planeta.)

[24] Consell de l'Audiovisual de Catalunya (2020), *Informe 71/2020. Observança del pluralisme polític a la televisió i a la ràdio. Maig-desembre 2019* <https://www.cac.cat/sites/default/files/2020-05/Acord_43_2020_ca.pdf.pdf>, p. 27.

- Private media: press, magazines, radio and television; the independent media have had an uncertain time.[25]
- Semi-governmental organisations such as the Catalan Association of Municipalities, Omnium Cultural, the ANC and their derivatives.
- Internet, social media and instant messaging *urbi et orbi*.

Many Catalans live in a counterfactual virtual reality from which they do not know when or how they will return.[26] Within separatist propaganda, special mention should be made of the so-called 'route maps' and the milestone of the 'referendum'. These are lists of the political aims of

[25] Subsidies to public and private media sympathetic to the separatist regime amount to €400 million per year. (Dolça Catalunya (2018), "La Generalitat compra a 533 medios de comunicación con al menos 310.000.000 € al año", 14 January <https://www.dolcacatalunya.com/2018/01/la-generalitat-compra-533-medios-comunicacion-al-menos-310-000-000e-al-ano/>.).

[26] On the changes to the cultural and political atmosphere in Barcelona due to the propagation of nationalism, see Federico Jiménez Losantos (2019), *Barcelona. La ciudad que fue: La libertad y la cultura que el nacionalismo destruyó*, Madrid, La esfera de los libros, 2ª ed. ampliada; Ramón de España (2013), *El manicomio catalán*, Madrid, La esfera de los libros; Joaquim Coll and Daniel Fernández (2010), *A favor d'Espanya i del catalanisme. Un assaig contra la regressió política*, Barcelona, Edhasa; Antonio Robles (2013), *Historia de la resistencia al nacionalismo en Cataluña*, Barcelona, Crónica Global; Juan Francisco Arza Mondelo and Joaquim Coll i Amargós (2014), *Cataluña. El mito de la secesión. Desmontando las falacias del soberanismo*, Córdoba, Almuzara; Pau Guix, (2017), *El hijo de la africana: Reflexiones de un catalán libre de nacionalismo*, Barcelona, Hildy; and Ernesto Martí Wetzel (2020), *La demencia catalana. El hundimiento de un país en 62 entradas, 2011–2020* <https://www.amazon.es/demencia-catalana-hundimiento-entradas-2011-2019-ebook/dp/B07N6FQ27S>; and Miriam Tey, Sergio Fidalgo, Juan Pablo Cardenal, and Pablo Planas (2021), *El libro negro del nacionalismo. La ideología totalitaria que ha conducido Cataluña al desastre*, Barcelona, Ediciones Deusto.

the Catalan separatists. Some of the many independence route maps[27] could be listed according to their final aim (independence), medium term aims ('economic agreement', 'referendum', 'negotiation, 'dialogue') and immediate aims (elections).

REFERENDUM

In this context the instrument most mentioned by Catalan separatists is a self-determination referendum. The term 'self-determination' is understood as being synonymous with secession, independence and the formation of a new state. A hypothetical self-determination for Catalonia has no juridical basis whatsoever either under Spanish or international law. Whether they be binding or consultative, in Spain referendums require the authorisation of the Cortes Generales (Spanish Parliament). Whatever the case, they must be held throughout the entire Spanish territory and be voted by the Spanish people as a whole.

A self-determination referendum for Catalonia consequently clashes head-on with the political system. That is why the separatists demand it.

---

[27] In the form of:

- Agendas (J. G. Albalat (2017), "Una agenda detalla la hoja de ruta del separatismo. La Guardia Civil intervino en el domicilio de Josep Maria Jové unas anotaciones claves sobre el plan soberanista", *El Periódico*, 11 December <https://www.elperiodico.com/es/politica/20171211/guardia-civil-halla-agenda-hoja-de-ruta-soberanismo-papel-de-los-principales-politicos-catalanes-6488665>).
- In Parliament (Artur Mas i Gavarró (2012), "Debat sobre l'orientació política general del Govern", *Diari de Sessions del Parlament de Catalunya*, Serie P, No. 67, 25 September <https://www.parlament.cat/document/dspcp/57786.pdf>).
- Web sites (Assemblea Nacional Catalana (2016), *Full de ruta 2016–2017* https://assemblea.cat/documentos/).
- Official publications (Generalitat de Catalunya. Consell Assessor per a la Transició Nacional (2014), *Llibre blanc de la Transició Nacional de Catalunya* <https://presidencia.gencat.cat/ca/ambits_d_actuacio/desenvolupament_autogovern/comissionat-de-la-presidencia-per-al-desplegament-de-lautogovern/llibre-blanc-de-la-transicio-nacional-de-catalunya/>). (Ver Víctor Porras and Santiago López (2015), "El proceso hacia la independencia según el CATN: una lectura crítica, I, II and III", <http://finestradoportunitat.com/catnlecturacriticaparteuno/>.)
- Many books (for all of them see Alfons Durán-Pich and Joaquim Torra i Pla (2012), *Catalunya, a la independència per la butxaca*, Barcelona, El fil d'Ariadna).
- To complete the agenda on their route map (to the coup) the separatists hardly required secrecy. The secessionist parties and leaders set out what they would do in great detail, they did it, and after their trial and sentencing, said they would do it again.

For that reason and because, as separatists—and terrorists—say, "We only need to be lucky once. They need to be lucky all the time". That is to say, terrorism tries and tries and at some time will achieve its specific criminal result. Even if it fails it will nevertheless succeed in terrorising. Separatism demands a referendum as if it were a right (a supposed and false one). Until it is held there is opportunity for separatists to sound off against democracy and the rule of law. If the pro-sovereignty movement were able to hold a referendum and win it, that would be that, no more referendums. If it were to lose, it would continue to call for another referendum as many times as it lost until it won one, and then the result would be irreversible.

The demand for a referendum, the campaign for a referendum and the result of the referendum constitute a very effective technique for social and political confrontation; it divides society into two. A plebiscitary referendum is the electoral technique preferred by dictators who, already in power, win them with 99% of the vote.[28] Finally, the profoundly sectarian, toxic, paranoid and despicable character of separatism continued to be seen during the first six months of 2020. The COVID-19 pandemic unleashed some despicable initiatives and some extremely lacerating words.

On 6 January 2021, supporters of President Donald Trump assaulted the Capitol Building during the confirmation of Joe Biden as winner of the election. Trump's putsch came as less surprising to the Catalans and all other Spaniards. We have a long and continued experience of coup-plotters and attacks on the rule of law!

In Catalonia we have had 40 years of dealing with separatists. We endured the full coup d'état they gave us in the autumn of 2017. We have had decades of great commotion, of hatred, of supremacism, decades indeed of what President Trump did. In these times of populism, everyone has fanatics in power. Here they were Artur Mas, Carles Puigdement, Quim Torra... Catalonia cannot, of course, be compared to the USA. Nevertheless, in spite of the colossal differences, when it comes to populism, the similarities between one case and the other are extraordinary.

---

[28] With regard to the impact of the 'referendum' of 1 October 2017, and of the referendum in general, see, respectively, Cercle d'Economia (2017), "Tras el 1-O. Para evitar los peores escenarios", Barcelona, 4 octubre <https://cercledeconomia.com/es/tras-el-1-o-para-evitar-los-peores-escenarios/>; and Col.lectiu Treva i Pau (2020), "¿Referéndum? No, gracias", *La Vanguardia*, 20 March. Both outstanding articles are compiled in Observatori Econòmic de Catalunya (ed.) (2021), *Consecuencias económicas del separatismo. 50 + 1 artículos*, Barcelona, OEC.

For all that, it is worth saying that the case of Catalonia, relatively speaking, is much worse than the case of the USA. In Catalonia (and in Spain), the assault on the state and the rule of law has been much more systematic, deeper and more complete than in the USA and other western countries. The process of wearing down democracy is also proving to be much longer. What is more, the separatists here continue their activities, and they will do it again!

Summary

- The repetition of separatist's mantras (right to decide, we want to vote, 'Spain robs us', freedom for the political prisoners) disseminated by the communication system and by the Catalan administration has proved very effective.
- The narrative for the independence rebellion keeps changing. It never stops. Like a hamster's treadmill and the theory of the bicycle, the passenger is the engine. After the separatist coup of autumn 2017, independence has disappeared from the discourse, which has now turned to a supposed democratic deficit in Spain and a virtual Catalan republic. In this reading, Spain would be a retrograde Francoist monarchy and the secessionists desirous of a true republic and democracy.
- The case of Catalan separatism provides convincing proof that when really implemented, 'ideas have consequences': the fragmentation of Catalonia and the disintegration Spain.
- In spite of the colossal differences between the USA and Catalonia, populism, which permeated separatism as much as Trumpism, gave rise to an incredible amount of convergence between these two processes. And it is worth saying that the case of Catalonia is, relatively speaking, much worse: it is 40 years in the making and, unlike in the States, the Catalan separatists would do it again.

CHAPTER 12

Language and Indoctrination in the Schoolroom

Look at them, look at them, they are full of the mud of propaganda.
They think they have invented and thought what has been stuffed into
their skulls. Within a few years, when the 'sense of history' has turned
around, their skulls will be full of the mud of another propaganda.
—Eugene Ionesco

EDUCATION, NOT IN THE MOTHER TONGUE, ONLY IN CATALAN

The Generalitat's 'education' policy sidelines the mother tongue of more than half of the schoolchildren in Catalonia, it violates the truth in the curriculums for history, geography and literature and is profoundly antisocial. The separatist Generalitat's educational policy practices what is known as 'linguistic immersion', which is to say, monolingual education in Catalan. This is contrary to children's rights to education in their mother tongue, it contradicts the real bilingualism of the Catalans, it contradicts the co-official status of Spanish and Catalan, and it contradicts numerous court rulings.

In particular, linguistic immersion only in Catalan is essentially discriminatory against more than half of Catalan children whose mother tongue is Spanish, and it is radically antisocial. Over the last years of severe confrontation, the schools of the Generalitat have become madrasas for independence, contrary to the rights of the children and those of their parents,

© The Author(s), under exclusive license to Springer Nature
Switzerland AG 2022
F. Brunet, *The Economics of Catalan Separatism*,
https://doi.org/10.1007/978-3-031-14451-6_12

as well as those teachers who believe in the applicability of the rule of law also in the schoolrooms of Catalonia.

This 'educational' policy serves the separatist cause and generates academic failure. Consider the results of the OECD PIRLS tests in Fig. 12.1. Spanish-speaking children have a 30% failure rate, for Catalan-speaking children it is 17.5%. The average failure rate in Catalonia is 23.7%. In Madrid it is 9.4% and is similar in other regions of Spain. There is, without doubt, a very serious problem. If we add indoctrination to linguistic and social discrimination,[1] we can understand the social and political function of the Generalitat schools. One language, one country.

As well as in academic failure, discrimination and the perverse effects of monolingual immersion in Catalan can also be seen when considering students' performance in specific subjects such as mathematics, the

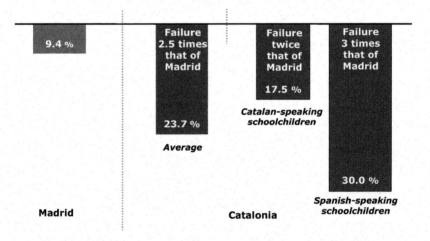

Fig. 12.1   The results of 'linguistic immersion': academic failure of Spanish- and Catalan-speaking schoolchildren in Catalonia. (Dropout rate/Source: Convivencia Cívica Catalana (2019), *Análisis de la PIRLS 2016 en Cataluña* <https://files. convivenciacivica.org/Analisisin%20dein%20losin%20resultadosin%20dein%20 PIRLSin%202016.pdf> on data from *PIRLS 2016 International Database* <https://timssandpirls.bc.edu/pirls2016/international-database/index.html>)

[1] Jesús Rul Gargallo (2019), *Nacionalismo catalán y adoctrinamiento escolar. Estrategia y práctica de control social and modelaje conductual*, Salamanca, Amarante.

sciences and reading. The performance of Spanish-speaking students is very much worse.[2]

The field of education exemplifies what has happened, and what is happening, in Catalonia, what the separatist challenge is, why and how it came about, and the consequences it has. The Autonomous Communities have transferred powers in education. The Spanish Constitution and the Statute of Autonomy of Catalonia establish that Spanish (also called Castilian) and Catalan are the co-official languages in Catalonia (in addition to Aranese, related to Occitan, spoken in a valley in the Pyrenees with a Catalan population of 10,372). The mother tongue of 55.1% of Catalans is Spanish; Catalan is the mother tongue of 31%, and other languages account for 13.9%.

Since the beginning of the transition to democracy, the Generalitat has imposed monolingual immersion in Catalan in the primary and secondary education under its control, as well as in private education that receives public subsidies. Spanish was relegated to the status of a foreign language to which three hours a week are devoted. It is worth pointing out that the governing classes in Catalonia send their children to private schools which do not practice monolingual education in Catalan, but have education in Spanish, Catalan and English, and/or German and French.

Given the blindness of the Catalan administration, the parents of school children were obliged to appeal individually before the courts to insist that Spanish too would be a language of instruction in Catalonia. Finally, in December 2020 the High Court of Justice of Catalonia determined[3] that education must be given, for a minimum of 25% of teaching hours, in each of the two official languages of Catalonia. This court decision invalidates the monolingual immersion in Catalan imposed for decades by the governments of the Generalitat on the pretext that the Catalan language was

[2] Ministerio de Educación y Formación Profesional (2022), *Resultados TIMSS de matemáticas y de ciencias, 2019* <https://www.educacionyfp.gob.es/inee/evaluaciones-internacionales/timss/timss-2019.html>; and Jorge Calero and Álvaro Choi (2019), *Efectos de la inmersión lingüística sobre el alumnado castellanoparlante en Cataluña,* Madrid, Fundación Europea Sociedad y Educación <https://www.sociedadyeducacion.org/site/wp-content/uploads/SE-Inmersion-Cataluna.pdf>.
[3] Tribunal Superior de Justícia de Catalunya. Sala Contenciosa Administrativa. Secció Cinquena (2020), *Sentència Núm. 5201/2020* <https://www.poderjudicial.es/cgpj/es/Poder-Judicial/Tribunales-Superiores-de-Justicia/TSJ-Cataluna/Noticias-Judiciales-TSJ-Cataluna/El-TSJC-obliga-a-un-minimo-del-25%2D%2Dde-ensenanza-en-castellano-dentro-del-sistema-educativo-de-Catalunya>.

in danger of extinction. Readers of this book already know the dire consequences of this monolingual immersion policy (see Fig. 12.1). As with other court decisions, this was ignored by the Generalitat, which then started a legal battle. Finally, in November 2021 the Supreme Court of Spain[4] confirmed this ruling and ordered its implementation within a maximum of two months. At the moment of writing (June 2022), this court ruling has still not been implemented and the Generalitat asserts that it will not do so. An indication of the extent of the rule of law in Catalonia.

FINES FOR SHOPS WHOSE SIGNAGE IS NOT IN CATALAN

Equally flagrant is the infringement of the law and, with regard to commercial signage, the rights of consumers and shop owners. In Barcelona, the Spanish language is used by 60% of citizens, but only 16% of signage is in Spanish (either Spanish alone or Spanish in combination with Catalan). In a linguistic situation that is much more confrontational than that of Catalonia, in Brussels, French is used by 69% of the population and commercial signage in French is 57% of the total.[5]

The Generalitat takes proceedings against, and fines, those establishments whose signage is not in Catalan. Forty-two per cent of the sanctions affect the hospitality sector, 21% the retail trade[6] and 6% transport. Neither, on the other hand, is the law observed with regard to road signage. At this stage of separatist absurdity and of the destruction of Catalonia, this could

---

[4] Tribunal Supremo. Sala de lo Contencioso Administrativo. Sección Primera Providencia (2021), *R. Casación 1676/2021* <https://www.poderjudicial.es/cgpj/es/Poder-Judicial/Tribunales-Superiores-de-Justicia/TSJ-Cataluna/Noticias-Judiciales-TSJ-Cataluna/El-Tribunal-Supremo-inadmite-el-recurso-de-la-Generalitat-sobre-el-25%2D%2Dde-castellano-en-las-escuelas-de-Cataluna>.

[5] Convivencia Cívica Catalana (2019), *Las lenguas de los comercios en Cataluña* <http://files.convivenciacivica.org/Las%20lenguas%20en%20los%20comercios%20de%20Catalu%C3%B1a.pdf>; y Convivencia Cívica Catalana (2018), *Las lenguas en las señales de tráfico en Cataluña* <http://files.convivenciacivica.org/Campa%C3%B1a%20por%20una%20se%C3%B1alizaci%C3%B3n%20biling%C3%BCe.pdf>.

[6] The separatists' stubbornness with the retail trade has been extraordinary. Language, days and hours of opening, permission to open and special taxes for large stores have all been the object of legal and political battles. With regard to the consequences of this obsession, see Autoritat Catalana de la Competència (2012), *Efectes del caràcter restrictiu de la normativa comercial sobre la competitivitat de l'economia catalana* <http://acco.gencat.cat/web/.content/80_acco/documents/arxius/actuacions/estudi_comerc_cat.pdf>.

perhaps be considered insignificant. Nevertheless, bilingualism is a key aspect of Catalonia's being and that of the Catalans. In contrast with this, only 5.2% of road signage is—as the law stipulates—in both of Catalonia's official languages, which are used equally by Catalans (well, Spanish slightly more than Catalan). 94.2% of road signage is only in Catalan while 0.7% is only in Spanish.

In spite of Spanish being an official language like Catalan, the Generalitat has banished the use of Spanish in the public administration of Catalonia. Spanish has been expelled from public life. In the Generalitat, the provincial councils, the town councils and in the many services and public bodies of Catalonia, everything is published in Catalan only, except the fines and taxes, which are published in both official languages to avoid any challenge to them or their nullity and non-payment.

And when you reach home, TV3 completes the linguistic and ideological indoctrination received in the schoolroom, while out shopping, on the bus, at the health centre and in the street. TV3 is essential for the separatist confrontation: 75.3% of those who get their 'information' from TV3 vote separatist; only 28.0% of those who get their information elsewhere vote separatist.[7]

SUMMARY

- Catalonia suffers from a nationalist regime guided by flagrant lies, contempt for Spain and a lack of respect for more than half of all Catalans. It is a regime sustained by indoctrination in the schools, in the media and in public life.
- The antisocial character of the secessionist Generalitat can be seen in the striking results of exclusion resulting from its 'education' policy: Spanish-speaking children have twice (!) the academic failure rate as Catalan-speaking children, and triple (!) the rate of those in Madrid.

---

[7] Societat Civil Catalana. Observatori Electoral de Catalunya (2017), *La Cataluña inmune al "procés". El referéndum: una falsa salida* <https://www.societatcivilcatalana.cat/sites/default/files/docs/La-Cataluna-inmune-vf.pdf>.

CHAPTER 13

Structure of the Separatist Narrative

If you can't convince them, confuse them.
—Harry S. Truman

THE SEPARATIST ARGUMENT

What can explain secessionism in advanced countries? An academic analysis of secessionist discourse provides us with very relevant keys to understanding and for reflection.[1] Four semi-structured questionnaires were carried out with people from the ages of 18 to 34 who identified as: middle class, university graduates, from Catalan families, Catalan speaking, very interested in politics, voters for ERC or CUP, and who considered themselves to be 'only Catalan' and who watched the news programmes on TV3.

The separatist consciousness displayed in the interviews was codified into: identity arguments, economic arguments, positive arguments and perceptions about all things Catalan and negative arguments and perceptions about all things Spanish. The arguments were structured as follows:

---

[1] Marc Collado-Ramírez (2016), *L'estructura del discurs independentista: una proposta d'anàlisi mitjançant la metodologia de xarxes,* end of degree project in Political Science and Public Administration, Facultat de Ciències Polítiques i Sociologia, Universitat Autònoma de Barcelona <https://ddd.uab.cat/pub/tfg/2016/163110/TFG_mcolladoramirez.pdf>.

87

- Identity arguments

  - Defence of Catalan culture
  - Language
  - Question of Catalans with Spanish identity who are not interested in politics
  - Being Catalan
  - Supporting independence on account of family or social influence
  - Own values/differential fact of being Catalan

- Economic arguments

  - Fiscal deficit/unfair distribution
  - Infrastructure administration
  - Bad economic management by the Spanish government
  - Lack of powers/the need for state structures
  - Economic stifling of Catalonia by the Spanish government
  - Economic viability of an independent Catalonia

- Institutional arguments/politicians/civic bodies in favour of Catalonia

  - Catalonia = political change
  - Confidence in institutions/government of Catalonia
  - Independence is left wing/to carry out social policies
  - Independence to make a more democratic state
  - Independence as not nationalism
  - Independence to decide everything
  - Catalonia's political system is different
  - Cross-section nature of the independence movement

- Institutional arguments/politicians/civic bodies opposed to Spain

  - Spanish government actions against Catalonia

- Character of Spaniards
- Centralism of Madrid
- Commentaries against Catalonia/Catalan phobia/anti-Catalanism of Spanish politicians
- Corruption
- Disconnection with respect to Spain
- Spaniards don't understand us
- Fatigue due to non-fulfilment by the Government
- Spain = no political change
- Being made Spanish
- Spanish media (coarse, vulgar TV/manipulation)
- Spanish nationalism
- Outdated Spanish political system
- Spanish-imposed uniformity

The secessionist narrative can be considered as a network of collective mental states. To find the structure of the narrative the various arguments were integrated and the relationships between them observed. From the qualitative and quantitative analysis of the interviews, it can be deduced that the most quoted and most central arguments in this network are the institutional arguments politicians/civic bodies in favour of/opposed to Catalonia, most important amongst which are the negative aspects of Spain and Spaniards and especially the actions of the Spanish government, perceived as attacks or aggressions against Catalonia.

Arguments concerning identity are channelled through references to the Catalan language. The explicit mention of Catalan identity as an argument for independence appears much less frequently in the discourse.

The institutional arguments/politicians/civic bodies in favour of Catalonia express confidence in the powers of the state being better administered by a Catalan state, and that independence is a way of implementing more social policies and of being able to decide everything.

The economic arguments in favour of independence have a secondary presence. The ones most alluded to are: 27% fiscal deficit/unfair distribution, 23% infrastructure administration, 19% lack of powers/the need for state structure, 15% bad economic management by the Spanish government, 6% economic stifling of Catalonia by the Spanish government and 10% the economic viability of an independent Catalonia. Other, different, analyses confirm the non-essential place of economic arguments for separatists.[2]

[2] J. Sorens (2005), "The Cross-Sectional Determinants of Secessionism in Advanced Democracies", *Comparative Political* Studies, No. 38, pp. 304–326 <https://doi. org/10.1177/0010414004272538>; Juan Manuel Sánchez Cartas (2015), *Herramientas económicas y secesión. Un enfoque heurístico para el caso catalán,* end of master project in Applied Economic Analysis, Universidad de Alcalá de Henares, 1st July <https://www. researchgate.net/publication/312811462_Herramientas_Economicas_y_Secesion_Un_ enfoque_heuristico_al_caso_catalan>; Jordi Muñoz and Raül Tormos (2015), "Economic expectations and support for secession in Catalonia: between causality and rationalization", *European Political Science Review,* Vol. 7, No. 2, pp. 315–341 <https://doi.org/10.1017/ S1755773914000174>; Juan Claudio de Ramón Jacob-Ernst (2018), *Diccionario de lugares comunes sobre Cataluña. Breviario de tópicos, recetas fallidas e ideas que no funcionan para resolver la crisis catalana,* Barcelona, Deusto; Josep María Oller, Albert Satorra and Adolf Tobeña (2019), "Secessionists vs. Unionists in Catalonia: Mood, Emotional Profiles and Beliefs about Secession. Perspectives in Two Confronted Communities", *Psychology,* Vol. 10, No. 3, pp. 336–357 <https://doi.org/10.4236/psych.2019.103024>; Josep María Oller, Albert Satorra and Adolf Tobeña (2019), "Evolución y legados de la aventura secesionista en Cataluña: fronteras lingüísticas, influencia delos 'media' e estratos económicos en una sociedad dividida", *Policy Network,* 14 October, <https://docplayer.es/168238376-Evolucion-y-legados-de-la-aventura-secesionista-en-cataluna.html>; Josep María Oller, Albert Satorra and Adolf Tobeña (2020), "Privileged Rebels: A Longitudinal Analysis of Distinctive Economic Traits of Catalonian Secessionism", *Genealogy,* Vol. 4, No. 1 <https://doi. org/10.3390/genealogy4010019>; and Adolf Tobeña (2021), *Fragmented Catalonia. Divisive legacies of a push for secession,* London, Policy Network.

THE SEPARATIST CYCLE

Would the separatist challenge form part of a cycle? Would it have a dynamic in which, after emergence and climax would come stagnation and decline?[3] As with the separatist narrative, an academic study provides us with a relevant analysis of the process of pro-independence Catalans.

Two different phases can be discerned in the dynamics of the secessionist process, "One in which the independence movement emerges from below and from the left, and another in which it becomes a mass movement, directed by the elite but with unprecedented mobilisation. The main leap forward for the independence movement occurred between 2011–2012, three years after the start of the crisis about the Statute. [...] The modification by the Constitutional Court of Catalonia's Statute of Autonomy, which had been voted for in Congress and in a referendum, generated a political and institutional crisis that provoked the collective indignation of a large part of Catalan society. The independence movement emerged in the streets, was later commanded by the elite, and led to a government agreement, reaching the institutions of the political system."[4]

SUMMARY

- Questions of identity are of fundamental importance in the separatist argument, followed by positive perceptions about all things Catalan, negative perceptions about all things Spanish and economic questions.

---

[3] "For two million nationalists in Catalonia who believe themselves to be Catalans locked in the body of a Spaniard, Spain is the problem and independence the solution. Nationalism has provided a foundational myth, a historical grievance, an exterior enemy and an anchor for identity: the Catalan language. [...] For such pro-independence Catalans, Spain is a parasite gestating in the belly of their country. This has been the real motive behind a process promoted by the rich, bourgeois, nationalist elites against the Spanish-speaking lower and middle classes. The Catalan problem is not a conflict between Spain and Catalonia, but rather two different conflicts. The first, between Catalans. The second, of Spain against its own historical phantoms. This book poses the revolutionary hypothesis that the solution to the Catalan problem is not less Spain in Catalonia, but more." (Cristian Campos Cura (2019), *La anomalía catalana ¿Y si el problema fuera Cataluña and España la solución?*, Barcelona, Deusto.)

[4] Martín Madridejos Muñoz (2016), *El ciclo de protesta del independentismo catalán: Un análisis del periodo 2009–2016*, end of degree project in Political Science and Public Administration, Facultat de Ciències Polítiques i de Sociologia, Universitat Autònoma de Barcelona <https://ddd.uab.cat/pub/tfg/2016/163129/TFG_mmadridejosmunoz.pdf>.

- Economic arguments are particularly pertinent for persons with ambivalent identity positions.
- The mass movement had a large influence on the evolution of the process. It inflated the separatist position in the opinion polls and in the elections.
- The mobilisation of the independence movement conforms to the classical pattern and theory of protest cycles.

CHAPTER 14

Spain, from a Model Transition to Democracy to Failed State?

The only thing necessary for the triumph of evil is for good men to do nothing.

—Edmund Burke

Totalitarian tyranny is not built on the virtues of totalitarians but on the faults of democrats.

—Albert Camus

SPANISH DEMOCRACY

Spain made a model transition from dictatorship to democracy, because of the way it was done, observing the law, without political violence and because of the result, one of the most advanced democracies where legislative power, executive power and judicial power work, with an effective party system and a free press. Spain established a complete state with the rule of law, a complete state with social protection, an extraordinary degree of political and administrative decentralisation and of the public services. The recently installed democracy overcame the coup d'état attempted by residual elements of the Franco regime on 23 and 24 February 1981. Only ETA terrorism, with 800 assassinations, cast a cloud over Spanish democracy. The first probing forays of Catalan separatism appeared over the last two decades, culminating in the coup d'état of the autumn of 2017.

© The Author(s), under exclusive license to Springer Nature Switzerland AG 2022
F. Brunet, *The Economics of Catalan Separatism*,
https://doi.org/10.1007/978-3-031-14451-6_14

For decades, from 1975 to 2004, the Spanish transition had been exemplary. It was the archetype for the transitions from dictatorship to democracy in central Europe, Latin America and numerous emerging countries. The Spanish transition was built on two foundations: a state under the rule of law (representation, separation of powers, rule of law), and the decentralisation of state powers to the regions, called Autonomous Communities and Autonomous Cities subject to the Spanish Constitution and their Statutes of Autonomy, endorsed in each Autonomous Community and approved by the Spanish Parliament.

The crisis in Spanish democracy is being caused by the violation of the rule of law by the autonomous Catalan government. This regional pillar of government declared itself sovereign and independent and undermined the constitutional pillar, which lacked the strength to overcome the centrifugal force.[1] The first (and the second, and the third...) probing forays of this confrontation were not curtailed by Spain's central government, whose immediate responsibility it is to guarantee the Spanish Constitution. Hence, the successive trials of strength of the separatist Catalan regional government consisted in raising the stakes until they culminated in the coup d'état of autumn 2017 (see Chap. 2).

Spain is amongst the leading democracies in the world, ahead of the USA and France. If we consider the various indicators in which Spain performs relatively poorly in comparison with better classified countries, it is in effective government. And, without doubt, the canker of the separatist challenge is due to this inability to make the Constitution and the rule of law applicable throughout the whole of the national territory. Does the Spanish state suffer from weakness in its actions? Perhaps the lethargic character of the Spanish democratic state is due to the historical proximity

[1] The Spanish Constitution establishes, "Article 2. The Constitution is based on the indissoluble unity of the Spanish nation, the common and indivisible country of all Spaniards; it recognises and guarantees the right to autonomy of the nationalities and regions of which it is composed, and the solidarity amongst them all."<https://www.boe.es/legislacion/documentos/ConstitucionINGLES.pdf>.

The Treaty on European Union establishes, "Article 4.2. The Union shall respect the equality of Member States before the Treaties as well as their national identities, inherent in their fundamental structures, political and constitutional, inclusive of regional and local self-government. It shall respect their essential State functions, including ensuring the territorial integrity of the State, maintaining law and order and safeguarding national security. In particular, national security remains the sole responsibility of each Member State". <https://eur-lex.europa.eu/resource.html?uri=cellar:2bf140bf-a3f8-4ab2-b506-fd71826e6da6.0023.02/DOC_1&format=PDF>.

and shadow of the Franco dictatorship. What would lead a state under the rule of law to be such a guarantor of the rights of delinquents that they persist and reoffend without end? Why was, and is, the Spanish state invisible in the face of separatist harassment? Why is it incapable of reacting? Perhaps the separatists could be hoping to obtain the property (sovereignty) of Catalonia by means of usucapion, that is to say, insofar as its legitimate owner (the Spanish state) has not claimed its legitimate property after 30 years of occupation by the separatists.[2]

ACUTE CONFRONTATION

The fratricidal tendencies of Spanish politics and of contemporary politics for acute confrontation have impeded the two dominant parties that alternate in democratic power, the PSOE and the PP, from reaching agreements about the separatist challenge. All this has, of course, led to a considerable constitutional crisis. The cost of the separatists' show of defiance grew exponentially on account of the inaction of the state and the rule of law.

The result is the destruction of Catalonia and the fragmentation of Spain. This has consequences and they are, and will be, very serious ones both for the Catalans and for all other Spaniards. It is well known that, in our global and digital world, the quality of the institutions is a key element for the development and well-being of nations. Competition, progress, the freedom of the peoples, depend on the effectiveness of the institutions. The governments of Spain, like ostriches burying their heads in the ground, practised a policy of appeasement, abandoning the Catalans to their fate. This had the usual result, kicking the ball forwards into the long grass, that is to say, more time and greater cost.

Have the Autonomous Communities stopped being one of the pillars of democracy to become one of its afflictions? Will they pass from being considered one of the great successes of the Spanish transition to being considered Spanish democracy's great failures? As we observed before,

[2] Juan Carlos Segura Just (2015), "La usucapión de Cataluña", *Crónica Global*, 28 November <https://cronicaglobal.elespanol.com/pensamiento/la-usucapion-de-cataluna_28829_102.html>; and Juan Carlos Segura Just (2015), *El libro negro de la independencia*, Barcelona, Reseda.

Spaniards' level of satisfaction with the Autonomous Community system is low, and decreasing.[3]

Could the push for separatism sweep Spanish democracy, and Spain itself, away? It could. Could Spain become a failed state? It could. Would it be possible for the Spanish state to die a slow death? Being so eaten away could it suddenly collapse? Although this is not very probable, it is possible, even quite possible. In fact, in order for Spain not to become a failed state in the coming years, very important changes are called for in Spanish politics.

SUMMARY

- Changes to the substance and crumbling of the second pillar of Spain's exemplary transition to democracy—decentralisation through the Autonomous Community system—is a serious threat to the first pillar, the rule of law.
- If the separatist challenge continues, Spain will become a failed state.

[3] Some relevant analyses of the challenges opened by the Catalan separatists done are: Santiago Muñoz Machado (2012), *Informe sobre España: Repensar el Estado o destruirlo*, Barcelona, Crítica; Santiago Muñoz Machado (2014), *Cataluña y las demás Españas*, Barcelona, Crítica; Francesc de Carreras (2014), *Paciencia e independencia: La agenda oculta del nacionalismo*, Barcelona, Ariel; Teresa Freixes Sanjuan, and Juan Carlos Gavara de Cara (coords.) (2018), *Repensar la Constitución. Ideas para una reforma de la Constitución de 1978: reforma y comunicación dialógica*, Madrid, CEPCBOE, 2 vols; Josep Ramon Bosch (2020), *Cataluña, la ruta falsa: El problema catalán: cómo solucionarlo y no sólo conllevarlo*, Barcelona, Deusto; José Rosiñol (2022), "Las tres Españas", *The Objective*, 16 August; and José Cuenca (2022), *Cataluña y Québec. Las mentiras del separatismo*, Sevilla, Renacimiento.

CHAPTER 15

Values and Qualities of Spain

POSITION IN INTERNATIONAL RANKINGS

Spain, Catalonia included, is an excellent place to live. Indeed, Spain is one of the best considered countries in terms of quality of life, health and well-being. The complicated indicators used in international rankings say it. Its citizens and visitors to the country say it.

This can be deduced also from the high level of net immigration. In spite of the Spanish employment rate being three times that of neighbouring countries, and the standard of living being lower, the country attracts many more immigrants, and they become much better integrated.[1]

The rankings need to be classified according to whether the indicators they use are especially political, social or economic. Amongst the political rankings, Spain occupies a place between the 10–20 most democratic countries in the world, be they large or small. Quite often, in a general political index and under many specific headings, Spain is ahead of countries more characteristically democratic, such as the USA and France (see Table 15.1). In the international rankings for democracy, Spain occupies a place between 13 and 27. Under some specific headers, it occupies positions between 5 and 32.

In international rankings on social aspects, Spain occupies first place as the healthiest country, position 26 with regard to the human development

---

[1] The Economist (2018), *The Strain in Spain. Special Report*, London, The Economist.

© The Author(s), under exclusive license to Springer Nature
Switzerland AG 2022
F. Brunet, *The Economics of Catalan Separatism*,
https://doi.org/10.1007/978-3-031-14451-6_15

Table 15.1   Spain's rankings in some international indexes on political aspects

	Indicator	Rank (better = 1)	Aspects	Year - Countries - Source
Politics	Democracy Index	24 (2021) 16 (2020)	Electoral process and pluralism / Functioning of government / Political participation / Political culture / Civil liberties	Year 2021 / 167 countries / The Economist / <https://www.eiu.com/topic/demo cracy-index>
	Liberal Democracy Index	26	Equality before the law and individual liberties: 11 / Limits of the judiciary to the executive: 7 / Clean elections: 7	Year 2022 / 179 countries / Varieties of Democracy Institute / <https://pol.gu.se/english/varieties -of-democracy--v-dem->
	Rule of Law Index	21	Respect for the rights of citizens / Restrictions on government powers / Absence of corruption / Existence of an open government / Fundamental rights, order and security, compliance with regulations / Civil justice / Criminal justice.	Year 2021 / 126 Countries / World Justice Project / <https://worldjusticeproject.org/si tes/default/files/documents/WJP_ RuleofLawIndex_2019_Website_ reduced.pdf/>
	Freedom in the World	20	Electoral Process / Political Pluralism and Participation / Functioning of Government / Freedom of Expression and Belief / Associational and Organizational Rights / Rule of Law / Personal Autonomy and Individual Rights	Year 2019 / 195 countries and 14 territories / Freedom House / <https://freedomhouse.org/sites/d efault/files/Feb2019_FH_FITW_2 019_Report_ForWeb- compressed.pdf>
	The Global State of Democracy	13	Representative Government: 9 / Fundamental Rights: 16 / Government Control: 14 / Local Democracy: 5 / Impartial Administration: 12	Year 2019 / 158 countries / IDEA International Institute for Democracy and Electoral Assistance / <https://www.idea.int/- publications/catalogue/global- state-of-democracy- 2019?lang=en>
	Worldwide Governance Indicators	27	Control of corruption: 32 / Government effectiveness: 23 / Regulatory quality: 26 / Rule of law: 25 / Voice and accountability: 22	Year 2020 / 215 countries / World Bank / <https://databank.bancomundial.o rg/Governance- Indicators/id/2abb48da>
	World Press Freedom Index	29	Pluralism / Media Independence / Environment and self-censorship / Legislative / Transparency / Abuses	Year 2020 / 180 countries / Reporters Without Borders <https://rsf.org/en/ranking>

Source: Author's compilation of data from the sources referred in the last column of this Table and listed in the references

index and 30th position on the happiness index. (See Tables 15.1 and 15.2.) Notable also is Spain's soft power position in aspects such as culture, cuisine and education. The influence of Spain can also be appreciated in the international presence indicator.

In the rankings based on economic indicators, Spain's position in the world is between 14th position for absolute GDP and 49th position for per capita GDP. In the global competitiveness index, Spain occupies position 23 and position 30 for ease of doing business. In specific indices, Spain's first position for both ease of cross-border trade and for health are outstanding, as is its 7th position for infrastructure provision. With regard to economic, military and soft power aspects, Spain occupies position 12 (Fig. 15.1).

Table 15.2 Spain's rankings in some international indexes on social and economic aspects

	Indicator	Rank (better = 1)	Aspects	Year - Countries - Source
Social	Human Development Index	26	Life expectancy at birth / Mean years of schooling / Gross national income	Year 2020 / 189 countries / United Nations <http://hdr.undp.org/en/content/human-development-index-hdi>
	Healthiest Country	1	Life expectancy / Access to clean water and sanitation / Tobacco use / Obesity	Year 2019 / 169 countries / Bloomberg <https://www.bloomberg.com/news/articles/2019-02-24/spain-tops-italy-as-world-s-healthiest-nation-while-u-s-slips>
	Life expectancy at birth (median age of dead)	23	81.8 years	Year 2020 / 223 countries and territories / US Central Intelligence Agency / The World Factbook <https://www.cia.gov/library/publications/the-world-factbook/geos/xx.html>
	Soft Power 30	13	Government / Culture / Enterprise Digital / Engagement / Education / Cuisine / Tech Products / Friendliness Culture / Luxury Goods / Foreign Policy / Liveability	Year 2019 / 30 countries / University of Southern California. Center on Public Diplomacy <https://softpower30.com/wp-content/uploads/2019/10/The-Soft-Power-30-Report-2019-1.pdf>
	Happiness	30	GDP per capita / Social support / Healthy life expectancy / Freedom to make life choices / Generosity / Perceptions of corruption	Year 2018 / 156 countries / United Nations <https://worldhappiness.report/ed/2019/>
	Global Presence	12	Economic / Military / Soft	Year 2021 / 120 countries / Real Instituto Elcano <https://www.globalpresence.realinstitutoelcano.org/es/>
Economic	Population	29	46,934,632 inhabitants	Year 2020 / 223 countries and territories / US Central Intelligence Agency / The World Factbook <https://www.cia.gov/library/publications/the-world-factbook/geos/xx.html> / and Eurostat <https://ec.europa.eu/eurostat/data/browse-statistics-by-theme>
	GDP total	14	1,202,193 M euros (2018)	
	GDP per capita	49	25,730 € (2018)	
	Competitiveness	23	Institutions: 28 / Infrastructure: 7 / ICT adoption: 19 / Macroeconomic stability: 43 / Health: 1 / Skills: 37 / Product market: 34 / Labour market: 61 / Financial system: 26 / Market size: 15 / Business dynamism: 34 / Innovation: 25	Year 2020 / 141 countries / World Economic Forum <http://www3.weforum.org/docs/WEF_TheGlobalCompetitivenessReport2019.pdf>
	Doing Business	30	Starting a Business: 97 / Handling Building Permits: 79 / Obtaining Electricity: 55 / Registering Property: 59 / Obtaining Credit: 80 / Protecting Minority Investors: 28 / Paying Taxes: 35 / Cross-Border Trade: 1 / Compliance with contracts: 26 / Resolution of insolvency: 18	Year 2020 / 190 countries / World Bank <https://openknowledge.worldbank.org/bitstream/handle/10986/32436/9781464814402.pdf>

Source: Author's compilation of data from the sources referred to in the last column of this Table and listed in the references

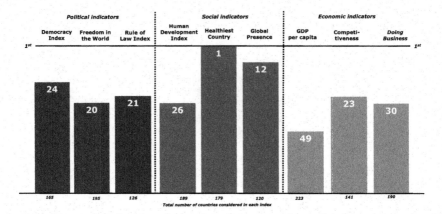

Fig. 15.1 Spain's rankings in some international indexes on political, social and economic aspects. (Source: Author's compilation on data from the sources referred in Tables 15.1 and 15.2.)

The Democracy Index, drawn up by *The Economist*,[2] considers five aspects. Ordered according to the rating achieved for them by Spain, they are: civil liberties, electoral process and pluralism, political participation, political culture and functioning of government. A comparison of the data for Spain with that of other nations, shows that, in effect, respect for civil liberties in Spain is greater than in other similar democracies, while the functioning of government is worse, except for Italy.

In the successive editions of the *Democracy Index*, Spain has occupied position 17 (2016), 19 (2017 and 2018), 16 (2019), 22 (2020), all of them as a full democracy, and 24 (2021) now as a flawed democracy. The damage caused by Catalan separatism to the rule of law in Spain is beginning to be seen.

SUMMARY

- Spain is frequently ahead of the USA, the United Kingdom, France, Italy and other advanced and consolidated democracies for the quality of its political system and institutions, both in some of the synthetic indices and in various sectorial indices.

[2] Economist Intelligence Unit. *The Economist* (2022), *Democracy Index* <https://www.eiu.com/n/campaigns/democracy-index-2021/>.

- All the political, social and economic indicators repudiate any grounds for Spain's black legend. Spain is a solid, healthy, capable, convincing, attractive and appreciated country.
- In the context of the political turbulence in more solid democratic countries (such as the presidency of Donald Trump in the USA, Brexit in the United Kingdom, the *gilets jaunes* in France and a populist government in Italy), Spain's position in the international rankings has risen in spite of the harm the Catalan separatist challenge is inflicting on democracy and integration in Spain.
- Spain has excellent positions in almost all aspects of democracy, except in the functioning of government. The Autonomous Community and Autonomous City system and the questions raised with regard to Catalonia probably explain a large part of this deficit.

CHAPTER 16

Corruption, Embezzlement, Profligacy and the Bad Government of the Separatist Generalitat

CORRUPTION

Absolute power corrupts absolutely. Who could doubt it? A regrettable confirmation of this truth is the case of Catalonia since 1980. One can remember when it was said that Catalonia was an oasis in comparison with what happened in the rest of Spain.[1]

Unfortunately, the Catalan oasis was not so. On the contrary, it was a pool full of very wily sharks. Could you smell them? Of course, they caused a considerable stench. But the corrupt were 'one of us' and the corruption was 'for the cause'. They had a right to be so, and they continue to have that right—they are corrupt for Catalonia. Behind every nationalist hides a crook.

Political corruption often starts with irregular party funding. Political funding is regulated, but that is always too little for the extremely high designs of politicians. And, of course, whoever manages to raise funds, keeps a part of them. Double corruption, therefore. That of the party and that of the leaders. Better still, triple corruption. The companies that are corrupted, and corrupt themselves, in order to gain public contracts,

---

[1] The expression 'Catalan oasis' appeared during the Second Republic. It was coined by Manuel Brunet i Solà (1936), "¿L'oasi", *La Veu de Catalunya*, 4 March): "Before and after 6 October [1934: separatist coup] I had said many times that Catalonia, with its Statute, could have become an oasis. [...] The blame lies not with the machine of autonomy, but with the men who operate it."

© The Author(s), under exclusive license to Springer Nature Switzerland AG 2022
F. Brunet, *The Economics of Catalan Separatism*,
https://doi.org/10.1007/978-3-031-14451-6_16

although this is often an indispensable condition for working for a public administration. Even quadruple corruption, that of the overseeing civil servant for the auditing of accounts and, specifically, for the abandonment of their duties, which are to control the use of money by politicians and that of the public administrations, according to the law.

In democratic Spain, corruption has mainly occurred in the Autonomous Communities. The new cantonisation of Spain is not unrelated to the rise in corruption. Corruption did not come from the central government, except that which affected the government of the PSOE, which even brought together the directors of the Guardia Civil and the Official Government Gazette, etc. There has been corruption in the political parties of nationwide scope when doing business in the Autonomous Communities, particularly in Andalusia under the PSOE regime and in Valencia and other communities with the Partido Popular. Judging by the number of people accused, the Autonomous Community of Catalonia has, by far, been the most corrupt of them all. In this list of title winners, no one else comes close.

In the case of Catalonia, let us be clear what came first, corruption or the *process*? Impunity, 3% [commissions] and independence.[2] Was the separatist *process* launched to avoid the legal consequences of corruption? It was probably not launched for this alone, but it was doubtless a reason. Covering up corruption was a powerful motive for Catalan leaders to unleash the separatist challenge.

After a very long police and fiscal investigation, Jordi Pujol confessed that, while he had governed Catalonia for three decades, he has

---

[2] In his fortnightly *El Triangle*, the journalist, Jaume Reixach, had pursued the particular *Catalan mafia* ever since the *Diari de Barcelona* newspaper censored an article that revealed the charging of 3% commissions by Convergència Democràtica de Catalunya. See, for example, Jaume Reixach (2019), "El porqué de todo", *El Triangle*, 15 October <https://www.eltriangle.eu/es/opinion/el-porque-de-todo_103864_102.html>; e Idem (2020), "Fills de Pujol", El Triangle, 1st September <https://www.eltriangle.eu/ca/opinio/fills-de-pujol_39457_102.html>.

Then, on 24 February 2005 (during a plenary session of the Catalan parliament on the collapse of the tunnel for line 5 of Barcelona's underground railway network in the heavily populated area of El Carmel), the then leader of the opposition, Pasqual Maragall, said to the president, Artur Mas "You have a problem, and this problem is called 3%". With regard to the size of this problem, it has been said that "it wasn't 3% because with only 3% we wouldn't have done anything".

accumulated a fortune.[3] His numerous family participated in the enterprise as a criminal organisation.[4] As an executive of Banca Catalana Pujol had already shown his capacity for appropriation. The 'process towards independence' was an attempt to cover up corruption. The *process* corrupted Catalan politics, society and the economy.[5]

Is the *process* corrupt in itself? Yes, in the sense that it hides the corruption of its leaders. But the *process* is also corrupt because it is founded on public funding, which is illicit, such funding being improper for the Generalitat administration. The *process* also receives private funding through donations, be they legal in the form of advertising or patronage, or corrupt as when, with a rake off by the leaders or their satellite organisations, companies improve their proximity to those who are responsible for allocating Generalitat government contracts.

In a material sense then, the *process* is corrupt without a doubt. It is also corrupt in a moral sense. Everything is false, the aims are impossible, the argument full of lies and the means immoral. Hence post-truth and boundless propaganda. Something that was sold as a process from bottom up turned out to be from top down. Something that was presented as peaceful, and it was, turned violent.[6]

Corruption is one of the criminal facets of the *process*, of the wastefulness and bad government of the Generalitat de Catalunya. Corruption, wastefulness and bad government are all linked together. When, instead of

[3] Anon. (2014), "Jordi Pujol confiesa haber tenido dinero sin regularizar en el extranjero", *eldiario.es*, 25 July <https://www.eldiario.es/catalunya/Jordi-Pujol-confiesa-regularizar-extranjero_0_285222219.html#carta>.
A biography of Jordi Pujol is available in Josep Guixà and Manuel Trallero (2019), *Pujol: todo era mentira (1930–1962). Desvelando el relato fundacional independentista*, Córdoba, Almuzara.
[4] Audiencia Nacional. Juzgado Central de Instrucción Número 5 (2020), *Diligencias Previas 141/2012. Auto de Procedimiento Abreviado*, 16 de julio <http://www.poderjudicial.es/cgpj/es/Buscadores/?categoria=&actuales=&text=Diligencias+Previas+141%2F2012.+Auto+De+Procedimiento+Abreviado%2C+16+de+julio+%3C%3E.+&paginacion=10>.
[5] Manuel Trallero (2012), *Música celestial: Del mal llamado caso Millet o caso Palau*, Barcelona, Debate; Parlament de Catalunya. Comissió d'Investigació sobre el Frau i l'Evasió Fiscals i les Pràctiques de Corrupció Política (2015), "Dictamen Tram. 261-00004/10", *Butlletí Oficial del Parlament de Catalunya*, X legislatura, N. 642, Sexto período, 16 July, pp. 1–128; and Manuel Ibarz (2019), *La corrupción en España: Un pozo sin fondo*, Barcelona, Ediciones del escarabajo.
[6] Miquel Porta Perales (2019), "Teoría, práctica and función de la desobediencia civil durante el proceso secesionista de Cataluña", *Cuadernos de Pensamiento Político*, N. 61, January-March, pp. 17–27.

governing in accordance with the legally established powers, the aims of the government of the Generalitat transformed into changing the law in order to achieve all the powers, the exercise of the actual powers (the only legal ones and the only ones that influence citizens' well-being) obviously became a secondary affair and a means to an end, the high aims of rebel secessionists. And, what is more, with Madrid paying the bill!

EMBEZZLEMENT

All of this was the result of the hijacking of the Generalitat de Catalunya, for four decades, by the autonomists-nationalists-sovereigntists-separatists.[7] This lack of neutrality by the administration of the Generalitat is one of Catalan separatism's most serious challenges to the rule of law.

So, everything was allowed. The 3%, and more, commissions for the crooked financing of the party and its exalted aims, and whoever was on the receiving end taking a cut to facilitate the thankless task of squandering through corruption, high prices, over pricing, useless purchases, subsidies for the outfits of likeminded fellow travellers, friends and followers. Basically, the trough, the manger, the feeding box. Financing for anything we have our fingers in. That is how the independence 'rebellion' was financed. From this point of view, the *process* is an industry. The interests of the independence clergy is not in the hypothetical final independence but in the immediate *process* itself.

During these decades of larceny and rebellion, the task of inspecting and authorising the accounts by the civil servants, the auditors and trustees of the Catalan administrations and the so-called Court of Audit (Sindicatura de Comptes) must have been really strenuous. So much to cover up! So long keeping the eyes firmly closed! The truth is that no infringement of the law was ever detected in the severe passivity of these heroic civil servants. That had to wait for the Guardia Civil and for people to spill the beans in a courtroom. Absolute power corrupts absolutely. Impunity magnifies and eternalises corruption, profligacy and the bad government of the separatist Generalitat.

---

[7] Marta Ferrusola, wife of Jordi Pujol, described her feelings when Pasqual Maragall was elected president of the Generalitat in 2003, "It's as if they've broken into the house and burgled it".

The Cost of Bad Government

Of course, profligacy, embezzlement and corruption have a cost. The total cost has two components: 1. the formal cost, the fragmentation of the state and the rule of law; and 2. the material cost, the resources removed from other tasks that are at the service of citizens and that do fall within the legal powers of the administration. The cost to the state and the rule of law is lethal for democracy.

The cost in terms of resources can be calculated from a microeconomic point of view (counting every item of the budget removed from its legitimate use), and from a macroeconomic point of view. The inventory of separatist fraud in the public budgets is calculated as €6300 million per year. (See later.)

From the macroeconomic point of view, the cost of profligacy, ideological subsidies, inappropriate powers, corruption and embezzlement can be calculated as 15% of the total budget of the Generalitat, even when it is doubtful that 85% is spent correctly. Given that the Generalitat's budget for 2020 was €46,057 million, that means that €6909 million a year, a figure similar to the one obtained from the microeconomic calculation.

Later we shall also see the cost of the separatist challenge insofar as it reduces the GDP (lower level of activity, reduced competitiveness). But what we can say now is that it is a reduction of 4.6% of GDP, that is to say some €10,894 million per year.

Impunity for profligacy and the improper use of powers is at the base of the bad government of the Generalitat. The administration of the Generalitat is not an administration, it is the promotion of rebellion, based on promoting hatred of Spain and giving out subsidies. In fact, what the separatist Generalitat leaders do really well, is pay themselves. Their lack of interest in administration explains the antisocial character of the Generalitat. Resources devoted to rebellion are subtracted from Education and health.

Summary

- Corruption flourishes when politicians and the administration think they have impunity. This has been the case with the Catalan nationalist and separatist regime since 1980.
- For 40 years, therefore, the hijacking of the Generalitat by separatists made this administration a distributor of money to their supporters and the maker and funder of the rebellion that culminated in the coup d'état of autumn 2017.

- Monetary corruption is based on the corruption of the political system and also on the moral corruption of people. It benefits the government political parties and their leaders and those of the administration. It harms the Treasury, which bears most of the costs and it harms the companies that pay bribes in order to obtain public contracts.
- Morally and legally, formally and materially, the *process* is corrupt, on account of its origin (there being no penal consequences for the separatist leaders' corruption, and because of their exclusive nationalism); on account of its means (public funding, distortions and misrepresentations of all kinds about the past, present and future), and on account of its consequences (the putrefaction of Catalan society and the decline of Catalonia).
- Embezzlement took resources away from the Generalitat budget for items that are essential from the social point of view: education and health. Hence, the Generalitat's reduced expenditure on these items and Catalonia's dreadful results in the education and health indicators.
- Hence the antisocial character of the separatist Generalitat. The separatists, the independence movement, couldn't give a damn about the Catalans.

CHAPTER 17

Surveys on Separatism

You cannot dissuade anyone with reasons about something they were convinced of without reasons.
—Jonathan Swift
Reasons are of no use for convincing people.
—Carlos Castilla del Pino

THE WISHED-FOR CATALONIA

If the world of surveys is effervescent, the one devoted to questionnaires about the political, social and economic situation of a Catalonia subjugated by the adventurers who govern the separatist Generalitat, is positively boiling.

A real state should have an official body for opinion polls (?!). The Generalitat de Catalunya's was created in 2005 and is called the Centre d'Estudis d'Opinió—CEO, (Centre for Opinion Studies). Since then, it has been what the separatists call a 'state structure'. Its most important task is to produce and disseminate a quarterly, multi-question barometer and omnibus.

The CEO's key question is, "Do you think Catalonia should be ...?" Support for the independence of Catalonia grew from 13.9% of the total surveyed in 2006 to 48.5% in November 2013 and fell to 34.5% in July 2019.

© The Author(s), under exclusive license to Springer Nature Switzerland AG 2022
F. Brunet, *The Economics of Catalan Separatism*,
https://doi.org/10.1007/978-3-031-14451-6_17

Respondents are also offered another three hypothetical options about what Catalonia should 'be'. That it should be a Spanish Autonomous Community fell from 38.2% in March 2006 to a minimum of 19.1% in October 2012 and has picked up a little slowly since then. That it should be a state within a federal Spain fell from 33.4% to 24.5% in July 2019. That it should be a region of Spain oscillated between 8.1% in March 2006, to 1.4% in October 2014 and 7.8% in July 2019.

The great polarisation of Catalan society and the persistent minority of the separatists can be seen in the replies to the question: "Do you want Catalonia to be an independent state?" Of the 17 polls carried out during the period 2014–2019, 'no' won 11 times and 'yes' won 6. Five of the six 'yes' wins were—according to this polling centre—between October 2017 and March 2019. In July 2020, the results were 'no' 50.5% and 'yes' 42%.[1]

YOUNG PEOPLE ARE LESS SEPARATIST

Age could be a relevant indicator for opinions about the separation of Catalonia from the rest of Spain. Are those born under the empire of the separatist Generalitat more separatist? The education system is in the hands of the Generalitat, with its 'linguistic immersion' policy of education only in Catalan, even for those school children whose mother tongue is Spanish (Spanish being the mother tongue of 55% of Catalans and an official language in Catalonia, like Catalan). Has this education system created separatists?[2]

We can see that, in effect, the cohort of people born after 1977 (the year the 'linguistic immersion' programme started) were, by 2010, 4.5% more separatist than previous cohorts. However, by the end of the 2017 series, this same age range was the least inclined to support independence. Basically, all the age groups considered in this CEO survey were, in 2017,

[1] Generalitat de Catalunya. Centre d'Estudis d'Opinió (2019), *Barómetro de Opinión Política. 2ª ola 2019* <http://upceo.ceo.gencat.cat/wsceop/7188/Dossier%20de%20 premsa%20-942.pdf>. The Spanish version of this report is full of spelling and grammatical mistakes, from the title to the last page. That it be published like this is an indication of the contempt for this language that the people responsible for it and its authors are proud to display.
[2] Generalitat de Catalunya. Centre d'Estudis d'Opinió (2017), *Baròmetre d'Opinió Política. 1a onada 2017* <https://ceo.gencat.cat/ca/barometre/detall/index.html?id=6168>.

around 7% more separatist than in 2010. To home in even further into the analysis of people's inclination for independence, it is necessary to take language and place of birth into account.[3] Catalans born in Catalonia are three and a half times more supportive of independence than Catalans born outside Catalonia.

SEPARATISM IS SOMETHING FOR RICH PEOPLE: THE RICHER, THE MORE SEPARATIST

According to a 2020 poll about remembering the vote in the Catalan elections of December 2017, CUP voters have a monthly family income of €2629; ERC voters €2485; JxC voters €2460; Cs voters €2341; CeC voters €2316; PPC voters €2143; and PSC voters €2036.[4]

The place of birth of each of the parents of those surveyed is also a factor that influences opinion about independence: 70.5% of those whose parents were both born in Catalonia would opt for separation as opposed to the 18.4% of those whose parents were not born in Catalonia. An analysis of the relationship between income, family origins and voting orientation shows that separatism is proportional to income and to having grandparents who were born in Catalonia. Similarly, the separatist parties obtain their votes in the wealthiest census areas, poorer voters prefer PSC, VOX, C's and PP.[5]

Indeed, separatism is something for rich people and the elites. When the CEO asked about support for independence[6]:

– 51% of those comfortably off say they would vote yes for independence in a referendum.
– 41% of those getting by say they would vote yes.
– 38% of those with difficulties say they would vote yes.
– 29% of those with great difficulties say they would vote yes.

[3] GESOP (2014), *Barómetro Político de Cataluña, marzo 2014* <https://cronicaglobal.elespanol.com/politica/ni-son-chonis-ni-son-independentistas_6506_102.html>.
[4] Generalitat de Catalunya. Centre d'Estudis d'Opinió (2021), *Baròmetre d'Opinió Política (BOP). 3a onada 2020* <https://ceo.gencat.cat/es/barometre/detall/index.html?id=7808>.
[5] Kiko Llaneras (2021), "Así se relacionan en Cataluña la renta, el voto, el origen and la independencia", *El País,* 20 febrero <https://elpais.com/politica/2021/02/19/actualidad/1613741557_146092.html>.
[6] Generalitat de Catalunya. Centre d'Estudis d'Opinió (2022), *Baròmetre d'Opinió Política. 1a onada 2022* <https://ceo.gencat.cat/ca/barometre/detall/index.html?id=8308>.

The wealthier and the elites are therefore the social groups that are most separatist. Income and education levels influence people's attitude to the separatist adventure, as Thomas Piketty saw.[7] Did Catalonia's economic situation, the severe crisis of 2008–2013, light the fuse of separatism?[8] Confining ourselves just to the data for unemployment, it is clear that there is a large correspondence between this and support for the separation of Catalonia from the rest of Spain. Unemployment and separatism grew in a parallel manner, the peaks of both were in 2013, and both also decreased in parallel.

LANGUAGE AND BEING CATALAN AND/OR SPANISH

There is also a correlation, albeit not as pronounced as the previous one, between the language usually spoken and the separatist vote: 68.9% of Catalan speakers would vote for the separation of Catalonia from the rest of Spain in comparison with 15.4% of Spanish speakers. There is a correlation between the mother tongue and a feeling of belonging. Feeling Catalan and/or Spanish, the combinations, and exclusions of that, are

[7] Thomas Piketty (2019), *Capital and Ideology* <http://piketty.pse.ens.fr/files/ideologie/pdf/G16.5.pdf> <http://piketty.pse.ens.fr/files/ideologie/pdf/G16.6.pdf>.

[8] "The Catalan independence movement is volatile. Separatism is in danger, in spite of the electoral law, since sufficient critical mass exists to achieve an alternative absolute majority. [...] The Catalonia that is loyal to the rest of Spain has an opportunity at the ballot box. A number has been repeating itself since 1999, to the torment of strategists, mainly those of ERC and JXCAT: 350,000 separatists easily stay at home, thereby reducing the electoral perimeter of this segment of the population. In fact, the absence of these 350,000 Catalans enabled, for example, the electoral victory of Pasqual Maragall [...]. In spite of 23 years of Jordi Pujol and his policies, the recent results (since 2012) and the intensity of the 'process', the separatist vote is less unconditional than it seems. The bases for alternation in Catalan autonomous power are solid and would make an alternative majority possible to that formed over the last four preceding decades, except for the years of the three-party alliance, by nationalist forces." (Carles Castro Sanz (2020), *Cómo derrotar al independentismo en las urnas*, Barcelona, ED Libros.)

A close analysis of the votes and seats by province would suggest that to alter the current separatist majority it would be enough to have 3500 votes in Lleida, 8000 in Tarragona, 13,500 in Girona and 20,000 in Barcelona. It is probable that there is a similar number of people who are not unilateralists.

related to the mother tongue and the language most commonly spoken.[9] In all linguistic groups (Catalan speakers, Spanish speakers and speakers of both languages) most people feel equally Catalan and Spanish. Most of those who feel equally Catalan and Spanish are Catalans who mainly speak Spanish; 48.2% of those who speak both languages indistinctly feel equally Catalan and Spanish. Those who speak Catalan and only feel Catalan are 47.7% of all Catalan speakers.

We can compare the situation in 2016 with that of 2006. In 2006 the proportion of Spanish speakers who felt equally Spanish and Catalan was 57.6%. In 2016 it was 60%. The *process* has only managed to radicalise the feeling of belonging of one sector of Catalonia: those who speak Catalan and only feel Catalan (not the majority). It is very noteworthy that the majority segment of Spanish speakers has remained immune to the *process*.[10]

Language forms part of belonging, but the big difference is in the channel of communication.

- Only 28.1% of those who do not receive their information from TV3 vote separatist. Little need be added to the role of TV3 and other Generalitat media in the manipulation of Catalans' feelings. Since the time of Goebbels and mass propaganda media at the service of manipulating states, a lie repeated a thousand times, becomes a truth. The *process* starts as propaganda and ends up burning Catalonia and Spain.
- From a historical perspective, since 1984, there has been a growth in the group that feels only Catalan from 9% to 21% at the expense of the group of those who feel equally Spanish and Catalan. On the other hand, since 2012, the proportion of those who only feel Catalan has dropped slightly, confirming the reduction in other indicators such as the separatist vote.

[9] Societat Civil Catalana. Observatori Electoral de Catalunya (2017), *La Cataluña inmune al "procés". El referéndum: una falsa salida* <https://www.societatcivilcatalana.cat/sites/default/files/docs/La-Cataluna-inmune-vf.pdf>.
[10] Ibid.

BILINGUALISM

Finally, let us consider the results of a survey into bilingualism.[11]

- Only 9% of Catalans say that Catalan should be the only vehicular language (monolingual immersion in Catalan).
- 64% prefer a trilingual model of education (Catalan, Spanish and English).
- Another 21% would prefer bilingual education in similar proportions of Catalan and Spanish.
- For 60% of those responding to the survey, the first language of educational contact for pupils in Catalonia's publicly funded and grant-aided schools should be the language usually spoken by the parents, be that Catalan or Spanish.
- 61% support a standard Spanish examination, the same throughout the whole of Spain, upon completion of compulsory secondary education.
- 82% reject the policy of fining establishments that do not have Catalan signage.

SUMMARY

- From the surveys about what Catalonia should be (an Autonomous Community, federal state, independent state, or region), a growth in separatism can be observed until it reached its peak in November 2013 with 48.5% of those surveyed by the CEO-Generalitat.
- Leanings towards constitutionalism or independence are broadly related with the place of birth and the language usually spoken. Catalan speakers born in Catalonia whose parents were born in Catalonia comprise the group in which separatism is largest and grew most.
- One's own language influences the feeling of belonging. Sixty per cent of those who feel equally Catalan and Spanish are Spanish speakers and 14% Catalan speakers.

[11] Observatori Electoral de Catalunya (2020), *Investigación sociolingüística en Cataluña. Encuesta realizada por GAD3*, 11 December <https://www.gad3.com/solo-uno-de-cada-10-catalanes-defiende-que-el-catalan-sea-la-unica-lengua-vehicular-en-la-ensenanza/>.

• The preferred TV channel for receiving information determines (or is determined by) the feeling of belonging. Only 28.1% of those who do not receive their information from TV3 vote separatist. Seventy-five per cent of those who receive their information from TV3 vote separatist.

• Since 2012 the proportion of those who feel only Catalan has dropped slightly, confirming the decrease in other indicators such as the separatist vote.

• Nine per cent of Catalans support monolingual immersion in Catalan, 64% would like trilingual education and 21% would like bilingual education.

CHAPTER 18

Separatism and Economic Crisis

CATALONIA'S IMAGE

The Catalan separatists' sustained push and their multifaceted attacks on the rule of law, democracy and the integration of Spain have damaged the image of Catalonia in the eyes of Catalans and all other Spaniards. In this regard we can summarise the findings of a survey conducted by GAD3[1]:

- Six of every ten Catalans think that the debate about independence has produced a negative image of Catalonia in the rest of Spain.
- The debate about the separatist *process* affects all Spaniards and is seen with concern and puzzlement within and outside Catalonia.
- Thirty-eight per cent of non-Catalan Spaniards have a relative who lives in Catalonia and 78% have been to Catalonia. Seven of every ten say they have been treated with respect and friendship. Similarly, 74% of Catalans feel at home when they travel to the rest of Spain.
- Eighty-seven per cent of Catalans think the diversity of languages enriches Spanish culture. Equally, 81% of Spaniards outside of Catalonia share this opinion.
- A large majority of Spaniards are against the boycott of Catalan products (70%) and say they do not bear in mind the Catalan origin of these products when making a purchase. Four of every ten citizens

[1] GAD3 (2017), *Encuesta sobre la imagen de Catalunya* <https://societatcivilcatalana.cat/sites/default/files/encuesta-gad3-2017>.

© The Author(s), under exclusive license to Springer Nature Switzerland AG 2022
F. Brunet, *The Economics of Catalan Separatism*,
https://doi.org/10.1007/978-3-031-14451-6_18

resident outside Catalonia have, or have had, savings in Catalan entities.

- A large majority of people, 79% of Spaniards, Catalans included, reject sport being mixed up with political demands. Most Spaniards want Catalan football teams to play in the Spanish league. In fact, one in four supports either Barça or Español.

- Hard workers, organised and cosmopolitan, and also imaginative and reliable, that is how most Spaniards view Catalans, a better image than Catalans have of themselves.

RELATIONS BETWEEN SPANIARDS

Fortunately, despite the depth of the Catalan separatists' nonsense and that of their regional government, it would seem that broad empathy prevails between Catalans and other Spaniards. In this regard, it is worth summarising some of the questions and answers in another survey on relevant socio-political questions concerning Catalonia under the *process*.[2]

- Do you maintain family, professional or any other kind of link with people in the rest of Spain (outside Catalonia)? 78.4% of Catalans maintain their links with the rest of Spain.

- Do you think the independence referendum divides Catalan society? More than half of Catalans think the independence referendum divides Catalan society. More than 70% of those who feel as Spanish as they feel Catalan, or more Spanish, think so, while 75.6% of those who feel only Catalan do not. A plebiscite is not a suitable instrument for settling issues that do not cover a large cross-section.

- With regard to the media in Catalonia, TV3 and Catalonia Radio, do you think...? 65.4% of Catalans think the public service media in Catalonia are favourable to separation.

- Do you think it is right or wrong for public administrations, such as, at the moment, some town councils, should fly the *estelada* (the name for the separatist flag: the Catalan flag with a triangle, usually blue, but red for leftists, that features a star) from their buildings? 86.3% of those who feel only Catalan think it is right, a proportion

[2] GESOP (2017), *Encuesta del GESOP para Societat Civil Catalana. Informe de resultados 2017* <https://www.societatcivilcatalana.cat/sites/default/files/docs/1034_GESOP_Informe_para_SCC_febrero_2017_castella.pdf>.

that falls to 30% amongst those who feel as Catalan as Spanish. Seven out of ten Catalan speakers approve. In contrast, only 34% of Spanish speakers do.

– How do you think compulsory education should be given in Catalonia? Three of every four Catalans think that compulsory education should be trilingual: Catalan, Spanish and English.

Unemployment and Separatism

To conclude with the sometimes boiling, sometimes effervescent world of opinion polls, let us pause to consider the relationship between separatism and the economic crisis. They evolved at the same time. (See Fig. 18.1.) It is said that the leaders of CiU fled to the hills—to flee Spanish justice on

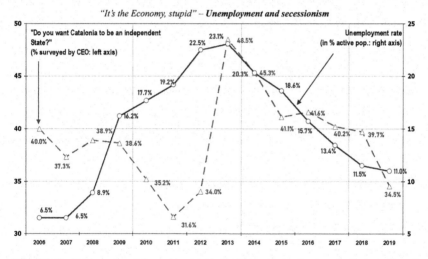

Fig. 18.1 Economic crisis and separatism. (Source: Author's calculations based on data from the Instituto Nacional de Estadística (2022), *Estadísticas territoriales* <https://www.ine.es/jaxiT3/###Table.htm?t=4247>; Generalitat de Catalunya. Centre d'Estudis d'Opinió (2019), *Baròmetre* <http://ceo.gencat.cat/ca/barometre/detall/index.html?id=6288>; and Bloomberg (2017), "Catalans Think Twice About Risks of Rupture as Good Life Returns", 9 August <https://www.bloomberg.com/news/articles/2017-08-09/catalans-think-twice-about-risks-of-rupture-as-good-life-returns>)

account of their corruption—and in the face of growing protests about the Generalitat's government cuts.

The independence movement has all the components of a populist, nationalist movement. An exterior enemy (perfidious Spain); the assumed people (although it is movement-driven from the top-down by a whole, legitimate government, which, although regional, has almost all powers (except pensions, foreign affairs and defence); indoctrination in schools; absolute propaganda; persecution of dissidents; rites (marches, candle-lit nights); imperialist pan-Catalanism (*Països Catalans);* and the falsification of the past, present and future, etc.

During the first three months of 2020, the coronavirus crisis hit Catalan society and brought into focus, for example, the Catalan people's appreciation for the army, once considered the standard bearer of the Spain the separatists hate. In April 2020, a survey revealed separatism's immovable base: 13% of Catalans, and 8% of Basques, were opposed to the assistance provided by the Spanish army. This is the implacable proportion of Catalan separatism.[3]

SUMMARY

- Separatism is for the rich, constitutionalism for the poor.
- Catalonia's image amongst Catalans and other Spaniards has deteriorated somewhat as a result of the separatist challenge.
- The independence movement grew alongside the economic crisis, unemployment and despair, reaching a peak in 2013.

[3] GAD3 survey in Mariano Calleja (2020), "Ocho de cada diez catalanes y vascos elogian al Ejército contra el coronavirus", *ABC,* 13 April <https://www.abc.es/espana/abci-ocho-cada-diez-catalanes-y-vascos-elogian-ejercito-contra-coronavirus-202004122035_noticia.html?utm_source=piano&utm_medium=email&utm_campaign=2257&pnespid=kLVmo_dHWwONvnfB_I4DRS1dAnTMYvttxKvB3X1x>.

CHAPTER 19

Constitutionalist and Separatist Votes and Deputies

Separatist Regional Government

The most specific thing about the Catalan separatist challenge is probably that it is orchestrated by a regional government. Successive governments of the Generalitat de Catalunya have been in favour of independence but have been elected legitimately at the ballot box and in parliament. Originally, they did not oppose the state, the rule of law and democracy, they did so with their praxis.

Limiting and correcting the universal tendency of individuals, politicians, and governments to take power, more power, and all power is something contemplated in the legal system (in the case in point, the Spanish Constitution, the Statute of Autonomy of Catalonia, and the laws), as well as through the division of powers, the justice system, checks and balances, individual and collective political liberties and civil rights. These forms of coherence and control are sufficient under ordinary political and administrative circumstances. In extraordinary circumstances constitutions envision state coercion or federal compulsion. (See Chap. 4.)

Minority of Votes and Majority of Seats

The second specific aspect of the Catalan separatist challenge is that its rebel government rests on a majority of seats in parliament produced by a minority of votes. The distortion between votes and seats is due to the

F. Brunet, *The Economics of Catalan Separatism*,
https://doi.org/10.1007/978-3-031-14451-6_19

non-proportionality of the electoral law which, in effect, overrepresents interior, rural, separatist, Catalan-speaking areas. Given the difficulty of changing this electoral law, the only way to have a rotation in the government of the Generalitat de Catalunya is for there to be an expansion in the constitutionalist vote. The constitutionalists must win very many more votes, a large majority of them, in order to achieve a majority of seats, which would hand them the government.

THE KEY TO THE AUTONOMOUS ELECTIONS IS THE LEVEL OF PARTICIPATION, AND ITS REVERSE, THE ABSTENTION OF THE CONSTITUTIONALISTS

In this way the Parliament of Catalonia is elected in accordance with the Spanish Constitution, the Stature of Autonomy of Catalonia and electoral law and regulations.[1] 53.5% of those registered on the electoral census took part in the Catalan autonomous elections held on 14 February 2021. This was the lowest turnout for democracy in any election in Catalonia.[2] The abstention of 46.5% of the census is due to three circumstances (see Figs. 19.1 and 19.2):

1. Holding the elections during the Covid-19 pandemic.
2. The despair of constitutionalist voters, abandoned and subjected for decades to a regional political regime that contradicts their identities.
3. The disenchantment of the separatist voters, whose level of participation was a third of what it had been in the elections held on 21 December 2017.

With an electoral census of 5,623,962 Catalans with the right to vote, on 14 February 2021, 1,360,696 people voted for constitutionalist parties and 1,332,137 for separatist parties, the difference between them being 28,559 votes. In the preceding elections held on 21 December 2017, there were 2,228,421 constitutionalist votes and 2,079,340 separatist votes, a difference of 149,081votes.

---

[1] Generalitat de Catalunya (2022), *Normativa electoral* <http://www.gencat.cat/gobernacio/parlament2015/es/normativa-electoral/index.html>.
[2] Ministerio del Interior (2022), *Resultados electorales* <http://www.infoelectoral.mir.es/infoelectoral/min/>; y Parlament de Catalunya (2021), *Parlament 2021* <https://www.parlament 2021.cat/es/inici/index.html>.

Constitucionalist vote
(vertical axis)

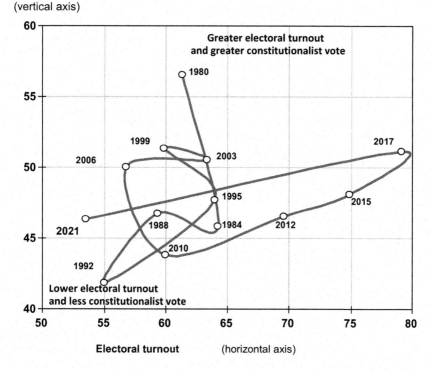

Fig. 19.1   Greater electoral participation generates a greater constitutionalist vote. (Source: Author's calculations on data from Generalitat de Catalunya (2022), *Eleccions al Parlament de Catalunya* <http://gencat.cat/economia/resultats-parlament2017/09AU/DAU09999>; and Parlament de Catalunya (2021), *Parlament 2021* <https://www.parlament2021.cat/es/inici/index.html>)

The main difference then is the level of participation: 53.5% in 2021 and 79.1% in 2017. This unprecedented fall in participation (25.6% of the census) meant that the constitutionalists lost 867,725 votes, and the separatists lost 747,203 votes.

On 14 February 2021, the Partit dels Socialistes de Catalunya (PSC) was the political group with the largest number of votes, 652,858, that is 23% of the total, 12.2% of the census and it won 33 seats. The PSC was followed by Esquerra Republicana de Catalunya (ERC), JuntsXCat, VOX,

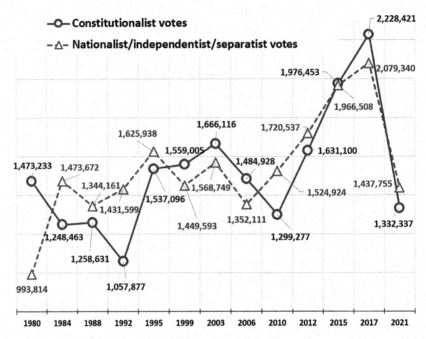

Fig. 19.2 Regional Catalan elections: Constitutionalist votes and separatist votes. (Source: Author's calculations based on data from Generalitat de Catalunya (2020), *Eleccions al Parlament de Catalunya* <http://gencat.cat/economia/resultats-parlament2017/09AU/DAU09999>; and Parlament de Catalunya (2021), *Parlament 2021* <https://www.parlament2021.cat/es/inici/index.html>)

CUP, En Comú Podem, C's and PP. Amongst the extra-parliamentary groups were PDecat and others.

As decentralisation of the Spanish administration became consolidated and the Autonomous Communities were given powers, the autonomous elections became more politically and socially important. In the case of Catalonia, the increased interest in the autonomous elections has also contributed to the rebellion of the Generalitat against the Spanish state and the rise of the independence movement as a mass movement.

DYNAMICS OF PARTICIPATION

There was a nationalist bias to the first elections to the Parliament of Catalonia, these elections seemingly the ones preferred by the nationalists. Inversely, it seemed that the separatists were less interested the general elections to the Congress of Deputies. Then these tendencies came together. Relatively speaking, the nationalist vote shrank in the autonomous elections and grew in the general elections, while the constitutionalist vote grew in the autonomous elections and shrank in the general elections.

The tendency of the constitutionalist vote to grow in the autonomous elections reached its peak in 2021. Constitutionalist voters started to perceive that the autonomous elections were important for their lives. The autonomous elections ceased being elections for only Catalan-speaking separatists and became elections for constitutionalists too, and their participation in the regional elections increased. For their part, the secessionists perceived that the general Spanish elections were important for their political visibility.

There is a double movement, therefore, of an increase in the constitutionalist vote in the autonomous elections and an increase in the separatist vote in the general elections leading to a convergence in the proportions of constitutionalists' and separatists' votes. With a very large proviso, it could be said that votes, which from 1980 had been for more or less right-leaning, conservative constitutionalist regionalists became, after 2012, 2013 and 2014, radical, revolutionary, separatist votes against the Spanish State. Previously, there was respect for the rule of law and coexistence in Catalonia was that of an advanced democracy, and the government of Spain enjoyed stability. Then the internal confrontation in Catalonia and that of the regional, separatist government with the government in Madrid, became the fuel for the nationalist-separatist vote.

Since the first autonomous elections in 1980, the electoral census has grown from 4.4 to 5.6 million Catalans and abstention has tended to reduce. Maximum participation was in 2017, minimum in 2021. The constitutionalist vote reached its peak in 2017 (2,228,421 Catalans) and the separatist one in 2015 (1,976,453).[3]

---

[3] Parlament de Catalunya. Departament de Comunicació (2022), *Eleccions al Parlament 1980–2017* <https://www.parlament.cat/document/composicio/150360.pdf>; and Parlament de Catalunya (2021), *Parlament 2021* <https://www.parlament2021.cat/es/inici/index.html>

There are parties with relatively stable votes, such as the PSC; parties with sustained growth, such as ERC; parties with a long decline, such as CiU; parties with very notable changes in fortune, such as PP; parties in persistent decline, such as En Comú Podem-PSUC; new parties, such as CUP and VOX; parties that peak and fall, such as C's; and there are also a couple of ephemeral parties.

Between 1980 and 2021, there were 13 autonomous Catalan elections. In terms of votes cast, the constitutionalist parties won 6 and the separatists 7. But in all 13, there was a majority of separatists' seats—sometimes with *sui generis* combinations—which enabled the formation of pro-independence, nationalist, secessionist, separatist governments.

GAP BETWEEN VOTES AND SEATS

This gap between votes and seats was to have serious consequences to the extent that, gradually, the dominant party in Catalonia, Convergència i Unió, underwent a U-turn in its political orientation, from an autonomist, regionalist party to a radical, revolutionary separatist party.[4] Madrid robs us, 'political conflict', 'right to decide the future of this land and this people', 'sovereignty', independence and a whole series of slogans and sophisms of this kind underscored this tendency. From this point we enter a period of political confrontation, social division and economic decline.

Since 1980, the constitutionalist and separatist votes in the autonomous elections grew more or less in tandem. The exceptions to this simultaneous progression are the elections of 1992, 2006, 2010 and 2021, years in which there was a drop in participation, one that was seriously pronounced in 2021 for reasons we have already mentioned at the beginning of this chapter (Covid-19, despair of constitutionalists and the disillusionment of the separatists).[5]

---

[4] The first president of the re-established Generalitat (1977–1980), Josep Tarradellas, was early to warn of the eventual separatist drift of Jordi Pujol and of CiU (Josep Tarradellas (1981), "Carta a Horacio Sáenz Guerrero, Director", *La Vanguardia*, 16 abril <http://hemeroteca.lavanguardia.com/preview/1981/04/16/pagina-10/32926422/pdf.html>). See Josep Maria Bricall (2017), *Una certa distància. Assaig de memòries*, Barcelona, RBA La Magrana.

[5] Generalitat de Catalunya (2020), *Eleccions al Parlament de Catalunya* <http://gencat.cat/economia/resultats-parlament2017/09AU/DAU09999>; y Parlament de Catalunya (2021), *Parlament 2021* <https://www.parlament2021.cat/es/inici/index.html>

Today's separatists managed to maintain their original share of the vote (and power) in spite of the U-turn they made from regionalism to secessionism. Even so, there is a constant drip of votes from CiU to ERC. But it is a fine achievement for the pro-independence leaders, and a surprise that this separatist and revolutionary change of direction should have taken place without losing hardly any votes. Without doubt, there was a flow of votes from CiU to ERC, both parties now trying to prove themselves more separatist than the other. Some new independence supporters prefer the original separatists (ERC) to the converted (CiU). Thus, between 2010 and 2017, the combined vote of CiU and ERC was well-nigh maintained, despite the separatist course taken, falling from 45.4 to 43%. If to this is added the 4.5% of the vote for CUP, we have the 47.5% of the minority separatist government of 2017, in comparison with the 48.7% of the similarly minority autonomist-separatist government of 2010.

The scramble between ERC and CiU for the electoral space, and the appearance of the extremist CUP party, has radicalised the regionalism-sovereignty-independence-separatism argument and this is one of the reasons for the degradation of politics in this region. The secessionist field, enlarged by the CUP, managed to maintain most seats, which is decisive, even though it did not achieve a majority of votes.

Vote and Preferred Language

In Catalonia, the vote is remarkably related to the preferred language. This would confirm that Catalan separatism is a linguistic nationalism. The proportion of votes for political parties according to the language most spoken by the voter in the Catalan autonomous elections of 2010 and 2017 may be summarised in the following manner[6]:

- Between the autonomous elections of 2010 and 2017, a relative reduction was observed in the vote of Catalan speakers and a relative increase in the vote of Spanish speakers.

[6] Cátedra José María Martín Patino de la Cultura del Encuentro (2018), *Informe España 2018*   <https://blogs.comillas.edu/informeespana/wp-content/uploads/sites/93/2019/05/IE2018Cap5-1.pdf> on data from Centre d'Estudis d'Opinió (2018) and from Centro de Investigaciones Sociológicas (2011).

- Similarly, between 2010 and 2017 the vote of those who speak Spanish and Catalan without distinction, grew from 6 to 8%. The vote of those who speak other languages rose by 1% to 5%.
- Between 58 and 84% of constitutionalist voters are Spanish speakers, depending on year and party, and between 59 and 74% of separatist voters are Catalan speakers.
- Amongst the constitutionalist parties, CeC-ICV is the one that receives the largest vote from Catalan speakers, between 36 and 23%. Eighty per cent of those voting for C's are Spanish speakers.
- Amongst the separatist parties, the main Spanish-speaking vote went from CiU to ERC. Sixty-four per cent of CiU voters are Catalan speakers and 25% are Spanish speakers.
- PSC and C's have the largest number of voters who usually speak a language other than Spanish or Catalan.

There is, therefore, a clear relationship between the party voted for and Catalans' preferred language. Consequently, apart from their linguistic nucleus, the parties have a large pool of votes if they manage to attract Catalan speakers, in the case of constitutionalists, and Spanish speakers, in the case of separatists.

- Let us analyse the relationship between the size of the municipality and the majority vote.[7] Barcelona and the other large Catalan cities have a mainly constitutionalist vote. In contrast, however, the smaller municipalities tend towards separatist hegemony, and the separatist vote is often more than 80% of the census. This is the separatist control of 'the territory'.
- Most of the municipalities in Catalonia are governed by JxCat (formerly CiU), and the others by ERC, or a combination of both. In the regional elections of 2021, on the coastal strip and in the Val d'Aran, the PSC was the constitutionalist party most voted for. The PP was in one town council and C's in none.

[7] El Confidencial (2017), *Elecciones catalanas* <https://www.elconfidencial.com/espana/cataluna/elecciones-catalanas/2017-12-22/resultados-municipios-comarcas-independentistas-constitutionalists_1497168/>

Vote and Standard of Living

To analyse the standard of living of the voters for the different political parties we can consider the results of the Catalan elections of 2021 according to the census division and level of income of those in the census.[8] The PSC is the party to have the most similar proportions in the four bands of income considered (very low, medium low, medium high, very high). C's also has a rather balanced structure of voters according to income.

The party with the highest proportion of very low-income voters is VOX. It also has the smallest proportion of very high-income voters. PdCat, which did not obtain seats in these elections, has the largest proportion of voters with very high income. In terms of income, Junts and CUP have similar proportions of voters and these two groups also have the smallest proportions of very low-income voters. ERC and ECP have similar proportions of voters in terms of income.

Non-proportional Electoral Law

Given that the electoral law is not proportional, a very relevant consideration in elections is the number of electors needed per seat in parliament, or the number of voters per seat in parliament. This is each party's 'price' for obtaining a member of parliament in each province. In the Catalan elections of 2021, it took, on average, 49,358 votes to obtain one deputy. In Tarragona, the figure was 32,301; in Girona 31,285 and in Lleida 21,019. In the elections of 2017, when there was a higher level of participation, there was a lower 'price', although it was equally unbalanced between provinces: in Barcelona 48,893 votes, in Tarragona 31,462, in Girona 30,463 and in Lleida 20,926. A deputy for Barcelona therefore 'costs' more than double that of a deputy for Lleida. A vote in Barcelona is worth less than half a vote in Lleida. Considered by party and province, the 'cost' of a deputy is even more uneven. For ERC, a deputy for Lleida 'cost' 8491 votes. For PP, a deputy for Barcelona (the only province in which it gained deputies in the 2021 elections) 'cost' 28,656 votes.[9]

---

[8] Kiko Llaneras (2021), "Así se relacionan en Cataluña la renta, el voto, el origen y la independencia", *El País*, 20 February <https://elpais.com/politica/2021/02/19/actualidad/1613741557_146092.amp.html>.

[9] Parlament de Catalunya (2021), *Parlament 2021* <https://www.parlament2021.cat/es/inici/index.html>; and Europa Press (2021), "Resultados elecciones Cataluña 14 de febrero de 2021, en datos y gráficos", *epdata* <https://www.epdata.es/datos/resultados-elecciones-cataluna-14-febrero-2021-datos-graficos/576>.

Thus, the electoral law applied to the elections to the Parliament of Catalonia produces a very different 'cost' in votes per deputy according to province and hence the party. In contrast, if the electoral law were proportional, each province would have, not a fixed number of seats as now, but a variable number according to the census. Before each election, the 135 seats would be distributed according to the census for each province. Moreover, if instead of provinces the electoral district were a single one for the whole of Catalonia, the result would require even fewer adjustments and the number of seats obtained by each party would be even more directly proportional to the number of votes obtained.

Had the current electoral law been replaced by a proportional electoral law, either in electoral districts at the province level or a single one for the whole of Catalonia, the majority of constitutionalist votes obtained in the autonomous elections of 21 December 2017 would have also produced a majority of constitutionalist seats. With a proportional electoral law, separatism would be playing a different tune and Catalonia's tragedy would have been avoided or shortened.

CONSTITUTIONALIST AND SEPARATIST POLITICAL SPACE

As a general consideration, in Catalonia as well as in the rest of Spain, the potential political space for constitutionalism is much broader and diverse than it is for separatism. Nevertheless, both obtain a similar number of votes. This contradiction is magnified when the difference between the proportion of votes and the proportion of seats is considered.

A contradiction can be observed between the broad political potential of constitutionalism and the reduced political potential of separatism. With respect to this, let us consider two of the main dimensions of politics:

- Degree of liberty and of public intervention: aspects to be regulated, orientation of politics and size of the public sector.
- Political, social and economic integration: narrative and practice of understanding or of confrontation.

All degrees of public regulation, from the smallest and most liberal to much larger degrees of regulation, as well as better political, social and economic integration find a place in constitutionalism. In contrast, separatism tends towards the most extreme state intervention and political, social and economic disintegration: this, precisely, is what the agenda, the road map, the deeds of secession consist of. These are, therefore, the potential spaces for constitutionalism and separatism. Constitutionalism, centred on and encompassing the various levels of state intervention, is bursting with political potential. Nevertheless, it receives a similar number of votes as the separatists.

Separatism, inclined entirely towards disintegration and total intervention, is lacking in political potential. Nevertheless, it receives a similar number of votes as the constitutionalists. The separatists obtain a proportion of votes similar to that of the constitutionalists and, what is more, they win more seats! The (relatively small) number of constitutionalist votes does not reflect the centrality of their political positions. The (relatively large) number of separatist votes does not reflect the marginal nature of their political position.

From the analysis of this paradoxical Catalan situation a conclusion must be drawn: the time will come when the reality of the constitutionalist and separatist vote reflects their respective political potential. Constitutionalism will expand to fill its vast potential and separatism will shrink to its diminutive potential.

Secessionist Rallies

The revolt of the Catalan separatists begins every 11 September. Since 2012, Omnium and the Assemblea Nacional Catalana have organised a rally, usually in the centre of Barcelona. Hundreds of coaches come from inland Catalonia with thousands of passengers wearing a T-shirt with this year's slogan on it. Families with children and grandparents out to spend the day in the capital and to march, from 17.14 hours, in honour of the 11 September of the supposedly infamous year of 1714.

Weeks before 11 September, TV3 announces the preparations, the itinerary and the slogans. On the day, the rally is broadcast from mid-morning to midnight. Then, in the following weeks, the separatists organisations provide some other performances: false referendums (9 November 2014 and 1 October 2017), autonomous elections (27 September 2015), large concentrations of over-excited enthusiasts in front of the regional parliament, the regional courts, other demonstrations, noisy protests against the King of Spain and the prime minister in universities, in front of consulates, in front of the headquarters of Societat Civil Catalana and of constitutionalist parties and so forth.

Every autumn is open season for the separatists. A significant aspect and a debatable one is the number of people attending these performances. [10] Two million! That is the outrageous figure they invented many years ago. Then there is the stubborn refusal to rectify the error. Calculating the number of demonstrators is something that is taught in police academies: surface area of the demonstration, minus street furniture, multiplied by density (up to four people per square metre, but usually one). Aerial photographs and computer technology to count the heads help too. In spite of the arithmetic, on every occasion, the number of demonstrators bandied about are as different as those announcing them, be they the organisers, the municipal police, the national police, the press, academic sources, etc.

It is known that, being a minority of the census and of the voters, the supporters of independence, along with the revolutionaries, obtain a majority of seats in parliament and therefore have a complete autonomous mini-state, parallel to the Spanish state, at their disposal. In this way, and thanks to the public service and publicly subsidised media, the secessionists can make as much, or more, noise than if they represented the majority of Catalans, or the enhanced majority, to change the Statute and the Constitution, proclaim their independent republic and impose it on the majority of Catalans and the majority of Spaniards.

A large number of people took part in the 11 September demonstrations of 2010–2020, but nowhere near two million, one and a half million or half a million. In the end there were 130,000 in 2019, 20,000 in 2020 (Covid) and 85,000 in 2021. The number of people taking part is ever smaller as different sources would confirm.[11] The tendency for the number of people attending or demonstrating at separatist performances coincides with, and confirms, the waning number of separatist voters.

[10] Álex Grijelmo (2017), "Nunca hubo un millón", *El País*, 3 octubre <https://elpais. com/elpais/2017/09/29/opinion/1506674781_614116.html>.
[11] Miquel Noguer and Ccamilo S. Baquero (2021), "Diada de división ante la mesa de diálogo", *El País*, 11 September <https://elpais.com/espana/catalunya/2021-09-11/el-independentismo-se-manifiesta-dividido-antes-de-la-mesa-de-dialogo.html>; Dolça Catalunya (2020), "Desplome apocalíptico de la Marmotada", *Dolça Catalunya*, 11 September <https:// www.dolcacatalunya.com/2020/09/desplome-apocaliptico-de-la-marmotada/>; Dolça Catalunya (2019), "Un vídeo i un gràfic que resumeixen la Marmotada 2019", *Dolça Catalunya*, 11 September <https://www.dolcacatalunya.com/2019/09/un-video-i-un-grafic-que-ensorren-la-marmotada–2019/>; El País (2019), "Resumen del 11 de septiembre", *El País*, 11 September <https://elpais.com/tag/fecha/20190911>; and Societat Civil Catalana (2020), "Informe sobre el recuento de individuos presentes en la gigafoto de la Vía Catalana", < https:// societatcivilcatalana.cat/assets/documents/informe-gigafoto-via-catalana-scc.pdf>.

SUMMARY

- In spite of the gradual, but radical, shift by CiU from being an autonomous party to being a separatist one, this group, and its reformulations, have held half of their voters. The other half has given its vote to ERC.
- In the elections held in Catalonia over the last two decades, there has been an increase in the constitutionalist vote in the autonomous elections and an increase in the nationalist vote in the Spanish general elections. The composition of the vote in the various elections converged.
- On most occasions, the constitutionalist voters are a majority, and even increase their lead, but the electoral system, which overrepresents the rural, Catalan-speaking areas, gives a majority of seats to the supporters of independence.
- The urban and coastal strip vote is predominantly constitutionalist, and the vote in rural, inland areas is regionalist (before) and separatist (now). The separatist parties, especially CiU and its reformulations, have very broad control over their estates.
- Constitutionalist voters are predominantly Spanish speaking and separatist voters are predominantly Catalan speaking.
- Participation in the elections is of key importance for their results, especially for the constitutionalists whose parties need to be overvoted to obtain a majority in the Parliament of Catalonia.
- Participation in elections in Catalonia is greater than the Spanish average. Participation in the autonomous elections grew from a minimum of 54.9% to 79.1% in December 2017, an election held after the attempted coup d'état of autumn 2017 and under the application of article 155 of the Spanish Constitution.
- The Catalan elections, like the false referendums and other separatist performances are called in the autumn, after the warm-up of the 11 September rallies and marches. The propaganda practised by the Generalitat de Catalunya, and its media stimulates the separatist vote.
- The higher the participation in the autonomous elections, the larger the proportion of the constitutionalist vote.
- Spanish-speaking voters tend to vote for PP, C's, PSC and ECP, and Catalan-speaking voters tend to vote Junts, CUP and ERC.
- Electoral participation in districts on the coastal strip is average and the vote is a majority constitutionalist one. Inland districts have a

very high level of participation, and the vote is a majority separatist one.

- The 'cost' of a deputy goes from four to one according to province and party. The highest price is paid by PP, the lowest by Junts-CiU and ERC.
- An electoral law proportional to the number of votes would have given a majority of seats to constitutionalist parties. Catalonia's tragedy would have been avoided.
- The rally held every 11 September marks the start of the new separatist season. The most numerous one was in 2013. The subsequent decline in numbers coincides with the decline observed in secessionist and revolutionary votes and seats.

CHAPTER 20

Hate and Separatist Violence, or Common Sense and Harmony

SECESSIONIST VIOLENCE

Is the violence an accident or is it part and parcel of the separatist challenge? From the conceptual point of view, violence, physical force over things or people to commit a crime or impose a belief or act, is an inherent part of the nationalist and supremacist discourse of the Catalan separatists. It shows the power of the separatists, and it is, specifically, the only way of achieving their aims, which consist of the subjugation of the population and the secession of Catalonia. The secessionists justify their violence on account of:

- A supposed moral superiority of the independence movement which, at the same time, is both victim and accuser.

- A supposed racial superiority of the Catalans[1] which legitimises phobia of the distinct, people who are different, the colonisers, immigrants to Catalonia from other parts of Spain, insultingly called *charnegos*, and this confirms their lack of respect and contempt for people.

Hatred forms part of the separatist narrative. Hatred of Spain, hatred of Spaniards, hatred of Spanish Catalans, hatred of anyone who thinks differently and hatred of anyone who does not share the same dreams and fantasies. Contempt, cancellation, the civil death of whoever disagrees, is a dissident, a traitor. And from there comes the silence of the lambs and the spiral of silence that the Catalan separatist regime has achieved. This conceptual violence of the secessionists is doubly empowered by the lack of contradiction of separatist ideas, which, at times, has even been non-existent, something that confers intellectual impunity, and by the penal impunity of secessionists for their violent actions.

The physical violence was not very visible in the separatist *process* until it entered a phase of decline, especially after the failed coup of autumn 2017. Previously there had been very sectarian, fascist-style independence groups (with their own black flags with white crosses, and they organised torch-lit marches attended by a significant number of people), there had

---

[1] To use his own terminology, in 2012, the animal in human form who became president of the Generalitat, Quim Torra, wrote, "Now you look at your country and you see talk of animals again. But they are a different kind of animal. Carrion eaters, vipers, hyenas. Animals in human form, without doubt, drooling hatred. A disturbed nauseating hatred, like mouldy false teeth speaking against everything the language represents. They are here, amongst us. They are disgusted by any expression of being Catalan. It is a sick phobia. There is something Freudian about these animals. Or a little glitch in their DNA chain. Poor people! They live in a country about which they know nothing: its culture, its traditions, its history. They are impervious to anything that has anything to do with Catalonia or being Catalan. It makes them come out in a rash. They recoil from everything that is not Spanish and in Castilian. They have names and surnames, these animals. We all know one of them. These animals abound". (Quim Torra (2012), "La llengua i les bèsties", *Catalunya Digital*, 19 December <https://tarragonadigital.com/opinio/5052/la-llengua-i-les-besties>.)

There you have it. Indeed, this is the level reached by the highest-ranking separatist 'intellectuals', these the beliefs that move them, this their hard-faced brazenness when they felt, as they still feel, legally and intellectually immune.

An anthology of racist Catalans can be found in Anon. (2021), *Racialistas catalanes* <https://racialistascatalanes.home.blog/2019/12/28/razacatalana/>.

also been communist-style groups (Arran, CUP Youth) and also terrorists.[2] Infecting everything with nationalist Catalanism has been the aspiration of the independence movement since the 2000 programme which Jordi Pujol launched in 1990 and which, since then, has been completely realised.[3] From football to all sports, from folk music to Catalan national classical music (sic), from supposed Catalan literature and philosophy to the complete distortion of history, including the invention of Catalan origins for outstanding historical personages such as Cervantes, El Cid, Santa Teresa de Jesús, Christopher Columbus, these were all Catalans according to the arch-subsidy-munching Institut Nova Història.

In this fervour, rather delirium, of 'everything is possible', of building castles in the air, fantasy, impunity, of playing poker, of bluffing and always increasing the stakes, of having behind you a regional government with its subsidies, you could be forgiven for thinking that, given the failure of the coup d'état of autumn 2017, some of the separatist forces would have had a difficult personal-psychological coming down to earth, as a group as well as politically, as contact with reality was made.[4] Or to put it another way, from the pleasure principle to the reality principle!

---

[2] Such as the Catalan Popular Army, Movement for the Defence of the Land, PSAN or Terra Lliure. Three hundred terrorist actions and a dozen murders. One of their leaders, Carles Sastre, spent 11 years in prison for the murder of the businessman, José María Bultó Marqués, for which he was pardoned in 1977, and for the double murder of the former mayor of Barcelona, Joaquín Viola Sauret and his wife, Montserrat Tarragona Domènech. This triple terrorist assassin is the leader of Intersindical-CSC, the separatist civil servants' union.

[3] On the task of turning the masses into a political actor, see the classic George L. Moss (1975), *The Nationalization of the Masses: Political Symbolism and Mass Movements in Germany, from the Napoleonic Wars Through the Third Reich*, New York, NY, Howard Fertig. On the place of native soil in regional identity and the task of nation building, see Eric Storm (2016), *La construcción de identidades regionales en España, Francia e Alemania, 1890–1939*, Madrid, Ediciones Complutense, 2019.

[4] The Comitès de Defensa de la República (CDR), successors to the Comitès de Defensa del Referéndum and Tsunami Democràtic, do not seem different from Junts per Catalunya (the former CiU) and ERC. The CDR coincide and compete with Arran (youth organisation of the Catalan pro-independence left) in subjugation, violence, barricades, public denunciation and terror. The police and the judicial system will determine the organisational structure—very strict and well supplied with technological resources—and everyone's responsibilities in the burning of Barcelona and the paralysis of Catalonia during the months of October and November 2019, and February of 2021.

The secessionist leaders had their 'astuteness' on show. They were, without doubt, astute. But not enough to deceive all the Catalans and the rest of normal Spaniards, nor the Spanish government or the Spanish judiciary. They were highly astute at deceiving their own separatist followers. That is why, in spite of the inevitability of the failure of the coup, it is taking such a long time for separatists to recognise the deception, and it will take all the longer if the post-coup Generalitat continues to be separatist and continues to stir up confrontation and if, furthermore, the government of Spain allows Spain to gradually fragment.

BARCELONA BURNS

Bearing all this in mind, it is not very surprising that the most senior secessionists should have been involved in serious incidents during the autumn of 2019, with the excuse of the court's ruling on the coup d'état in 2017, and in February and March of 2021, with the excuse of the imprisonment of a delinquent rapper. Of course, none of these disturbances were fortuitous or casual. Their reproduction in other Spanish cities is also very significant. This violence was possible due to the acquiescence of the government of the Generalitat and its police force, the Mossos d'Esquadra, Barcelona's local police, the Guardia Urbana and the absence of the National Police and the Guardia Civil, which the Spanish government did not deploy.

In effect what had happened is that, after the gradual falling off of various hundreds of thousands of peaceful separatist supporters and their families, and after the gradual decline in the number of pro-independence voters, a sediment of several hundred urban guerrillas rose to the fore. Pacifism and party were succeeded by rebellion and violence. Hatred and the discourse they manipulate opened the way for violence on the street and violent acts of increasing significance. Outrageous barricades proliferated, sudden blazes, havoc, destruction, vandalism and looting. Catalonia is a giant verbal bonfire, and sometimes it is a real bonfire with repeated calls for civil war. That is improbable, but terrorism is probable.

For separatists it is essential for there to be no manifestation of any opposition to their message. They must show the supremacy of the independence narrative in spite of its evident falsehood and in spite of their lack of respect for non-secessionists, their violation of people's rights and liberties, and of their minority position. They impose their supremacy in all possible ways, including, as is evident, violence, whether 'it is necessary' or, especially when 'it is not necessary'.[5] Hence the apparently random and gratuitous character of secessionist violence. To the conceptual violence of Catalan separatists, or soft terrorism, is added the physical violence of Catalan separatists, or hard terrorism. They aim to sow terror, fear, to subjugate, to impose, show who is in charge and who commands, and to establish a parallel world that is contrary to reason and the law. *Som república*, we are a republic.

Imposition of the credo, dogma, liturgy and separatist power is directed at:

A. People, basically through hate crimes, public denunciations, protests against

- Constitutionalists, be they leaders, work colleagues or members of the family.
- Constitutionalist political parties, their leaders, headquarters and events.
- Parents who request the law, which should ensure that 25% of education be in Spanish, be observed for their children.
- Judges.
- National police and Guardia Civil resident in their barracks and hotels in Catalonia during the autumn of 2017.
- The self-imposed signal of the yellow ribbon pinned to the lapel.
- Public denunciation, contempt, denunciation of artists, sports people, business people, teachers and writers.

B. Conquest and control of the territory, occupying it basically by

---

[5] During the first six months of 2019, there were 189 acts of political violence in Catalonia (Observatorio Cívico de la Violencia Política en Cataluña—Impulso Ciudadano (2019), *Informe sobre violencia política en Cataluña. Primer semestre de 2019* <https://www.impulsociudadano.org/wp-content/uploads/2019/08/Informe-sobre-violencia-pol%C3%ADtica-en-Catalu%C3%B1a_Primer-semestre-de-2019_Difusi%C3%B3n-online.pdf>).

- Flying starred flags, known as the *estelada*, from private balconies and from public institutions, in the streets, squares, roundabouts and any other public or visible space.[6]
- Yellow ribbons hanging from the facades of private and public buildings.
- Placards with their successive slogans: referendum, yes, yes, yes, independence, political prisoners, etc.
- Yellow crosses on beaches, squares and in parks.
- Occupation of urban space and the destruction of street furniture.
- Sabotage of infrastructure.
- Confrontation with the forces of law and order to show their capacity for control.

C. Control of the media and education through

- The orientation of all the programmes on TV and radio at all hours.
- Permanent presence of the Generalitat in public messages and information: 'The Generalitat by your side' (sic).
- Linguistic immersion only in Catalan.
- Indoctrination of school students.
- Intimidation of university students.

D. Control of all political institutions and of civil society

- Hijacking of each and every organisation, club and association and the imposition of separatist's dogma, credo, liturgy and power.

FROM VIOLENCE TO TERROR

For separatism, there is little difference between violence (good and cathartic) and terror, soft and hard, (necessary, imposed by the enemy). Both of them are key to showing who is in charge here and to make clear

---

[6] In the words of *Dolça Catalunya*: "[...] The ribbon wearing politicos enclose the neighbours in a spiral of silence: only what is seen exists, there is only space for the ideas expressed in the public space. If you don't see yours there, you are a bit weird, so either keep quiet or adopt the thought of the Regime." (Dolça Catalunya (2020), "A Tordera també resisteixen", *Dolça Catalunya*, 24 June <https://www.dolcacatalunya.com/2020/06/a-tordera-tambe-resisteixen/?fbclid=IwAR1dTzYbdu8hDmV5eU3LsOfZYhcUv41NVqlCeC AqVjkhZkXv41kIJgoirkY>).

the consequences of not communing with their credo, dogma, liturgy and power. It is the hijacking of the whole of society and the banality of evil.[7] The fine rain of hatred opens the spiral of violence: "[...] The most destructive violence for a society is not an isolated incident, no matter how terrible it may be. It is the fine rain of hatred: 'banal' events, small psychological aggressions (boycotts, threats, for example) or symbolic (ridicule, for example). Then vandalism and slander in the social media followed by physical aggression, apparently sporadic 'boys' fights'".[8]

Everything is legitimate to affirm the power of the separatists and part of this is control over people and the territory. Control over people and the territory is one of the requisites for a state to be recognised as such and independent. The presence of the general or central Spanish state Administration, its symbols and in its tasks, is inexistent in practically the entire territory of Catalonia. The Spanish state has been absent from Catalonia for three decades. Throughout the whole of Catalonia, the visibility of Spain is zero. The separatists have occupied Catalonia for more than three decades. Then it will be time enough for the usucapion of Catalonia by the separatists.[9]

The confrontation generated by the separatists enables them to show their real ability and danger. It gives them visibility in the media. In the end, it is the children of the Catalan separatist regime erected since 1980 who shake the tree, and it is the leaders, office holders and subsidised separatists who collect the fruit.

In the context of the political confrontation in Catalonia (and in the rest of Spain and in many other countries) the word 'fascist' has become one of the main terms of revilement: the term is thrown at anyone who thinks differently. It is the most odious and disparaging term in today's politics. It demonises the adversaries—who, of course, are normally not

---

[7] Hannah Arendt (1951), *The Origins of Totalitarianism*, London, Penguin, 2017.

[8] "Finally, the fine *rain* becomes a devastating storm that drags along with it the tormentors and the victims alike: methods of coercion and physical intimidation that become systematic and acquire potentially lethal danger levels. The process needs a catalyst: a yielding look, or the looking the other way of those who do not participate in these actions, and indifference, passivity and the incompetence of the authorities whose responsibility it is to protect the victims." (José Miguel Fernández-Dols (2018), "Fina lluvia de odio", *El asterisco. Notas and opiniones al margen*, 3 junio <https://www.elasterisco.es/author/aut_079/#.Xdl9Uuj0nBQ>).

[9] Regarding this, see Araceli Mangas Martin, (2014), "Cataluña: ¿No habrá independencia?" *El Cronista del Estado Social y Democrático de Derecho*, No. 42, pp. 54–65.

fascists at all—and it legitimises the use of violence against them, because they are 'fascists'.[10]

Hatred, intimidation, violence, soft and hard terror are essential ways of contributing to the confrontation between Catalans, and to the decline, decomposition, deconstruction, destruction, fragmentation, decadence and ruin of Catalonia.

SUMMARY

- *Barcelona no es crema!* "Barcelona is not for burning!" was the spontaneous cry of the people during the large, constitutionalist demonstration held on 27 October 2019.
- Hatred, verbal and physical violence, hard and soft terror, are inherent to separatist totalitarianism: they show separatists' ability to impose and the costs of opposing the new bosses. They create the appearance of unanimity and the ineluctability of independence, and demonstrate their control over people and the territory, all of which are elements of the sovereignty they wish to conquer.

[10] "Although fascism has almost disappeared, anti-fascism has not. An anti-fascism without fascism makes it possible to create or imagine exactly the right kind of enemy, one that, in reality, does not exist. This has the added benefit of apparently justifying a call to violence and the adoption of tactics that are ever more aggressive. This imposes an ever more centralised power, establishes censorship and achieves aims difficult to achieve through rational discourse and analysis. There is no simpler way of stigmatising and verbally affirming power over an opponent." (Stanley G. Payne (2021), "Antifascism without Fascism", *First Things*, 22 January <https://www.firstthings.com/issue/2021/01/january>).

CHAPTER 21

Quality of Democracy in Catalonia

THE CATALAN SEPARATIST REGIME

Is Spain a democracy? Obviously, yes. Is there rule of law in Catalonia? Obviously not. In spite of that, Catalonia is part of Spain, and the rule of law is part of democracy.

We are faced, obviously, with a contradiction. Spanish democracy has, for two decades, neglected the upholding of the rule of law in one of its regions. The non-application of Spanish legality in a part (and you could add, a very significant part) of Spanish territory, is a question of internal Spanish law suffered by 7.6 million Catalans. The non-application of the law eats away at the whole rule of law in Catalonia and the whole of Spain. Hence the crisis in Spanish democracy.

In the particular case of Catalonia, the quality of the regional government, the fiscal hell, as well as hatred, violence and hard and soft terror are analysed in other sections of this investigation. We shall, for now, summarise various aspects of the infringement of the law, the failure to uphold the rule of law (Spanish law, of course!) under the separatist regime that has emerged in Catalonia since 1980.[1]

A. No ideological liberty

---

[1] Societat Civil Catalana (2017), *Déficits de calidad democrática en Cataluña: La vulneración de los derechos fundamentales (2015–2017)* <https://societatcivilcatalana.cat/sites/default/files/docs/Informe-Deficits-2017.pdf>.

© The Author(s), under exclusive license to Springer Nature Switzerland AG 2022
F. Brunet, *The Economics of Catalan Separatism*,
https://doi.org/10.1007/978-3-031-14451-6_21

143

- Imposition of separatist's dogma, credo, liturgy and power by the administrations, corporations and associations
- Substitution of commonly held symbols for flags of independence
- Affiliation of the administrations to the secessionist process
- Partisan behaviour of corporations and associations
- Coercion of those who show themselves not to be nationalists

B. No right to education

- Nationalist indoctrination at school
- Nationalist indoctrination in the textbooks
- Nationalistic campaign in the school setting
- Nationalistic swaying of children's awareness in academic, cultural and leisure activities
- Linguistic immersion and harassment of the dissident

C. No right to free and impartial elections

- Infringement of the principles of impartiality, liberty and equality
- A non-proportional electoral law that favours the vote of more separatist rural areas
- Collaboration of Catalan public administrations in the flying of separatist flags from public buildings and in public spaces before and after electoral processes

D. No neutrality in the Generalitat administration

- Absence of pluralism in the public service media
- Administrations that act on the fringe of, or outside, the law and courts
- Creation of state structures
- Preparation of two self-determination referendums
- No right to effective judicial protection or juridical security
- General and total non-application of sentences against separatist practices
- No protection of privacy and discrimination on ideological grounds
- Illegal compilation of databases: census for the referendum and census for the Catalan tax Administration
- Lists of people who support or do not support the regime
- No guardianship of fundamental rights either by the justice system nor by the *Síndic de Greuges* (Ombudsman)

A Rebel Regional Government with Impunity

The secessionist challenge and the secessionist regime installed in Barcelona since 1980 would not have been possible without the backing of a regional government with wide powers and without the passive attitude of the government of Spain. The impunity enjoyed by separatist parties, separatist people and the separatist government encouraged acts that were ever more daring, wild, vehement and massive.

There is a simultaneous progression of impunity and the breakdown in the rule of law. And there is a symbiosis between the progression of the secessionist breakers of the rule of law and the indolence of the government of Spain. We know that the separatist challenge is consistent with the backing of a regional government that has impunity for its actions. We know less about the reasons for the indolence of the governments of Spain, whether it is the acceptance of the principle of appeasement or insecurity about the legitimacy of the state and the rule of law. The irresponsibility of both of them has destroyed Catalonia and led Spain to the verge of complete constitutional crisis.

Whatever the case may be, two notable milestones emerge from this conjunction between the impunity of the separatists and the indolence of the governments of Spain: false referendum I of 9 November 2014 and the coup d'état of autumn 2017 ('laws' of the regional government, of the regional parliament, false referendum II of 1 October 2017 and the declaration of the Catalan republic on 27 October 2017). The separatists' maximum programme having been totally realised, the central government, with its back against the wall, had no other option but to apply article 155 of the Spanish Constitution and assume direct control of the Generalitat de Catalunya.

Paradigmatic of the situation of Spanish justice is the case of the return by the persons convicted because organizers of the pseudo referendum I (November 2014) and of the pseudo referendum II (October 2017) of the public money with which the illegal acts they ordered were organized.[2]

---

[2] Manuel Miró (2022), "Auge y caída del Tribunal de Cuentas", *elliberal.cat*, 20 July.

SUMMARY

- Spain being a fully democratic country, the failure to uphold the rule of law in Catalonia represents a very important undermining of the country's capacities.
- Given that the electoral law eternalises the government of the Generalitat's rebellious position, the central government should take it upon itself to unblock this Catalan syndrome and put an end to the separatist rebellion. The risk, if it does not do so, is the disintegration of Spain.
- Postponing the resolution of the separatist challenge to the rule of law severely harms the rights of the Catalans and increases the social and political price that Spanish democracy will have to pay.
- It must surely be the case that the Catalans have some right for the central government to liberate them from the long confrontation they are suffering from and for the state to ensure the upholding of the rule of law in Catalonia, the upholding of their liberties and their progress. Catalans will place their trust in the Spanish state if it liberates them from the nationalist yoke.

PART II

Decline

CHAPTER 22

The Cost of the Separatist Challenge

THE COST OF SEPARATISM

The secession of Catalonia will not happen. Karl Popper said that our democratic societies are open: everything can happen. That is so, within limits, with respect for the law one orientation is possible, as is its contrary. One way or another everything is possible, but not everything is probable.

The probability of Catalonia ceding from the rest of Spain is vanishingly small, bearing in mind the real legal, national, and international context and, above all, in view of the fact that, at one of the separatism's most decisive moments, the false referendum I of 9 November 2014, their parties gained only 27% of the electoral census, and this according to their own figures! In the autonomous elections of 2017, they gained 37.4% of the census, a proportion that fell to 26.8% in 2021. (See Chap. 19.)

The markets have discounted the possibility of secession. Otherwise, how would the stocks of Catalan companies and those of the rest of Spain have remained almost stable? Nevertheless, the challenge of the separatists who are now badly governing Catalonia represents an essential threat to Catalans, to Spain and to the rule of law itself. It is an assault on Spanish democracy in particular, on liberty in general, and by extension, a threat to the other European states.

It is possible to think something similar might happen in any country. In fact, it has happened where the state was most decentralised and where

© The Author(s), under exclusive license to Springer Nature Switzerland AG 2022
F. Brunet, *The Economics of Catalan Separatism*,
https://doi.org/10.1007/978-3-031-14451-6_22

democracy found itself in some ways constricted on account of a previous dictatorship. To be a complete state, all that is necessary, especially for Catalonia, the Basque Country and Navarre is to have full control over raising taxes, over pensions, defence and foreign affairs.

The most characteristic feature of the Catalan independence movement is probably the fact that the challenge is articulated more by a regional government than by a legal political party or a mass movement. The separatist government of the Generalitat is legitimate in its origins, but has completely abandoned the principle of neutrality, does not recognise legality and exceeds its powers. On the other hand, in the face of all this— and without doubt it is very serious—there is little contradiction. The opposition and opponents to the separatist regime are not very visible and are still few and far between.

We can say that, fortunately, secession will not happen. But there is a very deep problem. There is a very high level of confrontation, led by a regional government and its public offices, where the separatist flags frequently fly and where the constitutional and statutory ones frequently do not.

There is a tremendous amount of confrontation, but secession will not happen. The consequences of a hypothetical separation of Catalonia are exactly that, hypothetical, they will not occur. But what is real are the consequences and the cost of the confrontation that stirs the Catalan separatists. We can consider three aspects of the price that has been paid for the separatist *process*:

A. Direct cost of the *process*: money invested. This is a tangible budget cost that today stands at some €6300 million a year. It consists of:

- Generalitat de Catalunya subsidies to entities and groups that organise the independence process, from the ANC to the most esoteric clubs. (€200 million).
- Subsidies to regional media, TV3 and its 6 channels, and all the local and regional newspapers, TV and radio stations, (€400 million).[1]
- Expenditure of the Departments of the Generalitat (devoted body and soul to subversion, 90% of the cost of the Presidential Office and 40% of the cost of the political Departments), organisations, insti-

---

[1] Xavier Rius (2020), "Toni Soler ve la luz", *enoticies.com* < https://www.youtube.com/watch?v=XLGPTLmV6HY>.

tutes and other agencies, (€200 million) and 10% of the government budget, that is, €5300 million.
- Improper powers that duplicate those of the state, amongst them, the embassies (€400 million).

B. Indirect cost of the *process*: negative consequences and lost opportunities. This is a current, tangible macroeconomic cost (for Catalonia and another, lesser one, for the rest of Spain) deriving from:

- Flight of investment and companies: during the period 2010–2018 the Community of Madrid received 3.5 times more foreign investment than Catalonia; in 2017, five times more, and in 2018 fifteen times more. (See Chap. 32.)
- A reduction in Catalan sales to the rest of Spain, in part due to the boycott practised by 23% of Spaniards and estimated to be 5% of sales to the rest of Spain (€2000 per annum).
- Serious and painful social fracture, contrary to the Catalan tradition of integration and the needs of a global economy based on knowledge and synergies.

C. Cost of the non-intervention by the central government in the face of the growing separatist challenge and the deterioration of Catalonia: the political, social and economic cost of the long-lasting separatist challenge over various decades and a serious level of confrontation. Although intangible, this cost is high and has profound effects in the medium and long terms. It can be seen, for example, in

- Lack of confidence, instability, risk and uncertainty.
- A fiscal hell that tempts people to flee to tax havens (the closest, Andorra, known well to the Pujol family), clientelism and corruption.
- A regulatory hell, as can be seen in the quality of regulation and economic freedom indices.
- Repudiation of Spanish in education and in the administration.

Furthermore, in the regional competitiveness analysis, we can see the impact of the secessionist scheme (see later in Chap. 24). Between 2010 and 2019, Catalonia fell from position 103 to 161 in the competitiveness ranking of the European regions. Madrid, meanwhile, occupies position 98. Separatist Catalonia expels; Madrid attracts people, companies and investment. Concentration of economic activity in Madrid is not the best thing for Catalonia, neither is it for Spain, nor for Madrid.

In the following chapters we shall analyse the components of the direct and indirect costs of the secessionist process of the Generalitat de Catalunya. That is to say, the tangible and intangible cost of the process expressed as a gap or deficit between the GDP of Catalonia with the *process* and the GDP of Catalonia without the *process*. This gap expresses the cost of the separatist challenge (undermining sales, activity and investment, causing political instability). It is estimated to cost around 4.6% of GDP (€10,626 million) and to have cost 117,000 jobs. (See the next chapter.)

THE LONG-LASTING NATURE OF THE SEPARATIST CHALLENGE

The accumulated costs deriving from the non-intervention of the central government to reduce and stop the challenge of the Catalan separatists and, in particular, the government of the Generalitat, is shown in Fig. 22.1. Four phases can be discerned in this challenge: 1980–2003, autonomous phase with increasing incidents of confrontation; 2003–2014, initial phase of the challenge with the first signs of disaffection with Spain, the Constitution and the rule of law; 2014–2016, sedition phase, with a war of attrition against the rule of law; and 2017, culminating phase of the rebellion and full realisation of the maximum separatist programme ('laws' of disconnection, false referendum and 'declaration of independence' and of the 'Catalan republic').

The central government only responded to the challenge of the separatist Generalitat in a proportional manner once the latter had realised its maximum programme. That was when it applied Article 155 of the Spanish Constitution and called elections in this Autonomous Community on 21 December 2017. Instead of preventing (1980–2003) and instead of treating (2003–2017), the response was delayed until there was a constitutional crisis, until it was impossible to ignore it except at the risk of destroying the rule of law in Spain.

Given that the governments of Spain were perfectly aware of the Catalan situation, their inaction over various decades of rebellion can only be explained by apathy, perplexity, incredulity, fear, paralysis, seizure, stagnation, exhaustion, terror, incapacity, disability, idleness, ineffectiveness, procrastination or something else equally serious, as the cause of their

A. High confrontation: In Catalonia ordinary laws are not fully implemented
B. Challenge: The Criminal Code can be applied to the separatist Catalan authorities
C. Sedition: Art. 155 of the Spanish Constitution can be applied in Catalonia
D. Cout d'etat: Art. 155 of the Spanish Constitution needs to be applied in Catalonia

Accumulative cost of the long-lasting separatist threat

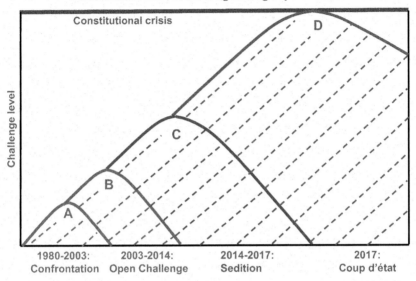

= Cumulative cost of the non-intervention against the separatist challenge to the rule of law in Spain

Fig. 22.1 Accumulative cost of the non-intervention of the Spanish state and of the long-lasting separatist threat to Spain's democracy. (Source: Author's conception)

absolute irresponsibility. The governments of Spain are characterised by inactivity in fulfilling the law and by the defence of individual, collective, political and civil rights. In Catalonia, there is exemption from central control over the upholding of the rule of law. They abandoned the Catalans to the whims of separatists.

Successive governments simply refused to assume the immediate political cost of intervening against Catalan separatism and a Generalitat that was experimenting with plotting a coup (a cost which today seems minimum), thereby passing a much greater political cost to the future. That is how the constitutional crisis of 2017, was achieved. And it is how a possible change of regime, a probable disintegration of Spain into 17 mini-states, remains on the horizon.

The blindness and self-deception of governments, of institutions and of the elites are amongst the main reasons for the collapse of political regimes. One need go no further than nineteenth- and twentieth-century Spain to find numerous examples of this. To put something of a psychological slant on it, you could say that not learning from history leads to the repetition of historic errors.

In Catalonia, the current regime of de facto authoritarian mini-state provides a taste of what would come if the separatists were to rule without restriction, which is exactly what they aim for. In a global world, the strategy followed by the separatists in Catalonia is probably the most harmful for this region. And this reflects their enormous irresponsibility. The challenge of independence therefore has a cost for Catalonia: a direct and indirect cost; tangible and intangible; in the short, medium and long terms; and it has some immediate beneficiaries, the separatist elite. With regard to this, a description of Catalonia made a century ago comes to mind, 'Catalonia, a declining people'.[2] At that time, the best contemporary period for Catalonia and for Spain, 1960–2000, was yet to come.[3] Now, in contrast, if the secessionist fracture continues, Catalonia will certainly see itself embroiled in a long recession and a steep decline.

THE ACCUMULATED COSTS OF NON-INTERVENTION BY THE SPANISH STATE

The challenge of the Catalan separatists continues, and lasts and lasts. Four decades of appeasement and feeding by the Spanish state have broken the virtuous balance between integration in Spain and in the European Union, and decentralisation, a virtuous balance of which the Autonomous Community and Autonomous City system was formerly a shining example.

One has to ask if the separatist challenge is reversible. Is the Autonomous Community system, whereby the Spanish state is made up of 17

---

[2] Josep Antoni Vandellós (1935), *Catalunya, poble decadent*, Barcelona, Biblioteca Catalana d'Autors Independents.

[3] See Joaquim Maluquer i Sostres (1963), *L'estructura econòmica de les terres catalanes*, Barcelona, Barcino; Joan Sardà Dexeus (1983), "Pròlogo", in Many authors (1983), *La economia de Cataluña hoy y mañana*, Barcelona, Banco de Bilbao; and Jacint Ros Hombravella (1991), *Catalunya: una economia decadent?*, Barcelona, Barcanova.

mini-states, reversible? Is the de facto situation of the disconnection of Spain from the citizens resident in the main part of Catalan territory reversible? Is the situation reversible in which the rule of law is not fully applied in Catalonia in fields such as people's rights, non-compliance with the law by regional and local administrations, lack of neutrality of the administrations and the non-execution of court judgements? Is the rebellion of the separatists and the current severe social and political confrontation reversible? Is the economic decline reversible?

Perhaps things could be reversed. There are two requirements sine qua non to re-establish the plenitude of the rule of law in Catalonia:

- A constitutionalist government of the Generalitat that emanates from a majority of votes and a majority of non-separatist seats.
- A government of Spain, of one or more constitutionalist parties, with the vocation, purpose and ability to implement the corresponding political, executive and legislative initiatives.

For the time being, the contagion of Catalan independence is infecting the rest of Spain. This is obvious in the Basque Country and Navarre. But Galicia, Andalusia, Valencia and the Balearic Islands are also showing symptoms similar to those of Catalan separatism. And the government presided over by Pedro Sánchez owes its existence to the separatists and revolutionaries in Podemos. So, very gradually, the rebellion—in Catalonia that of the separatists against Spain, in the rest of Spain against the right and against the democratic system—is spreading, progressing, lasting and becoming a task for government.[4]

In Spain as a whole, the initial collaboration between separatism and the extreme Catalan left has been reproduced, now as collaboration between separatism in various regions and the governmental extreme left to dismantle the Spanish democratic system. Perpetuate the challenge or resolve it.

There aren't really that many options for overcoming the challenge of the Catalan separatists and the incipient Spanish constitutional crisis and neither is there much time ahead. Indeed, if instead of one region (moved

---

[4] Joan López Alegre (2020), "La 'procesización' de la política española", *Economía Digital*, 13 June <https://ideas.economiadigital.es/joan-lopez-alegre/la-procesizacion-de-la-politica-espanola_20072130_102.html>.

to secession by an administration, but without the majority of the population) the rebellion expands in content and spreads to other places, the coup against Spanish democracy could be insurmountable.

SUMMARY

- Instead of secession and its proclaimed benefits, there is, in Catalonia, a process of fragmentation and decline that is already very costly in macroeconomic, budgetary and business terms, accompanied by acute social confrontation and institutional chaos.
- The absence of a response by Spanish democracy to the position it has been put in by the separatists has increased the cost the Catalans have already paid, and will continue to pay, along with all other Spaniards and Spain: instability, decline, fragmentation, constitutional crisis and disintegration.
- If the separatist challenge is not stopped, Catalonia's decline will be very steep.

CHAPTER 23

Dynamics of Catalonia's GDP under the *Process*

GDP GAP DUE TO THE *PROCESS*: -4.6%

How much has the *process* that the Catalan separatists have been implementing for decades cost and how much is it costing now? It is interesting to know the cost of the separatist challenge now, that is to say, how much is being lost on account of their cause, and how much has already been lost and invested in it? But, of course, the most pressing questions about the *process* are about its impact on the future and its future cost.

The cost of the separatist challenge can be expressed in terms of lost GDP, that is to say, the difference between Catalonia's real GDP (which unfortunately supports the synthetic cost of the process) and the estimated GDP of Catalonia without the *process* (on the assumption that this region would have grown in a manner similar to the weighted average of four regions of Spain whose economic structure is similar to Catalonia's: Madrid, Valencia, the Basque Country and Navarre).

The results of this estimate of the gap in GDP on account of *process* can be seen in Fig. 23.1. From 2005 to 2020 the gap in GDP is -4.6%. This is the cost of the *process*, the price paid by Catalan society. Catalonia's long-term permanent GDP is down by 4.6%. So far. That is minus €10,984 million per annum, or minus €1384 per Catalan (-4.6% of average income), minus €115 per month, minus €4 per day.

F. Brunet, *The Economics of Catalan Separatism*,
https://doi.org/10.1007/978-3-031-14451-6_23

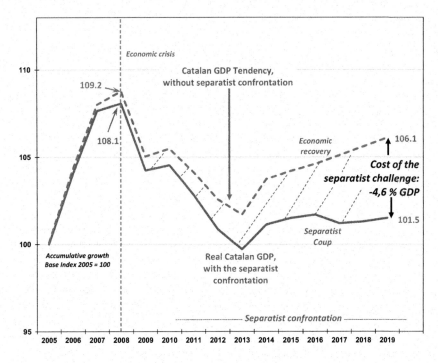

Fig. 23.1 The cost of the separatist challenge to the rule of law: -4.6% of GDP. (Source: Author's calculations based on data from the Institut d'Estadística de Catalunya (2022), *Producte interior brut (Base 2010). Oferta. Avanç* <https://www.idescat.cat/indicadors/?id=conj&n=10233>; and the Instituto Nacional de Estadística (2022), *Contabilidad regional de Spain* https://www.ine.es/dyngs/INE base/es/operacion.htm?c=Estadistica_C&cid=1254736167628&menu=res ultados&idp=1254735576581#!tabs-1254736158133)

Obviously, *the process robs us!* The separatist confrontation has robbed us, is robbing us and, if the Catalans and Spanish democracy are incapable of overcoming it, it will continue to rob us; it will rob us of our economic capacity, it will rob us of our jobs, it will rob our investment, it will rob us of understanding and peace. Something similar to this happened with investment. The dynamics of Catalonia's Gross Fixed Capital Formation (GFCF) is very negative: between 2007 and 2017, Gross Fixed Capital

Formation (GFCF investment) fell by 29.7%.[1] And since 2012, Madrid's GFCF exceeds that of Catalonia by 26.0%! The warning is clear, it is risky to invest in a Catalonia blighted by the *process*.

Gap in GDP Between Catalonia and Madrid: -11.2%

In 2019, Madrid's GDP exceeded that of Catalonia. The population of Catalonia is 14.4% larger than that of Madrid, the surface area of Catalonia is four times that of Madrid, but its average per capita income is 11% lower than Madrid's.[2] Figure 23.2 shows the dynamics of Catalonia and Madrid's GDP since 2005, as an accumulated growth index. At the end of 2019, Catalonia's GDP index stood at 101.5 and that of the Community of Madrid stood at 112.7. Between 2005 and 2019, there was: a) the crisis of 2007–2013, which was more profound in Catalonia; and b) the *process* of separatist confrontation, which only affected Catalonia directly.

This is the permanent gap in GDP arising from different rates of accumulated growth in Catalonia and the Community of Madrid: the gap between Catalonia and Madrid has opened to 11.2%. A comparison of Fig. 23.1 (difference between real Catalan GDP with the *process* and Catalan GDP tendency without the *process*) with Fig. 23.2 (difference between real Catalan GDP with the *process* and Madrid GDP) shows that 4.6 points of the 11.2 gap between Catalonia and Madrid are a direct result of the separatist *process*.

The decline of Barcelona and Catalonia, and the bias of Spanish economic dynamics towards Madrid, is a negative tendency for Catalonia and

---

[1] Instituto Nacional de Estadística (2020), *Contabilidad regional de España* <https://www.ine.es/dyngs/INEbase/es/operacion.htm?c=Estadistica_C&cid=1,254,736,167,628&menu=resultados&idp=1,254,735,576,581#!tabs-1,254,736,158,133>.

[2] See Table 5.1.

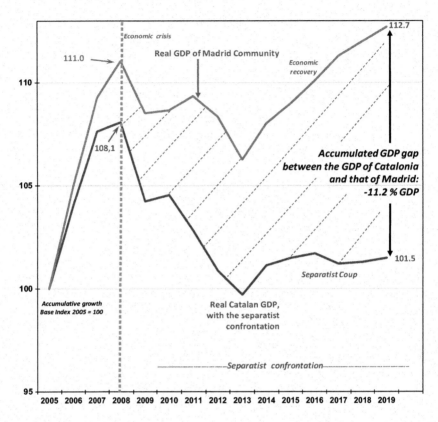

Fig. 23.2 Catalonia and Madrid GDP dynamics: Gap of -11.2%. (Source: Author's calculations based on data from the Institut d'Estadística de Catalunya (2022), *Producte interior brut (Base 2010). Oferta. Avanç* <https://www.idescat. cat/indicadors/?id=conj&n=10233>; and the Instituto Nacional de Estadística (2022), *Contabilidad regional de España* <https://www.ine.es/dyngs/INE base/ es/operacion.htm?c=Estadistica_C&cid=1,254,736,167,628 &menu=resultados &idp=1,254,735,576,581#!tabs-1,254,736,158,133>)

for Spain,[3] and even for Madrid itself, which supports the impact of metropolitan centralisation.

Obviously, because of its nationalist and separatist orientation, the Generalitat de Catalunya has done things badly, very badly. In contrast, the Community of Madrid, naturally orientated towards the unity of Spain, the single market, and economic freedom, achieved very good results. "Madrid overtakes Catalonia and becomes consolidated as the driver of GDP", was the headline in *El Economista*.[4] Between 1981 and 2019 Catalonia maintained its share of Spain's GDP. It rose from 18.3 to 18.8% of the total. Meanwhile, Madrid's rose from 15.7 to 19.1% of the total. At the same time, if in 1980 the per capita GDP of Catalonia was (Spain index = 100) 121 and that of Madrid was 119, in 2019 the GDP of Catalonia was 119 and that of Madrid was 135. Catalonia fell two points and Madrid rose 16 points.

Madrid's greater growth cannot be explained because *Madrid robs us*. On the contrary, Madrid's 'fiscal deficit' is double that of Catalonia. (See Chap. 28.) Neither is Madrid's greater growth due to debt. Catalonia's debt is 2.3 times larger than Madrid's. (See Chaps. 5 and 35.) So, if anything, *Spain robs Madrid!*

SUMMARY

- The cost of separatist opposition to the rule of law in Spain is 4.6% of GDP, €1384 per Catalan per year, €115 per month, €4 per day.
- The cost of the *process* has grown from levels we would now consider small to an astronomical level—the coup d'état of 2017, and an eventual future constitutional crisis.

---

[3] Catalonia ceased being the motor of Spain to become a 'burden': "Political uncertainty continues to undermine the evolution of the Catalan economy, and consequently the capacity for growth for Spain as a whole. The change of tendency in the evolution of the Catalan economy since the second half of 2017 has been a burden on the growth of Spain as a whole." (BBVA Research (2020), *Situación España*, First Semester <https://www.bbvaresearch.com/publicaciones/situacion-espana-primer-trimestre-2020/>)

Similarly, see Andrés Rodríguez-Pose and Daniel Hardy (2020), "Reversal of economic fortunes: Institutions and the changing ascendancy of Barcelona and Madrid as economic hubs", *Growth and Change*, Special Issue, pp. 1–23 <https://doi.org/10.1111/grow.12421>

[4] 23 December 2017, p. 15.

- Like other aspects of Catalan politics, society and the economy, investment plummeted with the *process*. The risks in Catalonia dissuade investors and expel companies, activities, and people.
- *The process robs us!*
- The accumulated gap of permanent GDP between Catalonia and Madrid is -11.2% of GDP.
- Catalonia is behind Madrid in almost all indicators.
- Madrid is the main beneficiary of the excesses of the Catalan separatists.
- Yes, *Madrid robs us*: it "robs" us of the companies, private investment, the GDP, employment that the separatists scare away with their challenge.

CHAPTER 24

Collapse of the Competitiveness of Catalonia

In Our Global World, the Quality of the Institutions Is the Key Element of Competitiveness

Ability to compete may be analysed by means of: a) pertaining conditions (pillars of competitiveness: infrastructures, productive system, legal regulation, education, etc.); and b) the results achieved (in the form of sales, exports, employment, profitability, etc).[1] These aspects are summarised in Fig. 24.1 where we can see that between 2010 and 2019 Catalonia drops from position 103 to 161.

Catalonia's competitive position worsened in the following fields: institutions (-68 positions), higher and continuing education (-82), labour market (-46, and drops to position 220!), market size (-80), technological ability (-100), business sophistication (-117). Catalonia improved in infrastructures (+55), health (+34, reaching position 12) and innovation (+41). A comparison of Catalonia with similar European regions shows that for road, rail, air and port infrastructures, Catalonia's facilities are always

---

[1] The *Regional Competitiveness Index,* published by the European Commission, is available for the regions of European Union Member States for the years 2010, 2013, 2016 and 2019. Different economic and social indicators combine to form the basis for competitiveness, and they are all grouped in a general index for each of the regions, their number varying between 268 and 281 NUTS2, in the terminology of the UE. See <https://ec.europa.eu/regional_policy/en/information/maps/regional_competitiveness/>.

© The Author(s), under exclusive license to Springer Nature Switzerland AG 2022
F. Brunet, *The Economics of Catalan Separatism,*
https://doi.org/10.1007/978-3-031-14451-6_24

163

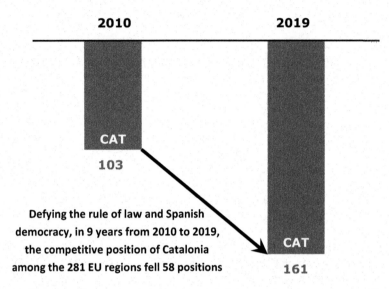

Fig. 24.1   Collapse of Catalan competitiveness. The most competitive European region is in position 1, the least competitive in the last position (NUTS2 regions were 268 in 2010 and 281 in 2019)./Source: Author's calculations based on data from the European Commission (2019), *European Regional Competitiveness Index* <https://ec.europa.eu/regional_policy/mapapps/regional_comp/rci2019.html>

superior to them as well as to the EU average. The opposite happens with institutions where Catalonia's position is amongst the lowest.

Let us compare the dynamics and competitive positions between Barcelona and Catalonia's main competing city and region, Madrid. Between 2010 and 2019 the Community of Madrid saw its general competitive position rise from position 56 to 98. Madrid improved in the same fields as Catalonia, as well as in market size. Madrid bettered Catalonia in each of the 11 competitiveness indicators. In the general ranking in 2010, Madrid was ahead of Catalonia in 47 positions and, in 2019, it was ahead in 63.

Madrid attracts. The severe and growing political instability that separatism has caused in Catalonia means that Madrid received and receives companies, investment, skills and talent that is fleeing Catalonia. Madrid received 80% of the 5682 companies that abandoned Catalonia between 1 October 2017 and 30 September 2019. (See Chap. 32). Aragon, Valencia and Andalucía also received a good number of the companies and skills fleeing Catalonia.

In the European regional competitiveness map for 2019, of the Spanish regions, only Madrid and the Basque Country exceed the EU average. Catalonia, relatively highly industrial, lost the best position it had a decade ago and is now amongst the lowest third of European regions.

In our global world, the quality of the institutions is a key element of competitiveness and in prime position, stability, precisely what separatism destroyed.

SUMMARY

- The collapse of Catalonia's competitiveness has been stunning: amongst the regions of Europe, it dropped from position 103 in 2010 to 161 in 2019.
- In 2019, Catalonia's main competitor, the Community of Madrid, occupied position 98.
- The collapse of Catalonia's competitiveness is the consequence of the separatist challenge and illustrates its effects very clearly.

CHAPTER 25

The Fall in the Attractiveness of Barcelona

THE BARCELONA BRAND

The ability of a city, a region or a country to attract people, skills, visitors, businesses, company headquarters and investment and, in brief, to generate employment, well-being, and quality of life for its citizens, is one of the key aims of territorial policies. Figure 25.1 shows this dynamic in terms of the attractiveness of Barcelona as a place for companies to have their headquarters. It combines real capacities with charm and appeal.

We can see Barcelona's laborious upturn to position 10 after the 1992 Olympic Games; the consolidation and expansion of the Barcelona brand in tourism and innovation that led the city to position 6 in 2000 and position 4 in 2010, and then came the unfortunate nosedive to position 11 in 2018.

In the Global Cities Index Barcelona occupies position 23, Madrid position 15.[1] In the 2013 Globalization and World Cities Index, Barcelona was in position 37 and Madrid in position 19 (out of 525 cities); in 2016, Barcelona was in position 47 and Madrid in position 18 (out of 707 cities); and in 2020, Barcelona was in position 62 and Madrid in position 21 (out of 707 cities).[2] Barcelona's employment attraction has also dropped.

[1] Kearney (2019), *2019 Global Cities Report* <https://www.atkearney.com/global-cities/2019>.
[2] Globalization and World Cities Research Network (2022), *The World According to GaWC 2021* <https://www.lboro.ac.uk/gawc/index.html>.

© The Author(s), under exclusive license to Springer Nature   167
Switzerland AG 2022
F. Brunet, *The Economics of Catalan Separatism*,
https://doi.org/10.1007/978-3-031-14451-6_25

Rise in Barcelona's attractiveness (because of the 1992 Olympic Games and other good work) and Fall (because of the *process* and chaos)

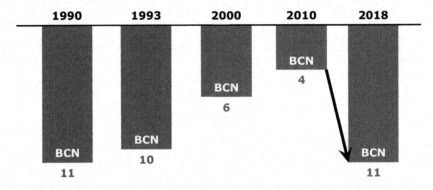

Fig. 25.1   Rise and fall of Barcelona's attractiveness. In this ranking, position 1 corresponds to the most attractive European city for locating company headquarters. Source: Author's calculations on data from Ferran Brunet (1994), *The Economics of Barcelona 1992 Olympic Games,* Lausanne, International Olympic Committee; and Global Power City Index (2022), *Barcelona in the Rankings* <https://www.barcelonaglobal.org/es/know-how/barcelona-en-los-rankings/>

According to the INSEAD Global Talent Competitiveness Index,[3] out of 114 cities analysed, Madrid occupied position 23, while Barcelona was in position 49. Madrid has a considerably better labour future than Barcelona.

With regard to the presence of large firms, Forbes 2000 gives Madrid 56 points and 36 to Barcelona. Large companies prefer Madrid to Barcelona.[4] In the European Patent Register, Catalonia keeps its better position relative to Madrid: in 2020, 559 and 378 new patents were registered from these two Autonomous Communities, respectively, from a total of 1791 for the whole of Spain.[5]

[3] INSEAD (2021), *2021 Global Talent Competitiveness Index* <https://gtcistudy.com/the-gtci-index/#gtci-country-comparison-view/Switzerland/CH>.

[4] Forbes (2022), *Forbes Lists* <https://www.forbes.com/lists/list-directory/#85e 8b69b274d> and Global Entrepreneurship Monitor (2019), *Informe GEM España 2018-2019* <http://www.gem-spain.com/wp-content/uploads/2019/05/GEM2018-2019.pdf>.

[5] European Patent Office (2022), *European Patent Applications* <https://www.epo.org/about-us/annual-reports-statistics/statistics.html>.

Barcelona's loss, on 20 November 2017, of the headquarters for the European Medicines Agency was a sharp blow to the Barcelona, Catalonia and Spain brands. It confirmed the enormous damage done by what should never have happened: the separatist challenge, institutional fragmentation, and an independence insurrection.[6]

IMPACT OF THE SEPARATIST CHALLENGE ON THE SPAIN BRAND

During the last week of November and the first week of December 2017, *Reputation Institute* surveyed thousands of people and hundreds of CEOs in eight European countries about the "impact on brand Spain of the events that have recently taken place there".[7] Here are two results from this survey:

- "It is a problem with a high degree of visibility. 85% of Europeans are familiar with the independence process on account of the high level of media coverage. [...] The internationalisation of the conflict has had a clear impact: 6 of every 10 Europeans think that Spain's image has been damaged because of the Catalan crisis. [...] Spain's reputation has broken the positive trend it has had since 2014. [...]"
- "The quality of Spanish institutions is the aspect to have been most prejudiced by the recent events in Catalonia. [...] The negative impact on Spain's reputation has been seen mainly in France and Germany [...]."

Even more than Spain as a whole, Catalonia and Barcelona have seen their reputations seriously affected. This can be seen in the significant reduction in tourism—national tourism to Spain has decreased drastically—in the flight of companies, in the first signs of boycott and in the lower number of sales of Catalan products, as well as in the drop in foreign investment.

[6] Apart from the moral damage, the damage of this particular loss for Barcelona can be quantified: 1359 jobs, 36,000 visitors per year for 500-600 meetings, in addition, for example, to services not rendered in trials and juridical acts. (Servimedia (2020), "El 'procés' hizo perder a Barcelona 100.000 visitantes y 230 millones al quedarse sin la Agencia Europea del Medicamento" <https://www.servimedia.es/noticias/1334923>).

[7] Reputation Institute (2017), *Informe sobre la reputación de marca España en el contexto europeo* <http://www.crones.es/pdf/Reputation_Institute_Marca_Espana2017.pdf>.

Moreover, if we consider the value of the 100 main brands in Spain,[8] we see that 10.9% correspond to companies whose headquarters are in Barcelona. Companies with their headquarters in Madrid make up 45.8% of the Spanish total. Galicia, the Basque Country, and Cantabria far outpace Catalonia with regard to the reputation of their emblematic companies.

SUMMARY

- From a model transition to democracy and the excellence of the Olympic Games to the separatist coup d'état of 2017 and the violence seen on the streets of Barcelona in 2019 and 2021, the city has passed from a peak of success and slid into decline. Without a doubt it is (was) a very long and difficult task to improve its attractiveness and it is (was) very easy and quick to lose it.
- The separatist challenge has seriously affected the attractiveness and brands of Barcelona, Catalonia and Spain.
- To recover its reputation, Spain's institutional reality needs to be proactively communicated and its political-economic normality and stability emphasised.
- The image and attractiveness Barcelona achieved thanks to the excellence of the 1992 Olympic Games, and which it was able to maintain and augment, has been shattered. For 25 years, we were 'Friends for ever!'
- Today, Barcelona and Catalonia are symbols of the assault on democracy, the failure to uphold the rule of law, political and institutional chaos, of a discriminatory and authoritarian regional government, and of juridical and personal insecurity.

[8] Brand Finance (2020), *España 100, 2020. Informe anual de las marcas más valiosas y más fuertes de España* <https://brandirectory.com/download-report/brand-finance-spain-100-2020-preview.pdf>.

CHAPTER 26

Regulatory and Fiscal Hell

Doing Business in Spain: The Hotchpotch of Regional Regulation

Doing Business is a World Bank publication that has been published yearly since 2004. Every year it reports on 50 indicators for economic freedom, and it contains thematic indices and general rankings on the competitiveness of each country. Given that regulation throughout the states is not implemented in a uniform manner throughout the territories, *Doing Business* also carries out occasional specific reports for regions and large cities. In 2015 it analysed the competitiveness of the Autonomous Communities and Cities, 17 cities and seven ports.[1]

Under consideration for the Spanish Autonomous Communities and cities were the number and the time and cost of four procedures: for opening a company; obtaining construction permits; obtaining an electricity connection and registering of property. For these four procedures, Catalonia occupies positions 9-11-1-16, respectively, and, in general, position 6. Catalonia's main competitor, Madrid occupies positions 2-14-5-3, respectively, and, in general, position 2. Another direct competitor, the Valencian Community, also scores better than Catalonia.

---

[1] World Bank (2018), *Doing Business in Spain* 2015 < https://subnational.doingbusiness.org/en/reports/subnational-reports/spain>.

© The Author(s), under exclusive license to Springer Nature Switzerland AG 2022
F. Brunet, *The Economics of Catalan Separatism*,
https://doi.org/10.1007/978-3-031-14451-6_26

The World Bank analysis highlights the great diversity that exists in the regulatory efficiency within Spain. The level of efficiency, in fact, is low. In only one of the four procedures does a region, La Rioja, exceed the EU average. All other Spanish regions fall below, sometimes very far below, the EU average for each of the four regulated procedures. The cost of obtaining building permission is three times higher than the European average.

CATALONIA, A REGULATORY HELL

The propensity of the Autonomous Communities to behave like a de facto mini-state can be seen through their regulatory intensity. They are the queens of the Official Gazette! Every year, the ebullient collections of the official gazettes of the state and the Autonomous Communities cover more than a million pages.[2]

The regulatory production of the central Administration was stable from the 1960s. It even decreased a little. That was until the appearance of the Autonomous Communities, which went into overdrive producing up to five times more legislative acts than the central Administration. The prize for regulatory intensity goes to Catalonia. In 2018, the official gazette of the Generalitat came to 104,042 pages. At a rough estimate that is 520 pages of official gazette per working day. The glory of the interventionist!

The other Autonomous Communities are not far behind Catalonia. The Community of Madrid produced more than 100,000 pages for some years, although it has recently reduced its output. Andalusia approaches 70,000 pages a year, and Galicia 55,000. In spite of the extent of its powers the Basque Country gets by with 6000 pages a year. "Since brevity is the soul of wit, I will be brief." If only! Given this level of regulatory inflation, give us smart regulation: smart, intelligent, brief, applicable, effective and perhaps even efficient. If, on the other hand, the intention is to have the instruments of statehood, in the manner of the Catalan separatists, what better to do than stuff the official gazette? But the official gazettes are not just a paper paradise, they are a very effective way of complicating people's activities.

---

[2] CEOE (2019), *La producción normativa en 2018* <https://contenidos.ceoe.es/CEOE/var/pool/pdf/publications_docs-file-601-la-produccion-normativa-en-2018.pdf>.

CATALONIA, A FISCAL HELL

Expenditure by the Autonomous Communities represents 49.2% of all Spanish public expenditure, it is greater than that of the USA, Germany and Australia, as we indicate in Chap. 6. The direct income of the Autonomous Communities represents 14.7% of the total income of the Spanish public administrations, a proportion similar to that of the USA, Germany and Australia.

This 15% of regional public income is collected by the Autonomous Communities in a very uneven manner. To analyse it we refer to the studies of the Autonomous Index of Fiscal Competitiveness (IACF).[3] The IACF is an index consisting of data concerning the autonomous bands, or extra charges, applied to taxes levied by the state central Administration (such as income tax, inheritance tax, transfer tax, stamp duty and hydrocarbon tax), and of the Autonomous Communities' own taxes, created and administered by them. In a list of the Autonomous Communities ordered according to their fiscal competitiveness, Catalonia comes last! In terms of tax, it is the least competitive, it is a fiscal hell, without doubt, the fiscal hell of Spain.[4] The Generalitat:

- Levies the highest autonomous bands and extra charges. For example, the minimum rate of income tax for residents in Catalonia (21.5%) and the maximum (48%), are the highest to be levied by the Autonomous Communities.[5]

---

[3] Cristina Enache (2019), *Índice Autonómico de Competitividad Fiscal (IACF) 2019*, Madrid, Fundación para el Avance de la Libertad <http://www.fundalib.org/wp-content/uploads/2019/10/IACF-2019-final-baja-resoluci%C3%B3n.pdf>; y Consejo General de Economistas de España. Registro de Economistas y Asesores Fiscales (2019), *Panorama de la Fiscalidad Autonómica y Foral, 2019*, Madrid, CGEE.

[4] Valentín Pich (2021), "Panorama sobre la fiscalidad autonómica en los tributos cedidos", in Instituto de Estudios Económicos (2021), *La competitividad fiscal de las comunidades autónomas. Condición necesaria para el desarrollo económico* <https://www.ieemadrid.es/wp-content/uploads/IEE-Opinion.-La-competitividad-fiscal-de-las-comunidades-autonomas.pdf>.

[5] Instituto de Estudios Económicos (2022), *Libro Blanco para la reforma fiscal en España. Una reflexión de 60 expertos para el diseño de un sistema fiscal competitivo y eficiente* <https://www.ieemadrid.es/wp-content/uploads/IEE.-LIBRO-BLANCO-para-la-reforma-fiscal-en-Espana.pdf>; y Consejo General de Economistas de España. Registro de Economistas y Asesores Fiscales (2020), *Panorama de la Fiscalidad Autonómica y Foral, 2020*, Madrid, CGEE.

- The Generalitat established 15 of its own taxes. These taxes are in addition to the taxes levied by the central Administration (on which the Generalitat had already established extra bands and charges). The next two Autonomous Communities in terms of voluntary taxation levied six of their own taxes, some of them quite small, and in the Basque Country no additional Autonomous Community tax has been levied.
- Catalonia's descent into fiscal hell—and its undermining effect on competitiveness—has been a persistent, voluntary, and vocational exercise of successive autonomist, pro-sovereign, pro-independence, and separatist governments of the Generalitat.

QUALITY OF GOVERNMENT AND SOCIAL PROGRESS

The influence of institutions in economic growth, social progress and people's quality of life is well known. In our global and digitalised world, the quality of the institutions is the most esteemed differential element of competitiveness.

For the analysis of the quality of government we refer to general studies, such as the World Bank's World Governance Indicators (WGI). These are based on the analysis of, and specific indicators for, the Perception of Corruption, considering International Transparency, the International Country Risk Guide, and the World Economic Forum survey of business leaders on corruption and bureaucratic efficiency. These reports are usually annual and refer to countries as a whole.

For the regions of Europe, we refer to the European Quality of Government Index. The various indicators of good government are grouped together in four, interrelated 'pillars': control of corruption, rule of law, government effectiveness, and voice and accountability. In the analysis of the data for 2017 for 174 European regions, Catalonia is in position 117, Madrid in 113.[6] In spite of the high level of decentralisation in Spain,[7] or perhaps because of it, the quality of government in Spanish regions is far from the European average.

[6] European Commission (2019), *European Quality of Government Index 2017* <https://ec.europa.eu/regional_policy/en/newsroom/news/2018/02/27-02-2018-european-quality-of-government-index-2017>.
[7] Real Instituto Elcano (2019), *The independence conflict in Catalonia* < https://www.realinstitutoelcano.org/en/work-document/the-independence-conflict-in-catalonia/>.

On the other hand, the European Union Regional Social Progress Index[8] aims to measure social progress for each region as a complement to traditional measures of economic progress. The Regional Social Progress Index follows the overall framework of the United Nations Global Social Progress Index whose indicators are grouped into three pillars: basic human needs, foundations of well-being and opportunity. In the European ranking, amongst 281 regions, the Autonomous Community of Catalonia occupies position 165 and the Community of Madrid position 110. For the analysis of regional well-being, we refer to the regional social indicators of the OECD. In 8 of the 11 indicators thereof, Catalonia is behind Madrid. Only in housing is Catalonia above Madrid.[9]

SUMMARY

- The Autonomous Communities have multiplied Spain's regulations by five. The Generalitat is the Autonomous Community that publishes the most pages of official gazette: 104,000 pages per year.
- There is great disparity between the Autonomous Communities with regard to economic procedures. Catalonia is in position 6, Madrid in position 2.
- The Generalitat levies 15 of its own taxes. Additionally, the autonomous bands and extra charges applied by the Generalitat on state taxes are also the largest.
- The Generalitat's fiscal hell diminishes the competitiveness of the Catalan economy, it restricts the activity in this region and limits its attractiveness, in prejudice to the Catalans.
- Catalonia is falling behind Madrid both in quality of government and social progress. For quality of government, they occupy positions 117 and 114, respectively, and for social progress they occupy positions 165 and 110, respectively. The well-being indicators show Catalonia to be straggling behind Madrid.
- The government of the Generalitat's scorn for economic laws has contributed to the flight of companies and people from Catalonia to other places that are more stable for business, for employment and where it is more pleasant to live.
- The more autonomous power there is, the less freedom for Spaniards.

[8] European Commission (2019), *European Social Progress Index* <https://ec.europa.eu/regional_policy/en/information/maps/social_progress>.
[9] OECD (2022), *Regional Wellbeing* <https://www.oecdregionalwellbeing.org/ES51.html>.

CHAPTER 27

Demographics, Immigration, Housing and Offices

CATALONIA, A DECLINING PEOPLE

As well as the *process*, Catalonia is also suffering from a significant demographic decline. Natural growth (births—deaths) is negative: -0.4% in 2018.[1] Since 2000 the number of inhabitants of foreign nationality (legal residents who maintain their foreign citizenship) has multiplied by five. The increase in the population of Catalonia, in a slightly smaller proportion to the growth of the population of Spain as a whole, is due to the increase in non-Spanish immigrants and their higher birth rate. Residents born abroad account for almost 20% of the Catalan population, a proportion that is amongst the highest of European Union countries.

Since 2002 the general birth rate has fallen from 10.6 to 8.1 per thousand. (See Fig. 27.1.) 29.6% of births in Catalonia are by mothers of foreign nationality, triple that of 9% in 2000. The birth rate of Catalonia is sustained by the birth rate of foreigners. The birth rate by mothers of foreign nationality (18.6 per thousand) is triple that of Catalan mothers (6.4 per thousand). 64.3% of legal residents in Catalonia are born in Catalonia, 16.6% in the rest of Spain and 19.1% in the rest of the world. 56.3% of the legal residents of Madrid are born in the Community of Madrid, 34.3% in the rest of Spain and 19.4% in the rest of the world.

---

[1] Instituto Nacional de Estadística (2022), *Cifras de población y Censos demográficos* <https://www.ine.es/dyngs/INEbase/es/categoria.htm?c=Estadistica_P&cid=1254735572981>.

© The Author(s), under exclusive license to Springer Nature Switzerland AG 2022
F. Brunet, *The Economics of Catalan Separatism*,
https://doi.org/10.1007/978-3-031-14451-6_27

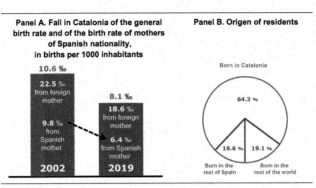

Panel A. Fall in Catalonia of the general birth rate and of the birth rate of mothers of Spanish nationality, in births per 1000 inhabitants

Panel B. Origen of residents

Panel C. Catalonia rise in the proportion of children born to foreign mothers

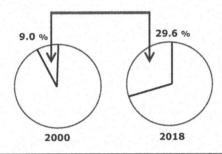

Panel D. Boom in residents with foreign nationality (only legal residents; non-legal residents cannot be counted), on p.100 of the total population

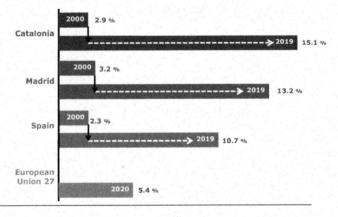

Fig. 27.1 Fall in Catalonia's birth rate and boom in immigration. (Source: Author's calculations based on data from Eurostat (2022), *Population on 1 January by sex, citizenship and broad group of country of birth* <https://ec.europa.eu/eurostat/data-browser/view/MIGR_POP5CTZ__custom_647694/default/table?lang=e>; Instituto Nacional de Estadística (2022), *Principales series de población desde 1998* <https://www.ine.es/jaxi/Datos.htm?path=/t20/e245/p08/l0/&file=02001.px#!tabs-###Table>; and Institut d'Estadística de Catalunya (2022), *Indicadors de natalitat* https://www.idescat.cat/pub/?id=aec&n=287&lang=es&t=2002)

Thus, Madrid is currently a region that is twice as open as Catalonia. In the city of Barcelona, the demographic tendencies of Catalonia and Spain are even more pronounced: 27.8% of residents were born abroad and the birth rate is 7.73 per thousand.[2]

Madrid attracts people. If, at the end of the 1990s, both received something more than 20,000 immigrants from the rest of Spain every year, after 2000, a gap began to grow between the two regions to the point where, in 2018, Madrid absorbed 41,500 more inhabitants than Catalonia. Furthermore, the immigrants to Madrid have better skills.[3]

HOUSING AND OFFICES

Let us also look at the dynamics of the property market. The housing and office markets are cyclical and very influenced by expectations. Housing, furthermore, is also very much influenced by regulations. In Barcelona and in Madrid, the policies regulating construction and home rentals have severely restricted the supply.

Housing is a social need and also a safe-haven asset. That said, the market is volatile. With regard to average prices, a maximum was reached in 2007, prices fell steeply until 2014 and recovered substantially and levelled off in 2019. The average price curves for house sales in the cities of Barcelona and Madrid have a similar profile, somewhat higher for the former. Restricting supply has been a keenly followed policy by the municipal and autonomous administrations.[4]

The property markets for rental and purchase of offices and other real estate for industrial use and the service and logistics sector are situation indicators of the first order. In Barcelona, there is 50% less investment in newly built properties and premises rented every year than in Madrid, and prices per square metre are 30% less.

---

[2] Ajuntament de Barcelona. Departament d'Estadística (2022), *Estadística i difusió de dades* <https://www.bcn.cat/estadistica/castella/dades/inf/pobest/pobest20/part2/nt11.htm>.
[3] Javier G. Jorrín, María Zuil and Jesús Escudero (2019), "La metropolización de Madrid vacía las provincias ricas de España", *El Confidencial*, 27 September <https://www.elconfidencial.com/economia/2019-09-27/exodo-urbano-espana-llegadas-madrid-ciudades_2240155>.
[4] Tinsa (2021), *Índice Tinsa IMIE Mercados Locales* <https://www.tinsa.es/precio-vivienda/catalunya/barcelona/barcelona/>; and Alba Brualla and Mónica G. Moreno (2019), "El alquiler de oficinas despunta y se situará este año en niveles precrisis", *El Economista*, 26 September <https://www.eleconomista.es/empresas-finanzas/noticias/10106942/09/19/El-alquiler-de-oficinas-despunta-y-se-situara-este-ano-en-niveles-precrisis.html>.

180   F. BRUNET

SUMMARY

• Catalonia, a declining people, is undergoing a demographic decline: -0.4% per annum. The population is being maintained by the increase in foreign immigration, foreign immigrants now accounting for 19.1% of the population. Since 2002, the birth rate has fallen from 10.6 to 8.1 per thousand.

• Mothers of foreign nationality have a birth rate that is triple that of Catalan mothers, and births by foreign mothers account for 30% of the total.

• Madrid attracts: migration to this city is far higher than migration to Barcelona and migration between Madrid and Barcelona is clearly favourable to the former.

• Property sales and rentals in the housing and office markets of Barcelona and Madrid follow a similar trend, but there is a gap of 50% in quantity and 30% in prices.

• The large amount of migration of people and companies from Barcelona to Madrid widens this gap, especially in the office market.

CHAPTER 28

Barcelona and Madrid

COMPETITION BETWEEN BARCELONA AND MADRID

Many of the countries of the world have two cities and regions where there is diversity, duality, rivalry, specialisation and complementarity: New York vs Washington, Milan vs Rome, Barcelona vs Madrid and so forth. But a comparison now of these two cities and regions of Barcelona-Catalonia and Madrid shows that one is in decline and the other is flourishing. There is a very serious problem in Catalonia and its economy, and its origins are not in perfidious Spain but in the huge excesses of the Catalan separatists and their regional (mis)government. The decline of Catalonia is due to the intense confrontation the separatists have been stirring up for 40 years and it has led to a steep decline. The slogan 'Spain robs us!' has become 'the process robs us!'

The contrast today between Catalonia and the Community of Madrid is, unfortunately, astonishing. The Catalan separatists banished stability, safety, understanding and good government, they scared investment, companies and people away. Madrid attracts. Anyone with legs and a head between their shoulders goes to Madrid. Madrid has benefitted from the Catalan secessionists' attack on the rule of law in Spain.

To put things in context: Catalonia and Madrid have different dimensions (the population of Catalonia is 7.6 million, that of Madrid 6.7) and have different antecedents and economic structures. Catalonia is still more

© The Author(s), under exclusive license to Springer Nature Switzerland AG 2022
F. Brunet, *The Economics of Catalan Separatism*,
https://doi.org/10.1007/978-3-031-14451-6_28

industrial, Madrid is mainly concentrated on services, including technological services. The orientation and political actions of their respective
regional governments stand in contrast.

BARCELONA AND MADRID COMPARED

Having said that, Madrid is better than Barcelona and Catalonia in each
and every aspect under consideration:

1. Absolute GDP: Catalonia €236,814 million, Madrid €240,130 million even though Madrid has a million fewer inhabitants.
2. Growth (annual average real GDP 2010–2019): Catalonia 1% and
   Madrid 1.6%.
3. GDP dynamic between 2005 (index 100) and 2019: Catalonia
   101.5 and Madrid 112.7. A gap, therefore, of 11.2% of GDP.
4. Level of employment (as a percentage of the population 16–64 years
   of age): Catalonia 61.6% and Madrid 63.4%.
5. Level of unemployment (as a percentage of the active population
   16–64 years of age): Catalonia 10.9% and Madrid 10.3%.
6. Per capita income (annual): Catalonia €30,572 and Madrid €34,641.
7. Regional competitiveness (over 281 European regions; best position is 1): Catalonia's position is 161 and Madrid's position, 98.
8. Doing Business (over 17 communities and 2 autonomous cities):
   Catalonia's position is 6 and Madrid's position, 2.
9. Autonomous taxes: Catalonia levies 15 of its own additional
   taxes, Madrid 4.
10. Fiscal competitiveness (over 19 communities and autonomous cit-
    ies): Catalonia's position is 19 and Madrid's position, 3.
11. Regulatory intensity: Catalonia—104,042 pages per annum of
    official gazette, Madrid—88,067.
12. Social progress index (over 281 European regions): Catalonia's
    position is 165 and Madrid's position, 110.
13. Regional quality of government index (over 174 European
    regions): Catalonia's position is 117 and Madrid's position, 113.
14. Migration: from all provinces, including Barcelona, migration is
    to Madrid.
15. Migration of companies: from Catalonia to Madrid, Aragon,
    Valencian Community, Balearic Islands and Andalusia. Companies

to avoid boycotts and legal insecurity, and banks to avoid bankruptcy, only regional, provincial or local companies remain in Catalonia.

16. Foreign investment (accumulated 2010–2018): Catalonia €27,644 million and Madrid €90,740 million.

17. Office and housing market: gap between Barcelona and Madrid of 50% in quantity and 30% in prices. Few town planning projects in Barcelona.

18. In the *Global Cities* index Barcelona occupies position 23, Madrid, position 15. Global Talent Competitiveness Index (INSEAD, employment attraction over 114 analysed): Barcelona position 49 and Madrid position 23.

19. Presence of large companies (Forbes 2000 Index, best = 100): Barcelona 36 and Madrid 56.

20. Bank deposits (as percentage of total Spain): Catalonia 14.6% and Madrid 28.6%.

21. Net contribution to the Spanish Treasury (annual 'fiscal deficit'): according to one method of calculation, Catalonia -€6934 million and Madrid -€12,304 million. With a million fewer inhabitants, Madrid's contribution is double that of Catalonia. 'Spain robs Madrid!'

22. Pensions (surplus or contribution paid to/or deficit or subsidy received from the Spanish social security system): Catalonia has an annual deficit (receives a net) of €3240 million and Madrid has an annual surplus (contributes a net) of €1527 million.

23. Autonomous public debt (2020): Catalonia €79,429 million and Madrid €33,692 million.

24. Birth rate, fertility index, death rate, life expectancy, gross rate of marriage, gross divorce rate, poverty index: again, in each and every one of the demographic indicators, Catalonia performs worse than Madrid.

25. The exact magnitude of the economy, companies, productivity and taxation in Catalonia and Madrid can be gauged from data on the tax levied on company profits. In 2021, in Spain, 1,645,353 companies paid this tax, contributing €30,415 million. In Catalonia, there are 328,658 companies (20% of the Spanish total) that paid this tax, contributing €6427 million (21.1%). In Madrid, there are 335,652 companies (20.4%) that paid this tax, contributing

€13,474 million (44.3%). That is to say, Catalonia and Madrid account for 40% of the companies in Spain, and contribute 65% of the total. Catalonia has almost as many companies as Madrid but contributes less than half.[1]

SUMMARY

- Everything is going quite a lot worse in Catalonia than in Madrid.
- The dreadful situation in Catalonia is a discredit to Catalonia. The good situation in Madrid is the merit of Madrid. Policies have consequences, delayed ones perhaps, but important consequences. The bonanza in Madrid is due to the better practice of its regional government, its strategic position and the chaos in Catalonia. The ills of Catalonia are not the fault of the Community of Madrid. Obviously. Consequently, with regard to autonomous policies, fiscal policies and planning policies, there is no way that the other Autonomous Communities should align themselves with the unruly rogue (Generalitat), it is much better for them to align themselves with the virtuous (Madrid).
- In the medium and long terms, the centralisation of economic activity in Madrid will be hugely detrimental for the whole of Spain.

[1] Registro de Economistas Asesores Fiscales and Instituto de Economía de Barcelona (2022), *Declaración de Sociedades, 2021,* Madrid, Consejo General de Economistas de España <https://reaf.economistas.es/estudios-e-informes/>.

CHAPTER 29

Catalonia's Trade with the Rest of Spain

CATALONIA'S EXTERNAL BALANCES

The balance of payments is the account of a territory's economic relations with the exterior, usually of one state with the rest of the world. This accounting practice can be applied to the analysis of relations of one region with the rest of the state, or of a city with the rest of its regions.[1]

Economic activity is not distributed uniformly around the territory. For geographical and historical reasons there are places, cities, regions, enclaves, clusters and relatively specialised centres of gravity that trade with each other, thereby forming part of the national chains, and today, global chains of supply and value. The flow of commercial activity to more and more territories (downwards) and globalisation (upwards) make integration and interrelation essential elements of growth. Geography aside, today countries' and territories' competitiveness, convergence and progress depend on the quality of the institutions.

---

[1] From, *The MacDougall Report* (*Volume I. Study group on the role of public finance in European integration,* Brussels: Commission of the European Communities, 1977 <https://www.cvce.eu/content/publication/2012/5/31/c475e949-ed28-490b-81ae-a33ce9860d09/publishable_en.pdf>) it is well known that the regions of the European countries that have a surplus in the trade balance have a deficit in the fiscal balance. And the contrary is true, the regions that have a trade deficit have a fiscal surplus. The trade and fiscal surpluses and deficits are of similar and inverse magnitudes. The same thing happens in the USA with the balances in the fiscal and commercial relations between the states. (Tax Foundation (2022), <https://taxfoundation.org/economic-analysis/taxes-economy/>).

A calculation of Catalonia's balance of trade helps in sifting through its relations with the rest of Spain.[2] To this end, two kinds of sub-balances are of great interest: (1) the trade balance, and by extension that of services and, perhaps, transfers; that is to say the current account balance, and (2) the fiscal balance with public income and expenditure. Catalonia's trade with the rest of Spain and the world is of interest as an explanatory element of the economic and social identity of both territories and also because, in the case of a hypothetical separation, the first thing to suffer would be just that trade. (See Chap. 40.) With independence everything that explains the being of the Catalan economy and society would come tumbling down. An economy such as the Catalan economy, disconnected from the rest of Spain, cannot be imagined.

SPECIALISATION OF CATALONIA

A third of Catalonia's production goes to the rest of Spain. In numerous sectors of production, a major part of the manufacturing is associated with sales to the rest of Spain. More than 60% of Catalonia's paper production goes to the rest of Spain, 57% of food products, 56% of pharmaceuticals, 55% of books, 48% of textiles, 48% of chemicals and 46% of freight transport. In total, the Catalan GDP resulting from production sold in the rest of Spain comes to €54,494 million and accounts for 973,000 jobs, 27% of the total.[3]

---

[2] The main analyses of the Catalan case in the twentieth century are: Carles Pi Sunyer (1927), *L'aptitud econòmica de Catalunya*, Barcelona, Barcino; Jaume Alzina (1930), *L'economia de la Catalunya autònoma*, Barcelona, Tipografía Emporium; Carles Pi Sunyer (1959), *El comerç de Catalunya amb Espanya*, México, DF, Club del Llibre Català; Ramon Trías Fargas (1960), *La Balanza de pagos interior: estudio relativo a la provincia de Barcelona*, Madrid, Sociedad de Estudios and Publicaciones; Ramon Trías Fargas (n.d. [1962?]), *Balance of payment studies for the region of Catalonia*, [S.l.: s.n.]; Ramon Trías Fargas (1972), *Introducció a l'economia de Catalunya: una anàlisi regional*, Barcelona, Edicions 62; Jacint Ros Hombravella and Antoni Montserrat Soley (1967), *L'aptitud financera de Catalunya: la balança catalana de pagaments*, Barcelona, Edicions 62; Jacint Ros Hombravella, Joan Clavera, Joan Esteban, Maria Antònia Monés and Antoni Montserrat (1978), *Capitalismo español: De la autarquía a la estabilización, 1939–1959*, Madrid, Edicusa.

[3] Convivencia Cívica Catalana (2019), *La aportación del resto de España a la economía catalana ¿Cuántos empleos, beneficios empresariales y riqueza genera el resto de España en Cataluña?* < https://files.convivenciacivica.org/La%20aportaci%C3%B3n%20del%20resto%20de%20Espa%C3%B1a%20a%20la%20econom%C3%ADa%20catalana.pdf>.

Since Catalonia has no borders with the rest of Spain, no tariffs, and does not have its own currency (fortunately!) it is not an easy task to calculate its exterior trade with the rest of Spain and the rest of the EU and the world. There are different measurements for Catalonia's external trade flows [4] and, from them, it is possible to extract some orders of magnitude concerning the destiny of sales by companies established in Catalonia.

A consideration of just the trade in industrial goods shows that 26% of production is destined for the Catalan market, 26% for the rest of Spain and 48% for the EU and the world. With regard to services, 60% of those produced in Catalonia are destined for the Catalan market, 23% for the rest of Spain and 17% for the EU and the world.

There is an inextricable interdependence between the Spanish regional economies. There is a good reason why Spain has been a national market for centuries. Catalonia was a factor in the historical make-up of the Spanish market because manufacturing industry that served the national market was concentrated in this region. Catalonia was the centre of gravity of the Spanish economy. Then, after Spain's industrialisation stage, and especially after 1959, industrial activity spread throughout the whole country. In addition to this, the service industries developed in Catalonia are today the backbone of the economy.

Let us consider the dynamics of Catalonia's trade in goods (see Table 29.1), its sales in Catalonia, in the rest of Spain and the world. It can be seen that since 1995 there has been

- Stagnation in Catalonia's production for internal consumption in Catalonia.
- A slight reduction of sales to and purchases from the rest of Spain.
- Strong growth in sales to and purchases from the rest of the world.

[4] C-intereg (2019) <https://www.c-intereg.es/informe-trimestral-de-c-intereg-julio-2019/>; Institut d'Estadística de Catalunya (2022), <https://www.Idescat.cat/indicadors/?id=conj&n=10,246&lang=es>; Cámara Oficial de Comercio, Industria y Navegación de Barcelona (2018), <https://www.cambrabcn.org/>; Foment del Treball Nacional (2017) <https://www.foment.com/wp-content/uploads/2017/11/Presentaci%C3%B3n-Nota-de-Econom%C3%ADa.pdf>; Pankaj Ghemawat, Carlos Llano, and Francisco Requena (2010), "Competitiveness and interregional as well as international trade: The case of Catalonia", *International Journal of Industrial Organization*, Vol. 28: 415–422; and Francisco Cabrillo (2021), *The Economic Cost of Catalonia's Hypothetical Independence and Departure from the EU*, Bruselas, European Policy Information Center <http://www.epicenternetwork.eu/publications/the-economic-cost-of-catalonias-hypothetical-independence/>;

Table 29.1   Geographical distribution of Catalan trade in industrial goods

M €	Sales in Catalonia	Sales ('exports') to		Bought ('imports') in		Balance	
		Spain	EU and rest of the world	Spain	EU and rest of the world	Spain	EU and rest of the world
2018	39,461	39,320	71,624	20,495	90,178	18,825	-18,554
2017	37,826	38,438	69,647	20,223	84,606	18,215	-14,959
2016	36,527	36,776	65,142	19,904	77,627	16,871	-12,485
Average 2013–2015	34,817	38,177	61,045	21,728	71,926	16,449	-10,882
Average 2008–2012	35,805	43,804	50,930	23,536	68,637	20,268	-17,707
Average 1995–2007	36,472	42,533	33,845	23,120	49,812	19,413	-15,967
Change between the average 2008–2012 and 2018	+10.2%	-10.2%	+40.6%	-12.9%	+31.4%	-7.1%	-4.8%

Source: Author's calculations based on data from C-intereg (2019), *Comercio interregional* <https://www.c-intereg.es/informe-trimestral-de-c-intereg-julio-2019/>

- In this way, the annual surplus with the rest of Spain has been maintained at €18,800 million and the deficit with the rest of the world has grown slightly to €18,500 million.
- Thus, the trade surplus with the rest of Spain finances the trade deficit with the rest of the world.

Catalonia's main competitor, the Community of Madrid, has a trade deficit with the rest of Spain of €9493 million and a trade deficit with the rest of the world of €31,334 million. As would correspond to a region that is specialised in selling industrial products to the rest of Spain, Catalonia has a large annual trade surplus of €18,000 million. Way behind are the trade surpluses of Andalusia (€8000 million) Galicia (€6500 million), Castilla y León, Castilla-La Mancha, Navarre, Murcia, and the Basque Country.[5]

[5] Convivencia Cívica Catalana (2020), *Análisis del comercio de Cataluña. Las ventas catalanas al resto de España y al extranjero* < https://files.convivenciacivica.org/Analisis%20del%20Comercio%20de%20Catalu%C3%B1a.pdf>.

Catalonia has a large trade surplus with the rest of Spain, but a large deficit with respect to the rest of the world due, to a large extent, to the cost of energy. Consequently, the surplus with the rest of Spain compensates for the deficit with the rest of the world. The reason why Catalonia is regarded as being somewhat richer is precisely because it is part of Spain. Likewise, the entity of Spain is in part due to the entity of Catalonia. More than rivalry, competition between Madrid and Barcelona is what is appropriate between two large cities and economic clusters, and it occurs in many countries around the world.

In order to appreciate the significance of the unity of Spain, the unity of the market and of the market of the rest of Spain for Catalonia, it is enough to compare the trade between Catalonia and the rest of Spain with Catalonia's trade with other countries. Thus, Catalonia's main market, as is natural, is Aragon! Sales to Aragon (population 1.3 million) exceed those to France (population 67 million). Catalonia sells double the amount to Castilla-La Mancha as it does to China. These greater sales are clearly not due only to geographical proximity but, and especially, due to the legal, political, social and language community Catalonia shares with the rest of Spain. Independence would shatter millions of customary social and economic relations between the Catalans and all the other Spaniards.

We could summarise the relations between Catalonia and the rest of Spain by saying that the income generated through sales to the rest of Spain amounts to €54,494 million per year, and that accounts for 973,000 jobs, 27% of the total number of Catalan workers.[6]

SUMMARY

- Importance and complexity of quantifying the exterior relations of a territory.
- Use of the balances of trade and external fiscal balances in the demands of regionalists, nationalists and supporters of independence.
- Catalonia buys from the world and sells to Spain. Catalonia compensates for its trade deficit with the rest of the world with its trade surplus with the rest of Spain.

[6] Convivencia Cívica Catalana (2019), *La aportación del resto de España a la economía cata-lana ¿Cuántos empleos, beneficios empresariales y riqueza genera el resto de España en Cataluña?* <https://files.convivenciacivica.org/La%20aportaci%C3%B3n%20del%20resto%20de%20 Espa%C3%B1a%20a%20la%20econom%C3%ADa%20catalana.pdf>.

- Catalonia's balance of trade is positive (5.5% of GDP) thanks to the flow of trade with the rest of Spain (which produces a positive balance of 9.7% of GDP), which more than compensates for the trade deficit with the rest of the world (-4.2% of GDP).
- Catalonia's trade with almost each and every one of the other regions of Spain is greater than that with any other country in the world!

CHAPTER 30

The Fiscal Balances: Accounts and Tales

GROUND ZERO OF THE SEPARATIST 'ECONOMY'

The fiscal balance is the ground zero of the separatist 'economy'. It is here that all the lies swirl around, along with all the supposed evils of the past and present caused by perfidious Spain, and it is here too where all the supposed benefits of a hypothetical 'independent' Catalan republic are concentrated. Put briefly, "Spain robs us, and when it stops robbing us, we'll be rich!"

With the large amount they rob us of we will be very rich. But there is a slightly inconvenient detail: an independent Catalonia simply would not sell what it sells now to the rest of Spain. It would sell very much less! Consequently, the 'enormous fiscal deficit' would not be such. Furthermore, the current trade surplus would be much reduced. Consequently, so much that would be supposedly gained with independence, the eventual current fiscal deficit, would simply have disappeared! And with it would have disappeared the supposed benefit of independence.

The accounts of the tales[1] and the tales of the accounts[2]: Let us see what is true and what is false in the secessionists' arguments story or narrative. The fiscal balances are a complementary aspect of the external balances,

---

[1] Ángel de la Fuente and Sevi Rodríguez Mora (2012), "Las cuentas de la lechera", *El País*, 24 September.

[2] Josep Borrell and Joan Llorach (2014), "¿Dónde están los 16.000 millones?", *El País*, 20 January. This article was followed by a bestseller: Josep Borrell and Joan Llorach (2015), *Las cuentas y los cuentos de la independencia*, Madrid, Los Libros de la Catarata.

F. Brunet, *The Economics of Catalan Separatism*,
https://doi.org/10.1007/978-3-031-14451-6_30

particularly the balance of trade, considered in the previous chapter.
Territories do not pay taxes. Taxes are paid by physical and juridical persons. Regarding fiscal structure and policy, the taxes paid in Catalonia are
paid according to people's ability to pay and the expenditure received is
received in accordance with people's needs.[3]

In the secessionist argument about the fiscal balance, two key elements
of separatist economics can be summarised:

- 'Spain robs us'. Hell. The reason for complaining about the problem: the autonomous funding of Spain gives Catalonia a bad fiscal
deal. The Generalitat de Catalunya is underfunded,[4] Catalonia needs
more public investment. (See Chap. 35.) We have tried to sort it out
with Madrid, but it has not been possible. Spain lives off Catalonia.
- Catalonia will be rich and plentiful. Paradise. The reason for wanting
independence, the solution: with independence, Catalonia will have
€16,000 million more a year. This is the fiscal dividend of independence, the manna of the new state.

[3] Just at the close of the Barcelona Olympic Games, in August 1992, Ernest Lluch, mur-
dered by ETA on 21 November 2000, professor of Economic Thought at the University of
Barcelona, founder of PSC-PSOE, and former Spanish government minister for Health and
Consumer Affairs, wrote about the fiscal balances and warned about the risks of taking a
victim's approach to the fiscal argument: "To talk about fiscal pillaging is therefore rather
difficult if you do not want to take the road to imprecision, or even the road to demagoguery.
I therefore very much regret that biased information, or information that is not calmly presented, can be causing, within Catalonia, what in my childhood was called 'sour milk'".
He continues: "[…] My position that nationalism in Catalonia has been basically democratic is well known. And I say so in the most positive and cheerful way in the world. But I
have also made it known that continued complaining can become an ideological explosive.
All terrorisms are nationalist or Marxist-Leninist. Not for nothing are most terrorist groups
formed with arguments of this kind [fiscal pillaging] that we have attempted here to modify
and qualify. Making it so that the peoples, and here I am referring to the peoples of Spain,
have their tensions, but without them spilling over because of ignorance or passion is the
great gift of peace and progress. I am aware that all the statistics I have cited here are debatable, but much less so than those which, in a partisan and unclear manner, have been stirring
up Catalan public opinion. Consequently, each one of us who participates in the formation
of public opinion must undertake to broach these questions studiously and without anger".
(Ernest Lluch (1992), "¿Cataluña expoliada?", *La Vanguardia*, 13 August <http://hemero-
teca.lavanguardia.com/preview/1992/08/13/pagina-12/33521851/pdf.html>.
[4] Like Valencia: Alto Consejo Consultivo de la Comunidad Valenciana. Comisión de
Economía (2013), *Informe sobre la deuda, déficit y financiación de la Comunidad Valenciana.
Propuesta de bases para un nuevo sistema de financiación autonómica* <http://www.presiden-
cia.gva.es/documents/80920710/80950149/Informe+Financiaci%C3%
B3n+Final+12+11+13.pdf/1f966b00-0147-42d9-bcd7-2c966afd9bcb>.

THE CALCULATION OF THE FISCAL BALANCE

Some analysis. The so-called fiscal balance of a territory, economy or country is an account of all the public income obtained and of all the public expenditure. A comparison of income and expenditure gives a balance that can be positive-surplus, zero-equilibrium, or negative-deficit. The options for calculating the fiscal balance, and its accuracy, depend on the registration of operations and the data available, whether a territory has borders, tariffs, and its own currency, or not, and finally the quality of the control exercised at the limit with other territories. There are two usual methods of calculation for this kind of public accounting[5]:

– The benefit flow calculation method: attributes income in the territory where the citizens live who bear the fiscal burden, and the expenditure in the territory where the citizens live who receive or benefit from the service or investment.[6]
– The monetary flow calculation method: attributes income where it is located and expenditure where it takes place.

In addition to these, two other aspects should be considered:

– The deficit (and the debt) of the Autonomous Communities and of the state, finance public expenditure, but are not calculated as fiscal income. When the deficit and the debt are borne in mind, or 'neutralised', options for calculating the fiscal balance are multiplied by two and there are now four methods: burden-benefit calculation without neutralisation and neutralised; and monetary flow calculation without neutralisation and neutralised.
– The beneficiary of public investments (apart from the territory where they take place, they benefit non-residents) and of general state expenditure (defence, foreign affairs).

[5] Carmen Alcaide (2014), "El debate sobre las balanzas fiscales", *El País*, 16 February <https://elpais.com/economia/2014/02/14/actualidad/1392390790_505427.html>.
[6] The Catalan government minister for the Economy in the government of Artur Mas, Andreu Mas-Colell ((2014), "El Estado obtendrá en el 2015 de Catalunya 3.228 millones más de los que gastará", *El Periódico*, 4 December <https://www.elperiodico.com/es/economia/20141204/el-estado-obtendra-en-el-2015-de-catalunya-3228-millones-mas-de-los-que-gastara-3744285>) calculated a fiscal deficit of €3228 million using the benefit flow method.

Table 30.1 Different options to calculate the fiscal balances of Catalonia with the rest of Spain

Calculation option	Fiscal balances in M €
Benefit flow and neutralized value	-11,261
Monetary flow and neutralized value	-16,543
Benefit flow and real value	+4015
Monetary flow and real value	-792
Benefit flow and social security flow	+1890
Monetary flow and social security flow	+1253

Source: Author's compilation based on data from Convivencia Cívica Catalana (2013), *El maquillaje de la balanza fiscal de Catalonia* <https://s.libertaddigital.com/doc/el-maquillaje-de-la-balanza-fiscal-de-cataluna-41912941.pdf>; Ministerio de Hacienda y Administraciones Públicas (2016), *Sistema de Cuentas Públicas Territorializadas* <https://www.hacienda.gob.es/Documentacion/Publico/GabineteMinistro/Notasin%20Prensa/2015/S.E.in%20administracionesin%20pin%c3in%9ablicas/21-07-15in%20pin%20cuentasin%20territorializadas.pdf>; and Verificat (2021), "D'on surt la xifra dels 16.000 milions d'euros de dèficit fiscal a Catalunya?" <https://www.verificat.cat/fact-check/don-ve-la-xifra-dels-16.000-milions-deuros-de-deficit-fiscal-a-catalunya>

Also, the following can and should be considered:

- The real value of the operations according to territory, with price and cost of living indices, that is, in parity of purchase power.
- Income and expenditure of the social security system (and of other public agents, such as public companies) (Table 30.1).

To the previous aspects should be added the availability of data and the complexity of their use. To the questions concerning the trustworthiness of the fiscal balances, there is the added inconvenience of the important gap that exists between the date of the data and the date the results of the analysis are presented. All this enables the separatists to cook the books through creative accounting: to count as fiscal income that of capital ("neutralisation"), to include taxes paid by non-Catalans (VAT on products sold by companies resident in Catalonia), to include negative fiscal flows with the European Union and to minimise state expenditure in Catalonia.

To reduce the limitations of the methods of analysing the fiscal balance, the Ministry of Finance and Public Administration introduced the

Territorialised Public Accounts System.[7] Since the 'Spain robs us' campaign opened the fiscal balance can of worms, dozens of approximations have been produced.[8]

- After all the empirical evidence about the territorial redistribution of the Autonomous Community system, some summary of the interpretation is called for:

  – Let us consider the order of magnitude of inter-territorial fiscal solidarity:
  – Madrid is the Autonomous Community that contributes the most: 10% of Madrid's GDP; in contrast, the Autonomous cities receive +25% of GDP.

[7] Ministerio de Hacienda y Administraciones Públicas (2016), *Sistema de Cuentas Públicas Territorializadas* <https://www.hacienda.gob.es/Documentacion/Publico/GabineteMinistro/Notas%20Prensa/2015/S.E.%20administraciones%20p%c3%9ablicas/21-07-15%20np%20cuentas%20 territorializadas.pdf>; Ángel de la Fuente, Ramón Barberán and Ezequiel Uriel (2014), *Informe sobre la dimensión territorial de la actuación de las Administraciones Públicas* <https://www.fundacionsepi.es/investigacion/publicaciones/otrasPublicaciones/Dimensi%C3%B3n%20territorial% 20Act.%20AAPP%20 propuesta%20metodologica.pdf>.

[8] These seven contributions constitute a sample of them: A. Castells, R. Barberán, N. Bosch, M. Espasa, F. Rodrigo, and J. Ruiz-Huerta (2000): *Las balanzas fiscales de las Autonomous Communities (1991–1996). Análisis de los flujos fiscales de las Autonomous Communities con la Administración Central,* Barcelona, Ariel; Almudena Semur Correa (2012), "La perversidad de las balanzas fiscales", in Many authors (2012), *La cuestión catalana hoy,* Madrid, Instituto de Estudios Fiscales, pp. 93–100; Antoni Zabalza (2014), "Measuring the Regional Incidence of Taxes and Public Expenditure: The Available Methodology and its Limitations", *Hacienda Pública Española,* No. 209, pp. 11–54; Xoaquín Fernández Leiceaga and Santiago Lago Peñas (2016), "Balanzas fiscales vs cuentas públicas territorializadas: Análisis y valoración de las diferencias", *Revista de Estudios Regionales,* No. 105, pp. 225–262; Francesc Trillas, Josep M. Vegara, Antoni Zabalza, M. Antònia Monés and Montserrat Colldeforns (2014), *Economía de una España federal: razones para una Europa sin fronteras,* Barcelona, Edicions i Produccions Multimedia Els Llums; Antoni Castells (coord.), Enoch Albertí, Francesc Amat, Núria Bosch, Ignacio Lago, Guillem López i Casasnovas, Toni Rodon, Albert Solé-Ollé and Maite Vilalta (2021), *Conseqüències econòmiques i financeres dels diferents escenaris de la relació Catalunya-Espanya,* Barcelona, Generalitat de Catalunya, Institut d'Estudis de l'Autogovern <https://presidencia.gencat.cat/web/.content/ambits_actuacio/desenvolupament_autogovern/iea/publicacions/01_IEAg/IEAg_arxius-i-vincles/IEAg-12.pdf>; and Montserrat Colldeforns and M. Antònia Monés (2022), "Apunts per a una reforma federal del sistema de finançament autonòmic", *Papers de la Fundació Rafael Campalans,* No. 172 <https://fcampalans.cat/uploads/publicacions/pdf/frc_papersdelafundacio172_web.pdf>.

- That means between −€2800 per year per inhabitant of Madrid, and +€3900 per inhabitant of Ceuta or Melilla.
- Catalonia's contribution is half that of Madrid: 'Spain robs Madrid!'
- The Balearic Islands and the Valencian Community are also important net contributors, something that attests to their economic strength and to one or other problem with the autonomous financing system.
- The regions in the north of Spain receive a large amount of net fiscal assistance, especially Asturias, Galicia, the Basque Country and Cantabria.

INTERTERRITORIAL SOLIDARITY

The analysis and interpretation of the fiscal balances of the Spanish regions can be expanded to include two aspects that are relevant for evaluating interterritorial solidarity.

- The first aspect is national, and we consider it as

- The relationship between the average per capita GDP of the regions and the fiscal balances (contribution or reception) of the Autonomous Communities. The richest regions of Spain are also those that transfer the most… except for the Basque Country.
- The comparison of per capita GDP and per capita Gross Final Disposable Household Income (GFDI) of the Spanish regions. Index Spain = 100. On the degree of redistribution between the Autonomous Communities, here are the Autonomous Communities that contribute and the ones that receive:

Contribute: Community of Madrid (10.6 of GFDI), Balearic Islands (5.6), Catalonia (4.6), Navarre (2.7), La Rioja (2.7), Murcia (1.9) and Aragon (1.6).
Receive: Principality of Asturias (14.3 of GFDI), Cantabria (9.5), Extremadura (6.3), Castilla y León (5.9), Ceuta (5.8), Castilla-La Mancha (5.6), Andalusia (4.5), Melilla (4.3), Galicia (4), Canary Islands (2.5), Valencian Community (2.1) and the Basque Country (0.3).

- The second aspect is international. Is the interterritorial redistribution of Spain similar or not to that of other highly decentralised and federal states? The Spanish case, and in particular the Catalan case, is totally normal in federal systems and is very similar, for example, to the USA.[9]

Given the wave of criticism for the slogan 'Spain robs us' and the inconsistency of the data it is based on, another slogan appeared, *Espanya ens frena* ('Spain holds us back'). This slogan, which you no longer hear, while just as false as the classic 'Spain robs us', sweetens the discussion and guides it towards a consideration of autonomous financing. To complete the daydream, it has even been asserted that, on account of the accumulation of successive fiscal deficits, the Spanish state owes a multi-billion historical debt to the Generalitat.

In the end then, the debate about fiscal balance has been much ado about nothing! More so than in the case of the Basque nationalists. Whatever the case, the long time spent ratcheting up the fiscal deficit fairy tale and tales about what one 'territory' would 'rob' from another has created an unprecedented discontent, confrontation and division in Catalan society, a serious constitutional crisis, large scale public disturbances, and all kinds of tales to stop you sleeping. As Goya wrote and painted, the sleep of reason produces monsters.

After the culmination of separatist defiance with the coup d'état of autumn 2017 and the separatist violence of autumn 2019, the slogan 'Spain robs us' has ceased to be the dominant one and, as we anticipated in Chap. 3, the evidence being clear for all to see, it has now been replaced with 'The process robs us!'

---

[9] Ángel de la Fuente (2014), "¿Maltrato fiscal?", in Ángel de la Fuente and Clemente Polo (2014), *La cuestión catalana II. Balanzas fiscales y tratamiento fiscal de Cataluña*, Madrid, Instituto de Estudios Fiscales, pp. 11–29. "With the numbers in the hand, Catalonia is not especially badly treated in terms of its financing or fiscal balance if we compare it to other regions with a similar income, both in Spain and abroad."

See also Ángel de la Fuente (2019), "La evolución de la financiación de las comunidades autónomas de régimen común, 2002–2017", *BBVA Research. Documento de trabajo*, No. 19/12.

SUMMARY

- The fiscal balances of the Autonomous Communities, those of Catalonia with the rest of Spain, have been submitted to every kind of analysis and debate. It needs to be said that Catalonia's fiscal deficit is neither as large, nor as exceptional, as the separatists claim. It is very usual in territories inhabited by fiscal subjects that are richer than in the rest of the country. In Spain, Catalonia is not in hell.
- On the other hand, the supposed fiscal deficit with the rest of Spain would disappear with a hypothetical secession because the flows of trade and the fiscal flows would have been reduced to an extraordinary extent. Outside of Spain, Catalonia would not be in paradise. Obviously, an 'independent' Catalonia would be somewhere close to hell.
- Despite the overwhelming empirical evidence of the falseness of the slogan 'Madrid robs us!', this slogan was essential for the Catalan separatists' challenge to the social and democratic state and the rule of law in Spain.
- After the coup d'état of autumn 2017 and separatism's subsequent decline into violence, the dominant slogan now for Catalans and Spaniards is 'The process robs us!'
- The *process* robs us all, it robs us of peace, understanding, employment, activity, investment and it robs us of the future.

CHAPTER 31

Social Security and Pensions

CATALONIA'S LARGE PENSION DEFICIT

The Spanish social security system is a single system, as is its Treasury. Nevertheless, an analysis of this system shows that in Catalonia, Social Security expenditure far exceeds income. Catalan pensioners are funded by the Spanish pension system.

There are two reasons for the regional Social Security imbalance: the north of Spain has a larger number of pensioners due to greater aging and deindustrialisation; and the average pension in the north of the country is higher than in the rest of Spain. The Social Security deficit in Catalonia is substantial and is financed by the rest of those affiliated to the system resident in surplus regions, in particular the Community of Madrid. Spanish solidarity benefits Catalan pensioners.

This situation occurs because of the relationship between the number of those contributing and the number of those benefiting from pensions (on account of incapacity, retirement, widowhood and orphanhood), the pensioners' contributory history, their sectors of activity and their average earnings. "In Catalunya in 2017, the cost of pensions was €2,848 million more than the amount contributed. In the Catalan region the average annual contribution by worker (€6,159.40) is amongst the highest in the state (€5,859.70). And the same thing happens with pensions: €13,383.20 per year in Catalonia as opposed to €12,888.40 for Spain. Since there are

F. Brunet, *The Economics of Catalan Separatism*,
https://doi.org/10.1007/978-3-031-14451-6_31

1.9 Catalan contributors for every pensioner, the deficit is €1,663.90 per pension, per year."[1]

As we will see later in Chap. 42, with a hypothetical secession of Catalonia, the deficit would be higher than the current €1664 per pensioner, per year. To this deficit would have to be added the reduction in revenue through contributions due to the drop in trade with the rest of Spain and the European Union, and the increase in benefit payments due to cessation of activity and increased unemployment. For Catalan pensioners, secession would be a good business!

Transfers through the social security system are a form of interterritorial transfer that completes the other taxes. Moreover, the dynamics of affiliation to the social security system have been very much influenced by the events of autumn 2017. In a year, the number of people joining the system fell by half. Between Catalonia and Madrid there is a gap of 30% in people joining the social security system.

SUMMARY

- Amongst the Autonomous Communities with a higher per capita GDP than the Spanish average, the Basque Country and Navarre are net receivers of income from the rest of Spain.
- Catalonia has an annual deficit with the Spanish social security system of €3000 million.
- Since the thwarted separatist coup d'état of autumn 2017, the number of people joining the social security system in Catalonia has fallen by half.

[1] Eduardo Magallón (2019), "Sólo Madrid, Baleares, Canarias y Murcia cubren el pago de pensiones", *La Vanguardia*, 25 March <https://www.lavanguardia.com/economia/20190325/461210858274/pensiones-espana-comunidades-autonomas-deficit.html>

CHAPTER 32

Flight of Companies, Capital and Bank Deposits

GOODBYE CATALONIA!

The constitution, closure, change of residence, capital increase or capital reduction are all indications of the development of companies and countries. A particular aspect of this business demography is a change of headquarters, company mobility, migration from a registered office, fiscal domicile, or centre of production, sales, logistics and research. There are many possible reasons for changing headquarters: proximity to the market or sources of supplies, tax regime (see Chap. 26), reputation, political stability, juridical security, as well as personal reasons of the owners and administrators of the company.

The change in headquarters becomes a sensitive issue when political and juridical risk is a consideration. The continual transfer of headquarters of companies' resident in Catalonia has been influenced by the long separatist confrontation and, very acutely, by the attempted coup d'état in the autumn of 2017.

A comparison of the absolute number of companies created and registered in Catalonia and in Madrid shows that since 2010, except for 2016, around 20% more companies were created every year in Madrid than in Catalonia. There is a strong tendency for large- and medium-sized companies resident in Catalonia, and which operate in the whole Spanish market, to relocate outside of Catalonia. Catalonia reached its peak of participation in the total number of Spanish companies in 2016 with 21.5%. The

F. Brunet, *The Economics of Catalan Separatism*, https://doi.org/10.1007/978-3-031-14451-6_32

years 2017–2021 were dreadful for the registration of new companies in Catalonia. The consolidation of Madrid's business leadership is confirmed.[1]

After the creation of companies, which shows the basic tendency, let us look now at the transfer of headquarters of already constituted companies to other Autonomous Communities. These data will show how, under different circumstances, mobility becomes more acute. From this we see: the negative balance sustained by Barcelona and the positive balance of Madrid. In the regions neighbouring Catalonia, in Valencia, Aragon and the Balearic Islands, the flow of arrivals of companies is greater than the flow of departures. This reflects the erosion of the Catalan business system because of the separatist confrontation, and the long abrasive friction that exists in political, social and economic relations.[2]

HELLO MADRID!

Let us consider some further aspects. As early as 2014 businesses were intrigued by the political instability. Most of the large Catalan companies consulted at the time by PricewaterhouseCoopers (PwC) could already see that the secessionist debate was having a negative (47.8%) or very negative impact (19.6%) on the economic and business relations between Catalonia and the rest of Spain. Nevertheless, 6.5% could even see a positive impact from the separatist challenge (Fig. 32.1).[3]

In the autumn of 2017 the following companies moved their headquarters from Barcelona and other locations in Catalonia to Madrid and other locations in the rest of Spain: Banco Sabadell, CaixaBank, Banco Mediolanum, Gas Natural Fenosa (today Naturgy), Dogi, Criteria, Agbar, SegurCaixa, Adeslas, Abertis, Inmobiliaria Colonial, Mahou-San Miguel, MRW, Torraspapel, Catalana Occidente, VidaCaixa, eDreams, Indukern,

[1] Colegio de Registradores de la Propiedad, Mercantiles y Bienes Muebles de España (CORPME) (2021), *Estadísticas Mercantiles* <http://www.registradores.org/>; and Javier G. Jorrín and Jesús Escudero (2019), "Catalonia falls behind in the race to lead the Spanish economy", *El Confidencial*, 28 September <https://www.elconfidencial.com/economia/2019-09-28/exodo-urbano-espana-cataluna-madrid-poblacion_2240171/>.

[2] Informa DB (2019), *Comparativa de Madrid y Cataluña* <https://cdn.informa.es/sites/5c1a2fd74c7cb3612da076ea/content_entry5c5021510fa1c000c25b51f0/5d81ee0e0d773500b2d55a88/files/Comp_Madrid_Cataluna_2019.pdf?1568796174>

[3] PricewaterhouseCoopers (2014), *Temas candentes de la economía catalana. Visión de los empresarios* <https://www.pwc.es/es/publicaciones/economia/temas-candentes-economia-catalana.html>.

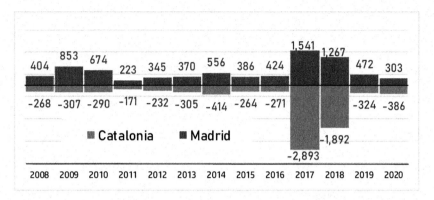

Fig. 32.1 Flight of companies: movement of companies to/from Catalonia and Madrid. (Source: Author's calculations based on data from the Colegio de Registradores de la Propiedad, Mercantiles y Bienes Muebles de Spain (CORPME) (2022), *Estadísticas Mercantiles* <http://www.registradores.org/>)

Gaesco, Applus, Bimbo, Grupo Planeta, Axa España, Codorniu Raventós, Gripo Gallo, Zurich Insurance, Cespa, La Bruixa d'Or, Cementos Molins, Global Payments, Allianz Seguros, Torrot, Hotusa, Pirelli…[4] On 19 October 2017 the largest number of changes of location of company headquarters from Catalonia to other Autonomous Communities was recorded.[5]

More than being called to leave, the companies had been expelled from Catalonia on account of juridical insecurity. They left to avoid bankruptcy (banks) and to keep their ratings (companies quoted on the stock exchange). With regard to the movement of companies included in the IBEX35 index and resident in Catalonia, before the separatist coup of autumn 2017, there were seven Catalan companies listed in this index. We

---

[4] Miriam Hermi Zaa and Manuel Blas García Avila (2019), "El intento secesionista en Cataluña (España) y la movilidad del capital", *Atelié Geográfico*, Vol. 13, No. 1, pp. 6–34. Employment, balance, market capitalisation, turnover and taxes paid by companies that have fled Catalonia are quantities that are difficult to specify, but, without a doubt, they represent a decisive fraction of the entire Catalan economy. The damage inflicted on Catalonia by the *process* is colossal and will have a long impact. And to think it could have been avoided…

[5] Foment del Treball Nacional (2017), *La movilidad empresarial derivada del contexto político en Cataluña*, 28 October <https://www.foment.com/wp-content/uploads/2017/11/Presentaci%C3%B3n-Nota-de-Econom%C3%ADa.pdf>.

should note that of the seven companies that resided in Catalonia, none were amongst the largest in the Spanish market. They represent somewhat less than the Catalan quota of 20%. After the coup, there remained only one company domiciled in Catalonia listed in the IBEX35. Be they companies quoted on the stock exchange, foreign companies, Catalan companies not quoted on the stock exchange but whose market is the whole of Spain, the tendency to locate the headquarters and subsequent activities outside Catalonia is gravely serious. For Catalonia. And for Spain. With the Catalan companies and multinationals that fled Catalonia and the Catalan companies sold to owners resident in other places, the business structure of Catalonia changed.

BANKS, DEPOSITS AND CREDIT IN TIMES OF REVOLUTION

Autumn 2017: pro-independence coup d'état. If you think secession will occur, then at least move the domicile of your bank deposits! Take your deposits, those of your family and of the company from a bank domiciled in Catalonia, that will be out of Spain and the EU eurozone and put them in another bank domiciled in a safer place.

Of course, as is well known, for years the separatist believers had had their money securely deposited in non-Catalan banks. For example, in Andorra! Or in the Paseo de la Castellana in Madrid! But this was not the case for 99% of Catalans. Any constitutionalist bank account holder was fearful in the autumn of 2017. October 1st, 2nd, 3rd... the message broadcast by His Majesty the King at 9 p.m.[6] The King put an end to the upheaval. The extraordinary gravity and complexity of the events of autumn 2017 showed that the separatist challenge was no joke. Hence the corresponding movement of bank deposits and bank credits from 2015 and during the revolutionary autumn of 2017. We can see that[7]

- Bank deposits in Catalonia are half of what they are in Madrid.
- During the 2017 coup d'état, between September 2017 and December 2017 bank deposits to the tune of €31,399 million left

[6] His Majesty King Felipe VI (2017), *Message*, 3 October <https://www.rtve.es/alacarta/videos/telediario/mensaje-integro-del-rey-tras-referendum-cataluna/4247341/>.
[7] Banco de España (2020, 2017 y 2015), *Boletín Estadístico* <https://www.bde.es/bde/es/secciones/informes/boletines/Boletin_Estadist/>

Catalonia, of them, €7000 million corresponding CaixaBank and €4600 million corresponding to Banc Sabadell. Credit fell by €15,982 million.

- From December 2017 until April 2020 bank deposits recovered by €22,000 million, but credit fell by another €6000 million.
- Growing funding gap.
- A slight tendency of reduction can be discerned both in bank deposits and bank credit in Catalonia, Madrid and in the rest of Spain. Between 2015 and 2020, bank deposits in Catalonia fell from 16.3 to 14.6% of the Spanish total, far from the quotas of 20% that bank deposits in Catalan banks represented as a proportion of the Spanish total in 1977. And far from the 28.6% of Madrid.
- CaixaBank's change of domicile to Valencia and that of Banc Sabadell to Alicante prevented their bankruptcy. Today, these banks have less than 30% of their business in Catalonia. The difference between deposits and credits (funding gap) is very large in Catalonia: -€32,304 million. In the Community of Madrid, the balance is +€772,000 million and in Spain as a whole it is +€36,324 million. It is as if all the credit surplus that Spain obtains from everyone were applied entirely to financing credit in Catalonia. In this way, the rest of Spain finances 15.6% of the credit granted to companies and people resident in Catalonia.

SUMMARY

- Madrid is consolidated as the domicile for companies to the detriment of Barcelona and Catalonia.
- During the separatist challenge, the tendency for companies to relocate their headquarters outside Catalonia became more pronounced. After the separatist coup of autumn 2017, this became a stampede.
- Reversing the flight from Catalonia of Catalan and foreign companies will be long and hard. This foreshadows a declining economic future for Catalonia.
- During the separatist coup of autumn 2017, bank deposits amounting to €31,399 million left Catalonia.

- Catalan banking operations are just 14.6% of Spanish banking operations when, in 1977, they represented 20%. It is half today's figure for Madrid at 28.6%.
- A significant part of bank credits obtained by people and companies resident in Catalonia (€32,304 million) is provided by bank resources from the rest of Spain.

CHAPTER 33

Collapse of Foreign Investment

FLIGHT OF FOREIGN INVESTMENT

The amount of foreign investment arriving in a territory is an indication of its present attractiveness and anticipates its future competitiveness. Foreign investments have a structural base in the existing productive fabric of the place they are destined and a volatile and circumstantial element, which includes an overview of the present, and expected future, institutional, social, economic and political stability. The dynamics of foreign investment, in particular, therefore reflect some of the consequences of the separatist challenge: not upgrading, closing down, moving the company headquarters, and choosing somewhere other than Catalonia for future investment, preferably Madrid. The case of Catalonia under the separatist cloud of confrontation is tragic: this region has gone from being the one preferred by foreign investment in Spain, to being a place to flee from, a place not to go.[1]

The investment fleeing Catalonia is mainly soaked up by Madrid. Madrid is the great beneficiary of the refusal of companies and foreign investors to expand, settle and invest in a place that was previously their preferred choice, as Barcelona was. In Catalonia, the stock of foreign capital provides employment for 24.5% of the workers; in Spain as a whole, 6.9%. Foreign

---

[1] Tesla's final decision not to install its European factory in Catalonia and Volkswagen's (the owner of SEAT, Catalonia's largest company) decision to install its third battery factory in the world, not in Catalonia, but in Valencia, show the persistence of the lack of confidence in Catalonia's future.

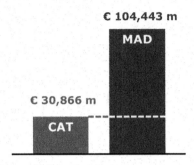

Fig. 33.1 Foreign investment in Catalonia and Madrid, 2010–2019. (Source: Author's calculations based on data from the Instituto Nacional de Estadística (2022), *Inversión extranjera directa en España* <https://www.ine.es/dyngs/IOE/es/fichaProg.htm?cid=1259946010777>; and Ministerio de Industria, Comercio y Turismo (2022), *Inversiones extranjeras* https://comercio.gob.es/Inversionesexteriores/Paginas/Index.asp)

investment in Madrid is triple the foreign investment in Catalonia! And that in spite of the fact that today both regions have a similar GDP, that Catalonia is more industrial than Madrid, and that it was the classic choice for multinational European companies to locate on the Peninsula (Fig. 33.1).

Brexit, Spain had the opportunity to attract large quantities of investment from the United Kingdom. "Between 2017 and the first nine months of 2018, Madrid had captured €4,574 million from Great Britain, representing 67% of British investment on the Peninsula during this period. […] Catalonia captured only €568 million of British investment. That is to say, €4,000 less. In spite of being the Spanish region with the largest GDP, it only managed to attract 8% of the investment that arrived in Spain as a result of Brexit."[2]

SUMMARY

- The foreign investment the separatists scare away goes to Madrid.
- The current level of foreign investment in Catalonia, 14.4% of all foreign investment in Spain, portends a steep decline in Catalonia's production system, level of employment and personal income.

[2] Ignacio Bolea (2019), "Madrid capta 71.807 millones más de inversión que Cataluña desde 2012", *Expansión*, 19 January <https://www.expansion.com/economia/2019/01/18/5c4181d222601d834d8b4589.html>

CHAPTER 34

Boycott of Catalan Goods and Services

THE BOYCOTT OF THE GOODS AND SERVICES OF COMPANIES RESIDENT IN CATALONIA REACHES 23%

The boycott of goods and services provided by Catalan companies, or companies resident in Catalonia, is one of the consequences of the extremely long challenge of the separatists against the rule of law and the unity of Spain. A hypothetical independence of Catalonia would double the current boycott.

The trade boycott is particularly acute in products of mass consumption, with reputed brands, such as those of food. The impact of the boycott might be limited if the origin of the seller is not recognised, or if the product is an intermediate one that is consumed by a company rather than an end consumer. The consumer boycott mainly affects products that are clearly Catalan such as cava, cured sausages and some multi-product brands, as well as services such as tourism. Two ways of reducing the impact of the boycott are to 'launder' the product labels with a non-Catalan address, and to issue invoices from places other than Catalonia. In these circumstances, Catalan companies have a double challenge: 1. maintain their sales to their usual customers, a difficult task, and 2. obtain new customers and new sales, a very difficult task.

The Spanish market is, of course, a key market for Catalan companies. Of the 23 markets in which Catalan companies sell for more than €1000 million per year, 13 of them are Spanish Autonomous Communities.

© The Author(s), under exclusive license to Springer Nature
Switzerland AG 2022
F. Brunet, *The Economics of Catalan Separatism*,
https://doi.org/10.1007/978-3-031-14451-6_34

Catalan companies sell more to Cantabria, a region with half a million inhabitants, than they do to the USA, the world's primary economy with a population of 300 million. Similarly, Catalonia sells more to the region of Murcia than it does to China, the world's second economy. And it sells more to La Rioja than to Japan, the world's third economy.

There are two ways of evaluating the magnitude of the boycott on Catalan products. One is to conduct consumer surveys. The other is from bilateral trade data. With regard to consumer surveys, we refer to the one on the boycott of Catalan products and relocation, conducted in November 2017 by the Reputation Institute.[1] It found

- 23% of Spaniards (without Catalonia) declare having stopped buying Catalan goods and services. Another 21% are thinking of doing so.
- In the event of a hypothetical independence, 49% of Spaniards (without Catalonia) would stop buying Catalan goods and services, with a potential loss of almost half of the national market, that is, €20,000 million.
- 65% of those surveyed in the rest of Spain think that companies with their headquarters in Catalonia should move their domicile to another region in the event of a hypothetical independence. The change of registered office and domicile for tax purposes meets widespread approval throughout the whole of Spain (77.5% of the total).
- Millennials (18–34 years of age) are the generation most critical of companies resident in Catalonia.

Finally, to appreciate the magnitude of the boycott of Catalan products and services, let us consider the bilateral trade data and, in particular, the sales of companies established in Catalonia to the rest of Spain. As we saw in Chap. 29, Catalonia's trade with the rest of Spain (sales and purchases) has fallen over the last decade. Average annual sales by Catalonia to the rest of Spain were €42,533 million during the period 1995–2007; €43,804 million (during the initial acute phase of the *process*); €36,776, €38,438 and €39,320 million, respectively, for the years 2016, 2017 and 2018 (economic recovery and secessionist coup).

---

[1] Enrique Johnson and Yeray Carretero (2017), "Informe sobre el impacto del desafío independentista", *Reputation Institute* <https://documentcloud.adobe.com/link/review?u ri=urn:aaid:scds:US:1341c361-86e3-4afa-b594-2fc06bd4515d#pageNum=32>.

For their part, the Assemblea Nacional de Catalunya (ANC) instigated a boycott of the products and services of non-secessionist companies in 2017. The "Strategic consumption. Connect with the Catalan Republic" campaign was reported by the employers' organisation (Foment del Treball) to the National Commission on Markets and Competition (CNMC), but a complaint was lodged about this by the Agència Catalana del Consum (Catalan Consumer Affairs Agency) about a conflict of competence in the matter. After an appeal to the Constitutional Court in December 2020, the matter was returned to the CNMC, which was obliged to make a judgement within 18 months.[2]

PLUMMETING TOURISM

Catalonia has great tourist attractions and tourism is an important economic activity in many districts. For their part, the 1992 Barcelona Olympic Games made the city an international landmark, a 'must visit' place. For 500 million Europeans, flying to Barcelona and spending a few days in Catalonia has been an easy and a very pleasant experience.

Receptive tourism in Catalonia accounts for the employment of more than 450,000 people and represents 13% of GDP. The centres of attraction and residence are the city of Barcelona, the Costa Brava, the Costa Dorada and the Pyrenees. Notable also are the number of people from the rest of Spain and abroad who, for seasonal tourism or retirement, have a residence in Catalonia.

The *process* had a strong impact on tourism. The Barcelona and Catalonia brands are in tatters. Tourist activity decreased in all fields, especially tourism from the rest of Spain, which fell by half.[3] Previously, foreign tourists accounted for 74.6% of the total number of visitors to Catalonia.

With the separatist coup of autumn 2017, everything contracted: reservations (down 60%), overnight stays and degree of occupation (down 23%), along with the prices for hotels and tourist apartments, airport traffic, the mooring of liners, purchases and so forth.

[2] EFE (2020), "Abren expediente sancionador a la Asamblea Catalana por su campaña de boicot a empresas no independentistas", *20 Minutos*, 21 December <https://amp.20minutos.es/noticia/4519473/0/abren-expediente-sancionador-a-la-asamblea-catalana-por-su-campana-de-boicot-a-empresas-no-independentistas>.

[3] Europa Press (2019),"Los jubilados evitan Catalunya: el 40% de plazas del Imserso, sin cubrir" (*La Vanguardia*, 13 November <https://www.lavanguardia.com/economia/20191113/471579113342/cataluna-imserso-viajes-jubilados-proces-disturbios.html>).

In 2018 and 2019, tourism continued to hobble along, affected by anti-tourist policies, actions of tourist phobia (noisy protests, performances, graffiti), and the stress caused by robberies and independence symbolism, such as yellow crosses on the beaches. In October 2019, with disturbances on the streets, there was a veritable outward stampede of tourists.

Finally, the icing on the cake for tourism in Catalonia came in March 2020 with the coronavirus pandemic. During the summer of that year, hotel occupancy hardly reached 10%, 75% of the city's hotels were closed and prices at those that were open fell by 50%. There is no a recovery of the tourism in Catalonia.[4]

SUMMARY

- The boycott of Catalan goods and services is already practised by 23% of Spaniards and a further 21% are thinking about it. In the event of independence, 49% of Spaniards would stop buying Catalan goods and services.
- The sale of Catalan products to the rest of Spain has plummeted by around 12%. Tourism was badly affected by the high levels of instability and the threats and violent actions resulting from the separatists' *process*.
- Catalonia was a very popular tourist destination. The *process* dealt it various serious wounds. Will the Covid-19 pandemic have dealt the final blow?

---

[4]Europa Press (2020), "La ocupación hotelera en Barcelona apenas llega al 10% este verano por la crisis del covid", *Catalunya*, 16 September <https://www.europapress.es/catalunya/noticia-ocupacion-hoteles-barcelona-apenas-llega-10-verano-crisis-covid-20200916120727.html>. José Ramón Riera (2022), "Cataluña sigue drenando la recuperación del turismo. España tiene un grave problema con la pérdida de ingresos en esta región", *El Debate*, 15 September.

CHAPTER 35

The Budgets of the Separatist Generalitat

Uncontrolled Budget

The budget of the Generalitat de Catalunya represented 18.4% of Catalan GDP in 2020 (€46,057 million). As part of a very extensive expansion, the government of the Generalitat systematically exceeded its own powers, broadened its responsibilities, and created, during a phase preparatory to the coup against the Spanish state, what the separatists called 'state structures'. Until the separatist leaders explain this in a court of law, we must suppose that the expenditure on 'state structures' are something like the meeting point between the revolution and the independence budget trough.

The administrative structure of Catalonia is composed of the Generalitat (with 14 departments with their corresponding directorates, etc.), 4 provincial councils, 946 town councils, 42 districts and district councils, 8 'veguerias', 2 municipal groupings, 82 commonwealths, 1 metropolitan area and 65 smaller municipal entities. In turn, these entities have created: 339 mercantile companies, 289 consortiums, 161 foundations, 75 autonomous organisations, 146 administrative organisations, 4 commercial organisations, 51 public entities, 31 public business entities, 14 other not-for-profit institutions and 7 public universities.[1]

---

[1] Ministerio de Hacienda (2021), *Informe sobre el impacto del sector público autonómico en la actividad económico-financiera de las Comunidades Autónomas* <https://serviciostelematicosext.hacienda.gob.es/SGCIEF/ISPANET/index.aspx?ejercicio=2020&periodo=01>.

© The Author(s), under exclusive license to Springer Nature Switzerland AG 2022
F. Brunet, *The Economics of Catalan Separatism*,
https://doi.org/10.1007/978-3-031-14451-6_35

Therefore, in the Generalitat budgets, it will be difficult to separate the wheat from the chaff. There is legal embezzlement (such as funding illegal referendums, the constant bombardment of propaganda, various performances, entities such as Diplocat and commissions for Independent Diplomat,[2] as well as a profusion of actions and structures beyond its powers and outside the law), and real embezzlement prevails (such as with juicy subsidies for separatist outfits), and with profligacy.

We know from Chap. 6 that public spending in Spain is highly decentralised (49.2% of the total is expended by the regions), while income generated by the Autonomous Communities and Cities represents 14.7% of the total, a proportion similar to that of federal systems. So, I spend, you collect! This is how, with money from Madrid, legal and illegal payments have been made to pay for the rallies, parties, fantasies, and rebellions. It is well known that the perfidious enemy's money is never enough to fund a people that shouts in unison with the good nationalist leaders, even more so if their deputies in Congress are necessary to form the Government of Spain.

Between 2000 and 2020 the, Generalitat budgets multiplied by 3.7, that is 370%. And this while the powers exercised remained the same, which is to say, without the legal powers increasing during these two decades, and in spite of the economic, financial and tax crises of 2008–2013. The main sources of income for 2020 were the autonomous band of state-levied income tax (IRPF), €11,587 million, participation in state-levied VAT, €7705 million), the Generalitat's own taxes (€2617 million generated through 15 different Generalitat taxes), and an annual increase in debt (€10,219, contracted with the Spanish Ministry of Finance Autonomous Liquidity Fund) (Fig. 35.1).[3]

The main expenditure items in the Generalitat budget are salaries for its own civil servants and those of Generalitat entities, consortiums, foundations, and companies (€12,816 million), the transfer to the Catalan Health Service (€9548 million), transfers to its own entities, consortiums,

---

[2] Antonio Fernández (2021), "Separatismo de talonario: Cataluña destinó miles de euros en comprar 'amigos' fuera", *El Confidencial*, 4 de mayo <https://www.elconfidencial.com/espana/cataluna/2021-05-04/cataluna-subvencion-onu-banco-mundial_3061675/>.

[3] Institut d'Estadística de Catalunya (2022), *Generalitat de Catalunya. Pressupostos* <https://www.idescat.cat/pub/?id=aec&n=535&lang=es>; i de Generalitat de Catalunya. Departament de la Vicepresidència i d'Economia i Hisenda (2020), *Els pressupostos de la Generalitat de Catalunya per al 2020* <http://economia.gencat.cat/ca/ambits-actuacio/pressupostos/2020/>.

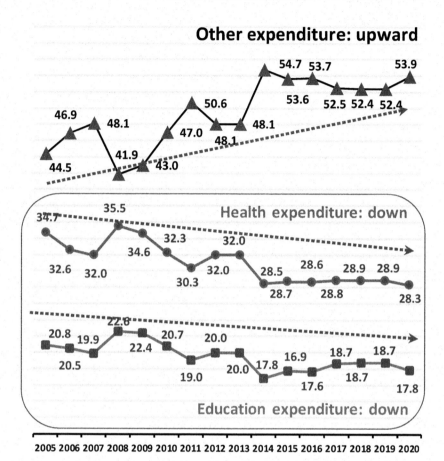

Fig. 35.1   Anti-social character of the separatist Generalitat: reduction of the budget in health and education and expansion in other expenditure. (Source: Author's calculations based on data from the Institut d'Estadística de Catalunya (2022), *Sector público Generalitat. Presupuesto. Gastos. Por áreas políticas de gasto* <https://www.idescat.cat/pub/?id=aec&n=683&lang=es>.)

foundations and companies (some €11,000 million) and debt repayment (€10,443 million). Considered by function, the main budget items for expenditure in the Generalitat budget for 2020 are Health (€12,501 million), Education (€6,698 million), local entities (€3,725 million) and police, Mossos d'Esquadra (€1,226 million).

THE ANTISOCIAL CHARACTER
OF THE SEPARATIST GENERALITAT

The dynamics of the Generalitat's expenditure on education and health are similar, they are falling. They reached their maximum in 2008, fell until 2014, recovered very slightly, and fell again until 2020. The antisocial character of the separatist governments of the Generalitat is dramatic and shameless. The results of this antisocial policy can be seen in the Catalan separatist education regime (as we saw in Chap. 12):

- In Andalusia academic failure is 19.4% in Madrid 9.4%. Consequently, in the Generalitat madrasas, even Catalan-speaking school students fail at double the rate of school students in Madrid.
- Academic failure of Spanish-speaking school students in Catalonia is 30% and 17.5% for Catalan-speaking school students.

Exactly the same thing happens in Health. Which 'national health service' of the 17+2 autonomous mini-states has the worst results? The separatist Generalitat of course. If the Generalitat wanted to be normal it could save many lives and avoid the ruination of many others.[4]

The Spanish Autonomous Communities have transferred powers for state services such as health, education and social services, but not (yet) pensions. Of all the Autonomous Communities, expenditure by the Generalitat de Catalunya on Health, Education and Social Services is the lowest in Spain and between 2009 and 2019 it fell by 21.1% (€2788 per inhabitant in 2009, and €2200 in 2019).[5]

PUBLIC INVESTMENT IN CATALONIA

The Autonomous Community of Catalonia represents 6% of the surface area of Spain, 16% of its population and around 15% of regional investment included in the general state Administration budget. During the period 2015–2021, the state invested €3970 million in Catalonia, ahead

[4] Expansión (2022), *Datosmacro* <https://www.epdata.es/datos/listas-espera-sanidad-publica-datos-graficos-comunidad-autonoma/28/cataluna/297>.

[5] Asociación Estatal de Directores y Gerentes en Servicios Sociales (2020), *Evolución de los presupuestos autonómicos en España* <https://www.directoressociales.com/images/Noticias/EvolgastoCCAA2018/GR%C3%81FICOS%20Evol.%20presupuestos%20auton%C3%B3micos%20_1.pdf>.

of Andalusia (€3386 million), Castilla y León (€3329 million) and the Community of Madrid (€3073 million).[6] Catalonia is therefore the Autonomous Community that receives the largest amount of investment from the Spanish government: 16.1% of the total, while Madrid receives 12.5%. Thus, the data completely disprove the existence of a supposed wrongdoing against Catalonia in the field of investment.

Public investment in Catalonia does not, therefore, seem to be scarce. Let us examine some of its characteristics:

- Spanish state investment in Catalonia is slightly inferior to the proportion of GDP (between 1 and 2% less, as is consistent with being a more developed region, specialised in the sale of goods to the rest of Spain), and is, naturally, much higher than the Catalan proportion of territory and similar to the proportion of the Spanish population.[7]
- State investment in Catalonia is far higher than state investment in other comparable Autonomous Communities, such as Madrid and Andalusia.
- Generalitat expenditure on infrastructures is 0.4% of its budget, while the other Autonomous Communities invest an average of 1.68%, and Madrid invests 1.95%.[8]

Given this real state of affairs with regard to public investment in Catalonia, the separatists come up with all kinds of distortions in the same manner as they do with the fiscal balance and foreign investment. In the case of public investment, the separatist drivel revolves around Spain's supposed mission not to invest in Catalonia. To this the separatists add their mantra about the Mediterranean corridor[9] and the nuisance of the

---

[6] Societat Civil Catalana (2022), *Las inversiones del Estado en Cataluña, Barcelona*, SCC; e Intervención General del Estado (2022), *Ejecución de inversiones reales del sector público empresarial por CCAA* <https://www.igae.pap.hacienda.gob.es/sitios/igae/es-ES/Contabilidad/ContabilidadPublica/CPE/EjecucionPresupuestaria/Paginas/isdistribucioninversion.aspx>

[7] Eduardo Magallón (2020), "Catalunya recibirá el 16.5% de la inversión estatal, menos que su peso en el GDP", *La Vanguardia*, 28 October <https://www.lavanguardia.com/economia/20201028/4959602249/inversiones-catalunya-GDP-regionalizable-presupuestos-estado-2021.html>.

[8] Convivencia Cívica Catalana (2018), *Las inversiones en infraestructuras en Cataluña. Licitación de obra pública. Análisis de los años 2011 a 2016* <http://files.convivenciacivica.org/Las%20inversiones%20en%20infraestructuras%20en%20Catalu%C3%B1a.pdf>.

[9] See the website El Corredor Mediterráneo (2022), *Quiero Corredor* <https://elcorredormediterraneo.com/estado-de-las-obras>.

motorway tolls. Except for the AP7 motorway, the tolls of the motorways of Catalonia are administered by the Generalitat de Catalunya. And, in order to avoid explicit tolls, other forms of financing, in collaboration with the road-building companies, known as 'shadow tolls', were introduced and applied for decades. Subrogated investments were also extended, with subsequent leasing by the Generalitat of the facilities built this way, as is the case with the huge network of stations for the regional police, the *Mossos d'Esquadra*.

The separatists accuse the government of Spain of something the government of the Generalitat does: it does not invest. Let us consider the Generalitat's enthusiasm for investment: "If, over the last six years, the Catalan government had invested the same proportion in infrastructure as the other autonomous governments in Spain it would have invested €1,971 million to this end instead of the 773 million it really expended. […] The autonomous government of Catalonia's failure to invest in infrastructure constitutes a notable prejudice for the Catalan economy and a burden for its competitiveness".[10]

From the dynamics of infrastructure in Catalonia, we can deduce:[11]

- There is a very large gap between budgeted investment and executed investment, within both the Catalan administration and in Spain as a whole.
- Between a level of investment of 2.2% of regional GDP, which would be a standard proportion, and the investment actually carried out in Catalonia from 2010–2020, there is an estimated deficit of €28,000 million.
- In 2020, public investment in Catalonia was €918 million, 38.1% less than the amount in 2019 (in Madrid it was €1386 million, 3.3%

[10] Convivencia Cívica Catalana (2019), *Las inversiones en infraestructuras en Cataluña. Licitación de obra pública. Análisis por administración* <http://files.convivenciacivica.org/Las%20inversiones%20en%20infraestructuras%20en%20Catalu%C3%B1a%202016.pdf>; and Societat Civil Catalana (2016), *La inversión en obra pública en Cataluña* <https://societatcivilcatalana.cat/assets/documents/InversionObraPublica.pdf>.

[11] Foment del Treball Nacional. Comissió d'Infraestructures i Equipaments (2020), *Catàleg d'infraestructures bàsiques pendents d'executar a Catalunya. CAT-100*, June <https://www.foment.com/wp-content/uploads/2020/07/Cataleg-infraestructures-basiques_-Actualitzacio_2020.pdf>; and Foment del Treball Nacional (2022), *El dèficit d'inversió en infraestructures a Catalunya 2009–2020* <https://www.foment.com/wp-content/uploads/2022/01/El-deficit-dinversio-en-infraestructures-a-Catalunya-2009-2020.pdf>.

less). According to agent: the state invested €284 million (also €284 million in Madrid), the Autonomous Community €324 million (€262 million) and the Local Corporations €309 million (€839 million).[12]

SUMMARY

- Between 2000 and 2020 the Generalitat budgets multiplied by 3.7. Debt grew at an annual average rate of 10.8%. The Generalitat is a machine for spending without measure and for accumulating debt. Madrid pays, and Madrid will continue to pay.
- The debt of the Generalitat is 26.6% of the total debt of the Autonomous Communities, a proportion to be compared with that of their GDP and population.
- Public investment by the central state Administration in Catalonia far outweighs investment received by other Autonomous Communities, notably Madrid.
- The Generalitat's investment deficit is exorbitant. It is the result of its priorities: not administration and well-being, but confrontation with Madrid and amongst Catalans.
- The expansion, creative accounting, indiscipline, and financial and budgetary defiance of the Generalitat have generated unsustainable Generalitat budgets, deficits, and debt, with ratios of illiquidity and insolvency that led to bankruptcy and bailout by the Spanish state.
- During a decade of the *process*, the sharp fall in expenditure on Health, Education and Social Services (-21.1%) demonstrates the profoundly antisocial character of the separatist Generalitat.

[12] Seopan (2022), *Licitación pública* <https://seopan.es/licitacion/>.

CHAPTER 36

Economic Policy of the Separatist Generalitat

FINANCIAL FANTASIES

In the context of the Generalitat's permanent rebellion against the Spanish state, budgetary creativity has, of course, flourished. All kinds of artifice and subterfuge are employed in the separatist Generalitat's income and expenditure budgets to expand them, even when lacking finance. This fiscal-financial engineering has two consequences: the deficit (total expenditure exceeds current income) and the debt (issued to finance the deficit). Let us analyse the Generalitat de Catalunya's debt:[1]

---

[1] Bearing in mind the budgetary cycle and the diversity of budgets (project, initial approval, implementation, settlement) and, especially, given the high level of budgetary creativity that characterises a rebel administration such as the Generalitat (which leads to the final deficit of the implemented budget always being much higher than the initial approved deficit), it is of no interest to consider the official deficits (it being the case that the information relating to them is void of any reliability) so we focus on the analysis of the capital debt (which accumulates the successive real final annual deficits), in accordance with data from the Banco de España.

© The Author(s), under exclusive license to Springer Nature Switzerland AG 2022
F. Brunet, *The Economics of Catalan Separatism*,
https://doi.org/10.1007/978-3-031-14451-6_36

- With relation to GDP
  - Comparing amounts: in 2000, the Generalitat's debt represented 8.3% of Catalonia's GDP, in 2020, it represented 33.7%.[2]
  - Comparing growth: the Generalitat's debt grew three times more than Catalonia's GDP.

- With relation to the approved budget
  - Comparing the volume of the debt with the volume of the budget: In 2000 the Generalitat's debt represented 81.5% of the Generalitat's budget; in 2020 it represented 187.9%.[3] During the decade of the *process* there was extraordinary growth in accumulated debt... which the government of Spain provided for.
- With relation to the debt of other Autonomous Communities
  - Comparing the Generalitat's debt with that of the Community of Madrid: in 2000 the Generalitat's debt was 2.5 times larger than that of Madrid, in 2020, it was 2.3 times larger. The debt of the Generalitat continues to double that of Madrid.
  - Comparing the Generalitat's debt with that of all the Autonomous Communities: in 2000 the Generalitat's debt represented 26.5% of the debt of all the Autonomous Communities; in 2020 it represented 26.6%. The values for the Generalitat maintain a proportion that is considerably higher than those of its population or GDP.

Generalitat Ratings, Risk Premium, Bankruptcy and Bailout

The budgetary and financial performance of the Generalitat de Catalunya has been really unusual and very expansive, as we saw in the previous chapter. Consequently, the ratings have been successively downgraded, increasing the Generalitat debt risk premiums and, to a lesser degree, those of the

---

[2] Of course, in a hypothetical scenario of secession from the rest of Spain, to this amount of the Generalitat's own debt must be added the quota for its share of the Spanish debt, as well as the other amounts attributable to the bill for independence. In this way, the debt of a hypothetically independent Catalonia would by far surpass 175% of its GDP, that is, 65% more than the debt of the rest of Spain. That would suppose an annual payment of more than 20% of GDP, completely impossible to finance given the lack of access to capital markets. A hypothetically independent Catalonia would significantly reduce Spain's financial costs.

[3] Banco de España (n.d.), *Boletín Estadístico* <https://www.bde.es/webbde/es/estadis/infoest/bolest13.html>.

companies resident in Catalonia, damaging the performance of the stock exchange and that of companies. The rating for debt issued by the Generalitat fell from Aa2 (high grade on Moody's rating scale) in 2009 to Ba3 (non-investment speculative grade quality) since 2016. The rating for Spain is four scales higher than Catalonia, with a rating of Baa1.

Even though the debt of the Generalitat is guaranteed by the Spanish state, with respect to Spanish debt, its risk oscillated between 50 and 652 basis points (that is to say +6.52% p.a.). The risk premium or differential between Spain's interest rate and the German *bund* has oscillated between 29 basis points in January 2000 and 97 basis points in March 2022, with a maximum of 536 in August 2012.[4] The chronic instability of Catalonia[5] was extrapolated to the profitability of quoted Catalan and Spanish securities. In the autumn of 2017 acute political risk became clear.

The capital debt of the Generalitat in the third quarter of 2021 was €82,936 million.[6] This represents 37.2% of GDP and €10,912 per Catalan. The composition of the Generalitat debt is as follows: debt to the state, €58,986 million[7]; loans from Spanish banks, €5858 million; loans from foreign banks, €5278 million; loans from other administrations, €4421 million; and finally, Generalitat bonds, €3837 million.

This capital debt in circulation of the Generalitat pays an average interest of 4.6%, which is 2% (200 basis points of risk premium) above the average interest paid on debt by the Kingdom of Spain. The securities of the Generalitat with the highest interest rates reach 6.35% and their date of maturity extends to 2041. Others have interest rates of 5.9% and 5.3%,

[4] Countryeconomy.com (2022), *Sovereigns Ratings List* <https://countryeconomy.com/ratings/spain>.

[5] Jakob Vanschoonbeek (2020), "Regional (in)stability in Europe a quantitative model of state fragmentation", *Journal of Comparative Studies*, Vol. 48, pp. 605–641.

[6] Banco de España (n.d.), *Boletín Estadístico* <https://www.bde.es/webbde/es/estadis/infoest/bolest13.html>. After Catalonia come Cataluña Valencia (€47,894 million), Andalusia (€36,356) and Madrid (€34,584). To these amounts should be added the debts of Autonomous Community public companies which, in the case of Catalonia, come to €1351 million.

[7] This is the amount pending reimbursement from the so-called Autonomous Communities Finance Fund, the Autonomous Liquidity Facility and the Finance Facility. Loans received from these funds and applied to the Generalitat's budget amounted to €88,296 million between 2012 and 2020, and the Generalitat obtained €8045 million even in 2019. (Ministerio de Hacienda (2020), *Financiación Autonómica* <https://www.hacienda.gob.es/esES/Areas%20Tematicas/Financiacion%20Autonomica/Paginas/Financiacion%20Autonomica.aspx>).

with due dates between 2024 and 2030. There are emissions with ingenious formulas for calculating the interest due that are referenced to inflation plus 3%, and others that are referenced to the Euribor. The periodicity of dates due oscillates between 12 and 3 months.

The emissions of the Generalitat were brokered by BBVA, Banco Santander, Crédit Agricole, Credit Suisse, Deutsche Bank, Goldman Sachs, JP Morgan, HSBC, Société Générale and Caixabank. It is worth mentioning that these 'patriotic' Generalitat bonds amounted to €22,540 million in 2011, after which time there were fewer, it being the case that the Generalitat, given its ratings, ceased having access to the financial markets.

Without access to credit, from 2012, the Generalitat met its financing obligations by having recourse to the Autonomous Liquidity Fund (FLA). This mechanism has prevented Catalonia falling into default. With a junk bond rating, the Generalitat could no longer issue more debt and it was the bailout from the FLA that prevented default, or the further cutting of services. The Generalitat is the Spanish administration that has received the most from this fund administered by the Spanish Treasury. Activated in 2012, it fixed interest rates between 0.3% and 0.7%, in line with the average interest of Treasury emissions. Most of the Generalitat requests to the FLA are applied to the repayment of previous loans.[8] Being insolvent, the Generalitat was bailed out by the central government by means of the creation of the FLA. Its resources were used to pay its civil servants' payroll, the exorbitant salaries of senior officials and to ease the payments to suppliers. Perfidious Spain came to the rescue of the rebellious Generalitat.

Economic Policy of the Separatist Generalitat

There was a time when people spoke about the Generalitat's economic policy. That was during the happy years of the 1990s. At that time, the immediate aims of the leaders of the Generalitat were still not the separation of Catalonia from the rest of Spain. Then the Generalitat, hijacked by the separatists, went about preparing a coup d'état, and then launched it.

---

[8] The International Monetary Fund has drawn attention to the impact of the Spanish regions' deficits on the sustainability of Spanish finances. (Mar Delgado-Téllez, Victor D. Lledó, and Javier J. Pérez (2017). "On the Determinants of Fiscal Non-Compliance: An Empirical Analysis of Spain's Regions", *IMF Working Paper*, WP/17/5.)

If, until the coup of 2017, the Generalitat was a wayward administration, since the coup, it has been a zombie administration that continues to turn to confrontation in a sectarian manner in spite of being responsible for the police, education, health and for 7.5 million Catalans.[9] It is a zombie administration, but it is not a small or lesser administration. Of the 2,597,000 people employed in Catalonia, 194,000 work in the autonomous public administration (5.3% of the total), 216,000 in autonomous education (8.3%) and 302,000 in the autonomous health service (11.6%). This amounts to 25.2% of people employed.

Characteristics of the separatist Generalitat administration are that

- It is sustained by a minority of Catalans' votes and by a majority of separatists and radical seats in the regional Parliament. (See Chaps. 17 and 19).
- It is not neutral: it disregards the obligation for the Administration to be neutral and to serve all Catalans, not just those with aspirations of independence.
- It is bankrupt and has been bailed out by the central government. (See previous chapters.)
- It spends money it does not have in abundance, and it does not invest.
- It provides subsidies without regard to its powers, and for ideological reasons (nationalism).
- It usurps state powers in foreign affairs that correspond to the central state administration in order to undermine the prestige of Spain and sell its separatist agenda.[10]
- It is morally corrupt on account of its lack of respect for more than half of Catalans and its use of the Generalitat only for confrontation. And it is financially and criminally corrupt, a) for the misuse of public funds for improper purposes; and b) because of the corruption scandals that blacken its leaders, the 3% commissions and more.

[9] This strong power is dressed in the 'soft' power of propaganda. *La Generalitat al teu costat* is the slogan (The Generalitat by your side) you hear at all hours of the day in all media. All the public and subsidised TV channels, radio stations and press denigrate Spain and Spaniards, (exterior enemy), and point to the baseness of constitutionalist Catalans (enemy within) even though these constitute the majority of Catalans, while pointing also to the goodness of independence.

[10] Juan Pablo Cardenal Nicolau (2020), *La telaraña: La trama exterior del procés*, Barcelona, Ariel.

- It disregards the laws it does not like, as well as the subsequent rulings that oblige adherence to them.
- It is opposed to bilingualism, something inherent to Catalonia,[11] and is completely unconcerned about the quality of education. The PISA reports show the dishonesty of the separatist Generalitat's educational policy.[12]
- Waiting lists in the Catalan health care service are amongst the longest of the larger Autonomous Communities and Cities.[13]
- Its police force, with 17,000 armed police, does not uphold the law.
- It is highly over-regulatory. (See Chap. 26).
- It is a mini- (or maxi-) state in embryo.
- It is the result of total confrontation and misgovernment.
- It is overpaid. Separatist leaders receive much higher salaries than those occupying similar positions within the central state Administration and most other Autonomous Communities.

CRONYISM, SECTARIANISM AND MISGOVERNMENT

Let us pause for a while to consider this last aspect. The trouble-making president of the separatist Generalitat is paid 81.5% more than the Spanish prime minister, the Generalitat ministers 55.1% more than Spanish government ministers, the secretaries general 21.2% more and the directors general 51.7% more. On average, high-ranking postholders in the autonomous Catalan administration are paid 43% more than high-ranking postholders in the central government administration. Two hundred and forty senior postholders in President Quim Torra's government are paid more than the Spanish prime minister. Altogether, the 413 senior separatist postholders are paid an average of €86,721 per year in contrast with the average of €25,553 per year paid to wage-earning Catalans, 3.4 times the

---

[11] *Vid.* Xavier Pericay (2007), *¿Libertad o coacción? Políticas lingüísticas y nacionalismos en España*, Madrid, FAES; and Sergio Vila-Sanjuán (2018), *Otra Cataluña: Seis siglos de cultura catalana en castellano*, Barcelona, Destino.

[12] Convivencia Cívica Catalana (2019), *Análisis de los resultados de PIRLS 2016 en Cataluña* <http://convivenciacivicacatalana.blogspot.com/p/informes.html>.

[13] Jessica Mouzo Quintáns (2019), "Las listas de espera se disparan desde que Torra está en el Govern", *El País*, 26 March <https://elpais.com/ccaa/2019/03/25/catalunya/1553541446_950963.html>.

average wage of a normal Catalan! High-ranking separatists are therefore very exploited by the Spanish state oppressor![14]

A breakdown of the figures reveals more succulent details. Women in senior posts represent only 37% of the total and, on average, they earn 9.5% less than men in similar posts. Only 14% of senior positions in the separatist, troublemaking Generalitat are held by Spanish speakers (we remember that 55% of Catalans are Spanish speakers), and this is without mentioning people's surnames... They undoubtedly do as they please, disregarding their compatriots and the law, and pay no heed to any good administrative practice.

Embezzlement, profligacy, confrontation with the Spanish state, scorn for more than half of the Catalans who are not supporters of their autocratic regime of misgovernment, bad government, and chaos. This is what the 'economic policy' of the Generalitat has been. The incapacity of the Generalitat's economic policy extends to all areas of its powers and actions. The separatist Generalitat exercises its own powers badly or does not exercise them. This is obvious in education, health and policing.

Right from the start the separatists took against the retail sector. They imposed opening hours that were contrary to those in the rest of Spain and contrary to the calendar for national holidays and Christian festivals; they imposed signage in Catalan and levied taxes on large stores and shopping centres. This unleashed a mini war with the Government Delegation in Catalonia and then between the courts and the Generalitat. Defending and maintaining the rule of law, insisting on compliance with it in a war of attrition between governments, one of which is clearly guided by disloyalty and finds its political energy in this kind of guerrilla war, is very ineffective and inefficient.

The Generalitat exercises its powers in a surrealist way. On the other hand, it always intends and endeavours to exercise powers it lacks to be a true state. Hence this vein of separatist provocation and verbiage: it aims to overwhelm the Spanish state, complaining about not having powers while trying to usurp the powers it (still) does not have in order to be a complete state.

---

[14] On the huge salaries in TV3 see Converses a Catalunya (2021). "In the middle of an economic crisis, these are the salaries in TV3. It would be difficult to find another professional post with the same employment conditions." <https://conversesacatalunya.cat/en-plena-crisi-aquests-son-els-salaris-de-tv3/>. Imagine the huge salaries in the myriad of entities, companies, agencies, foundations, and other outfits, that the separatists have awarded themselves from the budget of the Generalitat.

Meanwhile the Generalitat attributes its own shortcomings to the external enemy, Spain. This is the Generalitat's programme, this is the source of its perpetual challenge.

SUMMARY

- Given the unsustainability of the separatist Generalitat's finances, its ratings fell to junk status and its risk premium expelled it from the debt market.
- For this reason, the major portion of the Generalitat's debt is with the state of Spain, which it approached for a bailout.
- The separatist challenge has been dragging on for ages and with ever more undesirable consequences. In the elections to the regional parliament, the repeated majority of Catalan constitutionalist voters has not yet been sufficient to obtain a majority of seats due to the electoral law (see Chap. 19).
- Finally, on the other hand, in spite of having the highest legitimacy and complete legality (see Chap. 4), the state and Spanish democracy have not circumscribed the Generalitat to the proper exercise of its constitutional and statutory powers, with the result, in autumn 2017, of the separatist coup d'état.
- Everything that has happened since then, and what will continue to happen, makes it highly likely that Spanish democracy and Catalonia's progress will collapse.

CHAPTER 37

The Cost of 'Not Spain'

THE VALUE OF MARKET UNITY

In line with the so-called 'not Europe', due to the non-completeness of the process of European integration, it is worth pondering the cost of 'not Spain', due to the imposition of new regional regulations that would obstruct circulation and fragment the market with respect to the rest of Spain and the rest of the European Union.[1] The cost of not Spain, therefore, refers to the cost of over regulation, the reduction in the trade of goods and services, the flight of companies, capital and investment. This cost can be measured in terms of GDP: an accumulated impact of -4.6% on Catalonia's permanent GDP.

On the other hand, the size of the market is a relevant factor for competitiveness. Although markets tend to be global, for most activities, it is very different to have a market, such as the Spanish one of 47 million people (plus a market of 450 million in the rest of the EU) than to have one of 7.5 million, such as the Catalan market. Furthermore, another

---

[1] Various authors (2014), *El coste de la no-España*, Madrid, Fundación Progreso and Democracia; Gabriel Tortella Casares (2014), "Cataluña e España: el coste de la separación", in various authors (2014), *Cataluña en claro. Economía. Derecho. Historia. Cultura*, Madrid, FAES; and Fernando Sánchez-Costa (2014), "El coste de la no-España", *Claves de razón práctica*, No. 238, pp. 54–63.

F. Brunet, *The Economics of Catalan Separatism*,
https://doi.org/10.1007/978-3-031-14451-6_37

229

advantage to being part of Spain is to enjoy the benefits of sharing the Spanish language.[2]

Additionally, the cost that would be generated by a hypothetical separation of Catalonia from the rest of Spain and the European Union should be considered. Strictly speaking, this would be the cost of no longer forming part of Spain or of the European Union. In terms of GDP, the cost of 'not Spain' in a low-level secession scenario would be a fall of 9.3% of GDP, in a medium-level scenario a fall of 16.1%, and in a high-level scenario a fall of 24.4%. (See Chap. 41.)

Figure 37.1 shows both the cost of the separatist challenge and the cost of a hypothetical separation side by side. In the light of these two costs of

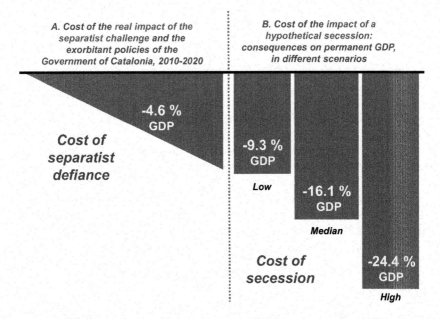

Fig. 37.1 The cost of 'not Spain' for Catalonia: cost of separatist challenge and cost of hypothetical secession. Source: Author's calculations based on data from Fig. 23.1 and Table 40.1

[2] José Luis García Delgado, José Antonio Alonso and Juan Carlos Jiménez (2012), *Valor económico del español*, Barcelona, Ariel and Fundación Telefónica.

the 'not Spain', what can be appreciated is the true and great value of Spain and of the single Spanish and European markets. This value is undermined by the separatist challenge and by the preposterous and anti-competitive policies of the separatist Generalitat.

THE SINGLE SPANISH MARKET

The European Commission has warned frequently about the necessity of a single Spanish market. Thus, as part of the European Semester, and within the annual revision of the member state's Stability and Reform Programmes, in this case the programme for Spain, the European Commission, in 2019, proposed to the Council of the European Union, which adopted it, the following Consideration 18 for the Spanish government:

- "The restrictiveness and fragmentation of regulation within Spain are preventing firms from benefiting from economies of scale and are holding back productivity. The Law on Market Unity remains an important tool to address these issues.
- Implementing that Law more decisively and removing identified restrictions on services, in particular for certain professional services such as civil engineers, architects and legal services, would improve growth opportunities and competition.
- As in other fields, where regions are key actors for the successful implementation of reforms, a stronger and sustained coordination between national and regional authorities could make policies in this area more effective."[3]

The European Commission deduced from the previous Consideration, and the European Council later adopted, final Recommendation 4 for the government of Spain: "To move forward in the application of the Law guaranteeing market unity, ensuring that at all levels of government the regulations governing access to economic activities and their exercise—particularly in the case of services—are coherent with the principles of that Law, and to improve cooperation between the Administrations".

[3] Council of the European Union (2019), "Council Recommendation of 9 July 2019 on the 2019 National Reform Programme of Spain and delivering a Council opinion on the 2019 Stability Programme of Spain, 2019/C 301/09", *Official Journal of the European Union*, Vol. 62, No. C 301 <https://eur-lex.europa.eu/legal-content/EN/TXT/PDF/?ur i=OJ:C:2019:301:FULL&from=EN>.

The quality of the institutions is therefore considered to be essential for competitiveness. Once again, the high value of Spain for Catalonia is very clear. In contrast to all this, we have seen the great instability generated by the separatist confrontation. We can imagine the hypothetical future confrontation Catalan separatists would have to organise to win the battle against the majority constitutionalist Catalans and against Spain.

Finally, we can also easily imagine what kind of institutions would emerge from such a secession of Catalonia. In the face of all this, the extremely high value of Spain, its social and democratic state and the rule of law is as clear as day.

SUMMARY

- A drop of 4.6% of Catalonia's permanent GDP is the amount lost due to the separatists' confrontation, and that of the regional government of Catalonia, with half of the Catalans and the rest of Spain.
- In a supposed separation of Catalonia from the rest of Spain, the cost of 'not Spain' would be a drop of 9.3% of GDP in a low-level secession scenario, a drop of 16.1% in a medium-level scenario and a drop of 24.4% in a in a high-level scenario.
- Spain has very high value for Catalonia. The stability and quality of its institutions, the size of its national market, the use of the Spanish language and the membership of the European Union are of major interest for Catalonia and for Catalans' freedom and progress.

CHAPTER 38

The Decline of Catalonia

STEEP AND LASTING DECLINE

As well as the social and personal confrontation between Catalans and political and institutional chaos, the separatist challenge has generated an economic downturn in Catalonia that anticipates its decline.[1] This decline shows all the signs of being long lasting. Moreover, should separatist defiance by any chance culminate in independence, Catalonia's current decline would turn into collapse.

The economic decline caused by the secessionist challenge can be seen in different indicators analysed in detail in previous chapters:

---

[1] In this regard, it could be said that the economy is slower than politics and society. The economic indicators (except, for example, the stock markets) are slower than political ones (where attack is the rule), but they act more deeply and have a longer-lasting effect. Economists are fond of saying that, in contrast with politics and politicians, the economy is resilient, resistant, stable, robust, structural... Thus, the misgovernment of the Generalitat continues for years, and while its economic impact is negative, it is not proportionate, it is less than the immense political impact. (See Jaime Malet Perdigó (2015), "¿Adónde vas, Catalunya?", *La Vanguardia*, 16 November.)

It has been said that it is as if the Catalan economy were a building affected by the slow degeneration of the cement used in its construction. The negative consequences of the situation caused by these years of challenge will be seen in a more pronounced way in the future. (Various authors (2019), "Conseqüències econòmiques del 'procés'", *Política i Prosa*, No. 7, May.)

- GDP: there is a gap of -4.6% between real GDP with separatist confrontation and the tendency of GDP without confrontation.
- Madrid is ahead of Catalonia in absolute GDP (in spite of having a population of 800,000 fewer) and, of course, in per capita GDP. Between 2005 and 2019, the gap in GDP growth between Catalonia and Madrid was -11.2%.
- Per capita GDP: the separatist challenge costs every Catalan €1384 per year, €115 per month or €4 per day.
- Boycott of Catalan goods and services and of companies resident in Catalonia: trade with the rest of Spain has declined.
- The competitiveness of Catalonia amongst the regions of Europe has fallen from position 103 in 2010 to position 161 in 2019. Catalonia's main competitor, Madrid occupies position 98.
- Barcelona's attractiveness amongst the cities of Europe has dropped from position 4 in 2010 to position 11 in 2019.
- Inward migration to Catalonia has declined. For its part, Madrid attracts people from all over Spain and, of course, even from Catalonia!
- Employment and number of people joining the social security system: Catalonia registers half the number in Madrid.
- Flight of companies and investment to Madrid, Valencia, Aragon and the Balearic Islands.
- Plummeting Spanish tourism and a fall in international tourism.
- Dearth of urban plans in Catalonia. The property market is way behind Madrid, and even further behind in the office market.
- Finance: Spanish state bailout of the Generalitat. Its deficit exceeds all fiscal rules, and its debt is completely unsustainable.[2] The process robs us!

---

[2] Three foreign résumés on how the *process* is ruining Catalonia: Charles Jaigu (2019), "Pourquoi la Catalogne est devenue folle", *Le Figaro*, 20 February <https://www.lefigaro.fr/vox/monde/2019/02/20/31002-20190220ARTFIG00238-pourquoi-la-catalogne-est-devenue-folle.php>; Nicolas Klein (2018). "Le séparatisme ruine la Catalogne", *Le Figaro*, 9 January <https://www.lefigaro.fr/vox/economie/2018/01/09/31007-20180109ARTFIG00122-nicolas-klein-le-separatisme-ruine-la-catalogne.php>; and Stefania Gozzer (2017), "Lo que pierden España y Cataluña si se separan", *BBC Mundo*, 27 October <https://www.bbc.com/mundo/noticias-internacional-41513571>.

Catalans are conscious of the decline of their economy (as well as the political chaos and the significant social confrontation). Surveyed in December 2020[3] about the 'independence *process*':

- Has the 'independence *process*' economically benefited or harmed Catalonia? 67.2% responded that it had harmed the economy.
- But, attention here! 6.1% of Catalans responded that the *process* had economically benefited the economy of Catalonia! 14.3% responded that it made no difference. These percentages are of cognitive distortion. Small but significant. To re-establish reality, there is a long road ahead.
- Has the *process* strengthened or weakened Catalan institutions? 57.1% responded that it had weakened them.
- Has it improved or damaged Catalonia's image? 65.1% responded that it had damaged it.
- Has it improved or damaged Spain's image? 67.7% responded that it had damaged it.
- Has it damaged coexistence and relations between Catalans? 53.6% responded that it had damaged them.
- Has it damaged coexistence and relations between Catalans and all other Spaniards? 64% responded that it had damaged them.

SUMMARY

- The current decline will have consequences in the medium and long terms, and many more still the longer it takes to stop what is stoking the flames, the separatist challenge, and the government of the Generalitat.
- 67.2% of Catalans believe, as has been shown throughout this investigation, that the *process* robs us. Truth will out.
- Enough of the *process*! Stop the decline of Catalunya! Let us remake Catalunya!

[3] GAD3 (2021), *Investigación sociopolítica en Cataluña*, Madrid, GAD3.

PART III

False Paradise

CHAPTER 39

Economic Consequences of a Hypothetical Secession

IMPACT OF SEPARATION

The secession of Catalonia from the rest of Spain will not happen. We Catalans do not want it and it would be extraordinarily prejudicial for everyone in all fields, political, social and economic. If it were to happen, a hypothetical separation of Catalonia would change all political, social and economic relations. With regard to politics, it would depend on how secession was brought about (degree of violence) and of the final result (separation only of the separatist areas of Catalonia, or separation of the entire territory of Catalonia).

Whatever the case, an entity outside of the Kingdom of Spain would automatically find itself outside the European Union, outside the customs union and out of the eurozone: the Treaties of the EU would not apply to the new state. Furthermore, after a successful rebellion against a democracy such as that of contemporary Spain, it would be difficult to reproduce and stabilise democratic order in the new separate entity.

With regard to society, we know the innumerable consequences of the confrontation generated by inciting secession, and in the event of that succeeding, that social confrontation would be complete. With regard to the economy, the impact of separation would also be very serious. Moreover, the consequences are more predictable and quantifiable. An entity separated from Spain would, indeed, have trade and investment relations different from those prevailing before separation.

© The Author(s), under exclusive license to Springer Nature Switzerland AG 2022
F. Brunet, *The Economics of Catalan Separatism*,
https://doi.org/10.1007/978-3-031-14451-6_39

What the pro-independence 'economic' argument has been selling is precisely the opposite. With separation, only good things will happen. For example, the hypothetical separation would be a way of saving the supposed 'fiscal deficit'. The much vaunted and imaginary €16,000 million … this would be the manna from heaven of independence. With this money, the country would leave the Spanish hell and enter separatist paradise.

Well, this pretended keystone of their argument is completely false. Of course, it is. In a scenario of separation, the €16,000 million—if they ever existed—would have disappeared because they derive from economic and trade relations that would also have disappeared. Consequently, the so-called fiscal benefit of independence is a fiction.

Ten Consequences

Analysts are unanimous on these matters. For example, according to Credit Suisse[1] ten economic consequences of an independent Catalonia would be:

1. Exit from the euro and absence of the European Central Bank: the ECB is the safety net that guarantees liquidity to the banking system in the eurozone. Thanks to its lines of support, numerous entities survived during the most severe stages of the 2007–2012 financial crisis. Financial entities domiciled in Catalan territory would lose access to these lines of finance.

2. No European banking supervision: Catalonia would be born outside the banking union. In an independent Catalonia, the relation between private and sovereign risk would remain intact with the following lethal consequences for public finance. Catalonia would be outside the European Stability Mechanism, the eurozone rescue fund of which Spain is a shareholder, with the ability to borrow up to €500,000 million to avoid default.

3. No access to any of the European Union funds: not the common agricultural fund, nor the structural fund, the Covid recovery fund or any of the other similar funds in operation. Catalonia would also be outside the European Investment Bank, of which Spain is the fifth largest shareholder.

[1] Credit Suisse (2012), «Catalonia's Choice», *Economics Research*, 19 November, <http://www.credit-suisse.com/researchandanalytics>.

4. Impact on the markets and on the risk premium: at one time during the separatist challenge, Catalan debt reached a surcharge of 1200 basis points.
5. Serious doubts about financing, the deficit, and debt: outside the European Union, the huge public debt of the new state would generate much more deficit and a huge debt.
6. Fall in trade and cost of tariffs: independence from Spain and an exit from the eurozone would oblige the payment of tariffs on account of leaving an economic zone with free movement of goods which, in turn, has signed free trade agreements with other nations. Payment of these extra charges would make Catalan exports much less competitive in comparison with the exports of other Spanish autonomous regions and other regions of Europe.
7. Less attraction for foreign investment: instability and risk would substantially reduce industrial, equity and portfolio investment.
8. Risk of relocation: if there were closures of international factories and many resident companies moved their head offices out of Catalonia on account of the *process*, after an eventual secession, there would be bankruptcies, closures, and a stampede of companies out of the country.
9. End of the tourist goose that lays the golden egg: tourism, one of the main pillars of the Catalan economy, would see the number of visitors from the rest of Spain and third countries, as well as the amount they spent, reduced by up to 60%.
10. Cost of creating a new country: the day after independence, the Catalan government would have to grapple with the huge costs of guaranteeing public services of all kinds.

That is a summary of the Credit Suisse report. For their part, an analysis by Sociedad Civil Catalana[2] indicated that the secession of Catalonia would imply: a large drop in the flow of trade with the rest of Spain and the world, the excision and relocation of companies, a substantial rise in unemployment, an increase in the deficit of the pension system, a drop in GDP, a large increase in the debt of the Generalitat, as well as putting the liquidity of the financial system in total risk.

---

[2] Societat Civil Catalana. Comissió d'Economia i Empresa (2014), *Consecuencias económicas de una hipotética secesión de Cataluña* <https://societatcivilcatalana.cat/assets/documents/informe-economia-hipotetica-secesion.pdf>

The secession of Catalonia would, therefore, be a very costly process and one that was full of uncertainties.

SUMMARY

- The political, social, and economic changes that would come about as a result of a hypothetical separation of Catalonia from the rest of Spain have been analysed in numerous reports. There is consensus amongst them about their depth and negativity.
- In the following sections, we shall analyse these various aspects.

CHAPTER 40

Impact of a Hypothetical Secession on Trade

CHANGES TO TRADE IN INDUSTRIAL GOODS WITH THE REST OF SPAIN, EUROPE AND THE WORLD

The secession from Spain of a territory corresponding to the former Catalonia, and its recognition as an independent state, would naturally affect its economic relations with the rest of Spain. The trade in imports and exports would seem to be the aspect most susceptible with regard to the imposition of borders. After an analysis of the impact of a utopian separation on trade, we shall evaluate the impact on GDP, employment and per capita income.

Let us suppose that the entity that came into being after separation from Spain corresponds to all of present-day Catalonia. In Chap. 29, we examined Catalonia's trade with the rest of Spain We saw how it is made up there and how it has already been weakened by the separatists putting the rest of Catalans and Spaniards in check.

Here we shall go on to consider the impact of a hypothetical independence on trade between Catalonia and the rest of Spain in three areas: bilateral trade of the new independent Catalonia with the rest of Spain; trade with the rest of the EU and the world; and sales to the Catalan market; and we shall do this while considering three scenarios of low, medium, and high impacts of independence. In view of the analysis referred to in Table 41.2 (see below), as well as the experiences of other countries' disintegration, such as the former Soviet Union, Czechoslovakia and

F. Brunet, *The Economics of Catalan Separatism*,
https://doi.org/10.1007/978-3-031-14451-6_40

Yugoslavia,[1] we can formulate the impact of an eventual secession of Catalonia on its exterior trade in industrial goods:

- A reduction in imports and exports of the hypothetical independent Catalonia with Spain of -25%/-35%/-50%.
- A reduction in exports to the EU and the rest of the world of the utopian independent Catalonia of -20%/-30%/-40% and of imports of -10%/-15%/-20%.
- An increase in production for the interior Catalan market of +5%/+10%/+15%.
- When these proportions are applied to the real data for sales and operations in Catalonia, the rest of Spain and the rest of the world, the results can be seen in Table 40.1.
- Without secession, the surplus with the rest of Spain (+€18,825 million) finances the deficit with the rest of the world (-€18,554 million).
- With secession, a Catalonia out of Spain would have an industrial trade deficit with the rest of the world of -€9742 million in the low impact scenario, a deficit of -€14,279 million in the medium impact scenario and a deficit of -€19,755 million in the high impact scenario.

The virtuous balance between the surplus with Spain and the deficit with the rest of the world prior to separation would turn into an abysmal deficit with the rest of the world. There would not, of course, be sufficient foreign investment to finance such a deficit given that investment would have flown anywhere in the world rather than staying in an independent Catalonia.

CHANGES TO TRADE IN NON-INDUSTRIAL GOODS WITH THE REST OF SPAIN, EUROPE AND THE WORLD

The industrial sector is the most open sector in the economy and is therefore the largest importer and exporter. Quantitatively too it is the sector most susceptible to a hypothetical secession. For its part, the service sector finds itself more protected given that it includes health, education and public administration. Nevertheless, non-protected activities within the

[1] A. Rodríguez-Pose and M. Stermšek (2015), "The Economics of Secession: Analysing the Economic Impact of the Collapse of the Former Yugoslavia", *Territory, Politics, Governance*, Vol. 3, No. 1, pp. 73–96.

Table 40.1 Impact on trade of a hypothetical secession of Catalonia

M € per year		Sales and operations in Catalonia	Sales (exports) to		Bought (imports) in		Balance = Exports−Imports			Total	
			Spain	EU and the rest of the world	Spain	EU and the rest of the world	Spain	EU and the rest of the world	Total	Trade of goods	Change from the no secession data
		1	2	3	4	5	6=2−4	7=3−5	8=6+7	9=1+8	10
Trade in industrial goods Year base: 2018		39,461	39,320	71,624	20,495	90,178	18,825	−18,554	271	39,732	/
Scenarios	Low	+5%	−25%	−20%	−25%	−10%					
	Median	+10%	−35%	−30%	−35%	−15%					
	High	+15%	−50%	−40%	−50%	−20%					
	Low	41,434	29,490	57,299	15,371	81,160	14,119	−23,861	−9742	31,692	−20.2%
	Median	43,407	25,558	50,137	13,322	76,651	12,236	−26,515	−14,279	29,128	−26.7%
	High	45,380	19,660	42,974	10,248	72,142	9413	−29,168	−19,755	25,625	−35.5%
Trade in non-industrial goods[a] Year base: 2018		175,567	26,468	22,354	24,020	11,418	2447	10,936	13,383	188,950	/

(continued)

Table 40.1 (continued)

M € per year	Sales and operations in Catalonia	Sales (exports) to		Bought (imports) in		Balance = Exports—Imports			Total	
		Spain	EU and the rest of the world	Spain	EU and the rest of the world	Spain	EU and the rest of the world	Total	Trade of goods	Change from the no secession data
	1	2	3	4	5	6=2-4	7=3-5	8=6+7	9=1+8	10
Scenarios Low	−4%	−35%	−15%	−20%	−15%	/	/	/	/	/
Median	−9%	−45%	−30%	−30%	−20%	/	/	/	/	/
High	−15%	−60%	−50%	−40%	−25%	/	/	/	/	/
Low	168,439	17,204	19,001	19,216	9705	−2012	9296	7284	175,723	−7.0%
Median	159,479	14,557	15,648	16,814	9134	−2257	6514	4257	163,736	−13.4%
High	148,470	10,587	11,177	14,412	8563	−3825	2614	−1211	147,259	−22.1%

aServices, tourism, construction and agriculture. Estimations based on the last real data available (2018) and on the Input-output table of Catalonia 2014 (the last published, + 7%)./Source: Author's calculations based on data from C-Intereg (2019), *Comercio interregional* <https://www.c-intereg.es/informe-trimestral-de-c-intereg-julio-2019/>; Institut d'Estadística de Catalunya (2022), *Marco Input-Output de Cataluña 2014* <https://www.idescat.cat/pub/?id=mioc&lang=es>; and Table 29.1

service sector, such as tourism, transport, and other company services, are indeed open and susceptible to a hypothetical secession. We shall now formulate the impact of an eventual secession of Catalonia on the exterior trade in non-industrial goods (all the services, tourism, construction and agriculture[2]):

- Reduction in non-industrial exports of a hypothetical independent Catalonia to Spain -35%/-45%/-60%
- Reduction in non-industrial imports of a hypothetical independent Catalonia from Spain -20% /-30%/-40%
- Trade in services is more inelastic with relation to the rest of the EU and the world than it is with the rest of Spain, and so the reductions are somewhat lower, around -15%/-30%/-50%.
- Reduction of production of services for the internal Catalan market of some -10%/-15%/-20%.

When these proportions are applied to the real data for sales and operations in Catalonia, the rest of Spain and the rest of the world, the results can be seen in Table 40.1, which shows the changes in the trade of non-industrial goods on account of a hypothetical secession. To summarise the effects of secession, we can refer here to the balance of non-industrial trade of a hypothetical separated Catalonia (column 8 of Table 40.1):

- An independent Catalonia would go from having a surplus in non-industrial trade with the rest of Spain (+€2447 million) and the rest of the EU and the world (+€10,936 million) to having a deficit with the rest of Spain of between €-2012 million and €-3825 million (depending on the scenario) and its current surplus with the rest of the EU and the world would be reduced to between +€9296 million and +€2614 million.
- With this, the combined balance of a Catalonia separated from the rest of Spain and the EU would go from the current +€13,383 million per annum, to between +€7284 million and €-1211 million.

[2] Institut d'Estadística de Catalunya (2020), *Marco Input-Output de Cataluña 2014* <https://www.idescat.cat/pub/?id=mioc&lang=es>.

SUMMARY

- The hypothetical separation of Catalonia would reduce the bilateral trade in industrial goods with the rest of Spain by between 25% and 50%, depending on the scenario of secession. With regard to the rest of the EU and the world the trade of an independent Catalonia would fall by between 20% and 40%.

- The hypothetical separation of Catalonia would reduce the bilateral trade in non-industrial goods with the rest of Spain by between 35% and 60%, depending on the scenario of secession. With regard to the rest of the EU and the world, the trade of an independent Catalonia would fall by between 15% and 50%.

- The secession of Catalonia from the rest of Spain and the European Union would turn the current exterior trade balance into a large deficit, impossible to finance with reluctant foreign investment. Similarly, the surplus in the service trade would become a deficit.

CHAPTER 41

Impact of a Hypothetical Secession on GDP

FROM TRADE TO GDP

Since foreign trade is the most susceptible to the imposition of borders, the key element in the evaluation of the economic impact of a hypothetical separation is the extent to which bilateral trade is affected, and in particular, Catalonia's sales to the rest of Spain.

We know that trade with the rest of Spain produces a large surplus for Catalonia. On the basis of the data set out in the previous chapter on the impact of an eventual separation of Catalonia from the rest of Spain, we can formulate Table 41.1 that shows the changes to Catalonia's GDP in the three scenarios of a hypothetical separation from the rest of Spain.

We arrive, therefore, at an important conclusion: a hypothetical separation from the rest of Spain would generate a reduction in GDP of 9.3% in a low-level scenario, a reduction of 16.1% in a medium-level scenario, and a reduction 24.4% in a high-level scenario.

In the medium-level scenario, €38,000 million disappear from the annual permanent GDP, although, strictly speaking, they would not be euros because Catalonia would no longer be in the eurozone. That is equivalent to a reduction in per capita income for every Catalan of 4868 'euros', that is, 406 'euros' every month, or 14 'euros' per day.

F. Brunet, *The Economics of Catalan Separatism*, https://doi.org/10.1007/978-3-031-14451-6_41

Table 41.1 Impact on GDP of a hypothetical secession of Catalonia

M € per year	Sales and operations in Catalonia	Sales (exports) to		Bought (imports) in		Balance = Exports—Imports			Total	
		Spain	EU and the rest of the world	Spain	EU and the rest of the world	Spain	EU and the rest of the world	Total	Trade of goods	Change from the no secession data
	1	2	3	4	5	6=2-4	7=3-5	8=6+7	9=1+8	10
GDP	215,028	65,788	93,978	44,515	101,596	21,272	-7618	13,654	228,682	/
Year base: 2018										
Scenarios Low	209,873	46,694	76,300	34,587	90,865	12,107	-14,565	-2458	207,415	-9.3%
Median	202,886	40,115	65,785	30,136	85,785	9979	-20,001	-10,022	192,864	-16.1%
High	193,850	30,247	54,151	24,660	80,705	5588	-26,554	-20,966	172,884	-24.4%

Source: Author's calculations based on data from Table 40.1

COMPARATIVE ANALYSIS

We can compare the results obtained in this investigation with previous ones. Interest in Catalonia's case, especially after the first separatist attempted illegal referendum of 9 November 2014, produced numerous analyses of the impact of a hypothetical secession. Table 41.1 summarises the main results with respect to GDP, trade, debt and other significant aspects. We observe that (Table 41.2):

- Import-export trade between Catalonia and the rest of Spain would be reduced within a range of 10 to 50% on account of a hypothetical secession.
- Catalonia's GDP would drop by up to 25%.
- The Generalitat's public debt would increase by between 100% and 184% of GDP.

As far as the economy is concerned, therefore, there is clarity about the impact of a separation. The establishment of borders would mean bilateral trade between the new independent entity and Spain and the rest of the world would not be the same as it was with Catalonia integrated with the rest of Spain and the world. Catalan, Spanish, and foreign investment and activity would all have fallen notably, demolishing the GDP and Catalans' well-being as they fell.

SUMMARY

- A hypothetical separation of Catalonia from the rest of Spain would reduce the GDP by 9.3% in a low-level scenario, it would reduce it by 16.1% in a medium-level scenario, and by 24.4% in a in a high-level scenario.
- In a medium-level scenario the average annual income of every Catalan would fall by 4868 'euros', equivalent to 406 'euros' every month, or 14 'euros' per day.

Table 41.2 Estimates of the impact of a hypothetical secession of Catalonia

Source	Trade with the rest of Spain	GDP	Public debt/GDP	Other relevant aspects
Brunet (this research)	-18.8%/-30.0%/-42.4%	-9.3%/-16.1%/-24.4%	184%	El procés ens roba Decadence and collapse of Catalonia
Comerford and Rodríguez Mora (2019)		-11%		
Fitch Ratings (2019)			120%	
Natixis (2017)			105.5%	'An impossible divorce"
DBRS Morningstar (2017)	-50%	-20%		
Reynaerts and Vanschoonbeek (2016)		-20% long term GDP		
CIDOB (2015)		+3.3% to -1.1%		
Barclays (2014)			100%	
Cámara de Comercio de Barcelona (2014)	-10% to -50%	-1.1% to -5.7%		
Generalitat de Catalunya. Consell Assessor per a la Transició Nacional (2014)		-1%		
FAES (2014)	-50%	-19% to -24%		
Feito (2014)	-50%	-10% to -20%		
Fitch Ratings (2014)		-19%		
Moody's (2014)		-20%		
Morgan Stanley (2014)		-22%		
Ministerio de Asuntos Exteriores y Cooperación (2014)		-20 to -25%		Transaction costs: +13%
Polo (2014)		-20%		

Societat Civil Catalana (2014)	-10%/-25%/-50%	-7.4%/-15.4%/-23.5%	118%	More unemployed: 447,000/ unemployment rate: 34%
Comerford, Myers and Rodríguez Mora (2013)		-9%	110%	
de la Fuente (2013)		-9%		
Antrás and Ventura (2012)		-2%		
Credit Suisse (2012)		-20%		
JP Morgan chase Bank N.A (2012)	-50%	-18%		
UBS (2012)		-21%		
Guinjoan and Cuadras (2011)		-4%		
Buesa (2010)		-25%		

Source: Author's compilation based on data from this research and from the analyses referred to in the first column of this table and listed in the references

Impact of a Hypothetical Secession on Employment, Pensions, Health and Education, and on the Deficit and Debt

IMPACT ON EMPLOYMENT

As a consequence of a supposed independence of Catalonia, bilateral trade with Spain, the rest of the European Union and the world would change substantially. The establishment of trade, regulatory, juridical, monetary, and fiscal borders would naturally lead to a drop in trade, activity, the GDP, employment and well-being.

An estimate of the reduction in employment can be made from the reduction in GDP. Supposing that the levels of employment, trade and GDP lost on account of secession are similar to the economy average, there would be a drop in employment of 9.3% in a low-level scenario, a drop of 16.1% in a medium-level scenario and a drop of 24.4% in a in a high-level scenario. In terms of jobs lost, an eventual independence would generate an extra 322,003 unemployed in a low-level scenario, 557,446 in a medium-level scenario and 844,826 in a in a high-level scenario.

In terms of the rate of unemployment, a hypothetical secession would increase the rate of unemployment, which stood at 13.2% of the active population aged 15–64 in the third quarter of 2020, to 19.2% in a low-level scenario, 25.3% in a medium-level scenario and 32.7% in a high-level scenario, as shown in Fig. 42.1.

© The Author(s), under exclusive license to Springer Nature Switzerland AG 2022
F. Brunet, *The Economics of Catalan Separatism*,
https://doi.org/10.1007/978-3-031-14451-6_42

255

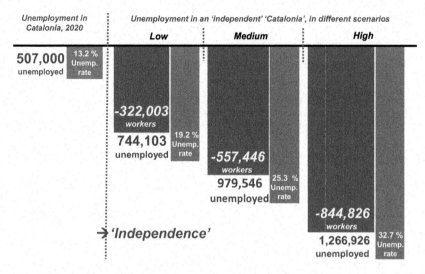

Fig. 42.1 Impact on employment and unemployment, in different scenarios of a hypothetical secession of Catalonia. (Source: Author's calculations based on data from Tables 41.1 and 41.2; and the Institut d'Estadística de Catalunya (2022), *Població ocupada. Per sectors d'activitat* <https://www.idescat.cat/indicadors/?id =conj&n=10204>)

IMPACT ON PENSIONS, EDUCATION AND HEALTH

In Catalonia, the amount paid out in pensions exceeds the amount contributed by €3000 million per year. Catalonia's deficit is the largest of all the Autonomous Communities and is today covered by the Spanish Social Security system. In the case of hypothetical independence, this deficit would not be covered by Spain. Furthermore, the deficit would be significantly higher due to increased unemployment caused by the drop in trade with Spain, the rest of the European Union and the world and the consequent collapse of GDP. Independence would be economic suicide for Catalonia.[1]

A comparison of the situation regarding pensions between Catalonia forming part of Spain and the situation after a hypothetical independence shows the profound consequences of secession. In a secession scenario,

---

[1] Derblauemond (2017), "La economía de guerra y el problema catalán", 9 October <https://www.elblogsalmon.com/>.

the number of people contributing falls along with income from social security contributions, while the number of people receiving a pension rises along with expenses for the provision of services. Furthermore, the subsidy from the rest of Spain disappears. Thus, if at the present time the average monthly pension drawn by a Catalan pensioner is €1031, after secession, it would 634 'euros'. The outcome could not be worse. Every kind of misfortune awaits the Catalan pensioners. Fortunately, secession will not happen!

Secession would produce the following string of events:

1. Less trade with Spain, the EU, and the rest of the world
2. Less activity, smaller GDP, and less employment
3. More unemployment and more pensioners
4. Less income from fewer contributors
5. Greater expenditure on pensions
6. End of the subsidy from the Spanish social security system
7. Fewer resources available to pay more pensioners
8. Smaller pensions for pensioners

Under these circumstances, in order to maintain the level of pensions and avoid an uprising by pensioners, an 'independent' Generalitat would be obliged to make very large cuts to other items of budget expenditure. The largest ones would be the most affected, that is health and education, precisely the most social items in the budget. A hypothetically independent Catalonia would have very serious social and economic implications. Depending on the scenario, there would be between 322,003 and 844,826 more people unemployed and the rate of unemployment would be between 19 and 33%.

The total irresponsibility of the separatist leaders is manifest. What is also manifest is the intellectual and moral depravity of those who have spent years living from, inventing and crowing about the completely false advantages of a secession of Catalonia from the rest Spain. Even though secession will not happen, the separatist confrontation has already generated political chaos, the economic decline of Catalonia, severe social confrontation, and the loss of a great deal of activity and employment (-4.6% of GDP).

THE SEPARATIST GENERALITAT'S FINANCES

With independence the finances of the Generalitat de Catalunya would suffer a severe blow. At present the deficit of the Autonomous Community of Catalonia is €8000 million, which represents 3.5% of GDP. To this amount, given independence, must be added

- 15,000 million 'euros' for the annual payment of the proportion of Spain's debt that would correspond to Catalonia upon secession.
- 10,000 million 'euros' for increased expenditure on greater expenses caused by the exercise of new powers.
- 9000 million 'euros' extra expenditure caused by the post-independence economic crash.
- 3000 million 'euros' for the expenses of the new treasury and loss of revenue.

The annual deficit of the independent Generalitat would therefore amount to €45,000 million, that is, 19.5% of Catalonia's current GDP and 25.6% of the GDP of an eventual independent Catalonia, in a medium-level scenario. On account of independence the deficit would have multiplied by 7.

For its part, the initial debt of an eventual Catalan republic would be multiplied by 5 to amount to 415,000 million 'euros', 178% of current GDP or 184% of the GDP of an eventual independent Catalonia, in a medium-level scenario. This amount is obtained by adding the autonomous debt at the third quarter of 2021 (€82,936 million), the proportional part of the debt of the central Administration of Spain, the value of assets transferred by the central Administration, the proportional part of the debt of other central Administration entities, the proportional part of the debt of the Spanish social security system, the debts of local Catalan corporations to the central Administration and pending Generalitat payments to suppliers.[2]

Such a level of debt would in turn imply that the annual payment corresponding to the Generalitat's financial burden (the annual maturities for repayment together with interest) would be 11 times higher (from the

---

[2] In this regard, see the separatist literature of the Economy Committee of the Col.legi d'Economistes de Catalunya, coordinated by Oriol Amat and Modest Guinjoan (2014), *Economia de Catalunya - Preguntes i respostes sobre l'impacte econòmic de la independència*, Barcelona, Profit Editorial.

current 2.3% of GDP to 25% of the GDP of an eventual independent Catalonia, in a medium-level scenario), very far from admissible financial levels, a circumstance that would cause insoluble financing problems, and consequently exclusion from the markets.

SUMMARY

- It is high time to stop the destruction and decline of Catalonia and to start reconstructing the economy, society and Catalan and Spanish politics.
- With a hypothetical independence Catalonia would cease receiving from Spain the current subsidy of €3240 million for the payment of pensions. Together with the increase in the deficit for social services (-5993 million 'euros') this brings the total social deficit to 9233 million 'euros'.
- Revenue would be reduced, there would be more pensioners, it would not be possible to cover rocketing expenses. Thus, the average monthly pension drawn by the Catalan pensioner, which stands today at €1031, would drop to 634 'euros' after secession.
- To avoid the collapse of pensions, the hypothetical independent Generalitat would have to introduce very large cuts. The main cuts would be in health and education, the most social items of expenditure.
- Independence would be catastrophic for Catalan pensioners. And for health and education too. This, then, is the real antisocial nature of secessionism and the independence movement.
- After a hypothetical secession of Catalonia, the income of the Generalitat would fall greatly and expenses would rise greatly. Consequently, the budget deficit would go from the current annual €8000 million to 45,000 million 'euros'. That would represent 25.6% of GDP, a non-financeable magnitude.
- The Generalitat's public debt would rise to 415,000 million 'euros', that is, 184% of GDP. The annual payments (repayment plus interest) would be more than 40,000 million 'euros' per annum, or 25% of GDP, an unacceptable magnitude.

CHAPTER 43

Impact of a Hypothetical Secession on the Financial System and on Spain

End of the Euro, Measures to Protect the Banks and *Pujoletes*

One of the most delicate questions concerning secession is about the serious consequences this would have on the financial system. Due to the juridical insecurity caused by the separatists' attempted coup d'état of autumn 2017, banks with registered head offices in Catalonia transferred them to other regions to avoid the bankruptcy that would ensue after a run-on deposit.[1] Since then, those banks have not returned to Catalonia and bank deposits have recovered a little. (See Chap. 33.)

Even so, a large funding gap persists in the Catalan financial system. Thus, since there are fewer deposits than credits, some of the credit granted to juridical and physical persons resident in Catalonia is financed by deposits captured in the rest of Spain.

---

[1] Javier Santacruz (2017), "El sistema financiero catalán ante el riesgo secesionista", *El Economista*, 6 October.

F. Brunet, *The Economics of Catalan Separatism*,
https://doi.org/10.1007/978-3-031-14451-6_43

HYPERINFLATION AND FALL IN THE VALUE OF SALARIES, RENTS AND PROPERTIES

With effective Catalan independence, the new independent state would automatically and effectively be outside of Spain, outside the European Union and outside the Eurosystem. Consequently:

- Consequence I: The euro would not be the legal currency in the new Catalan state that would now not be part of Spain, not be a member of the European Union and not a member of the Eurosystem.
- Consequence II: A hypothetical Catalan central bank, and banks resident in Catalonia, would not have access to the European Central Bank (ECB), would not receive bank notes or coins in euros from them, either in cash or as bank deposits.
- Consequence III: Outside the Eurosystem, without the protection of the ECB, systemic risk coverage would be lost, access to ECB lines of credit and liquidity would be lost, bank deposits would lose the coverage of the Deposit Guarantee Fund, and access to the European Stability Mechanism for bailouts and assistance for financial entities would be lost.
- Consequence IV: Euros in the hands of the public would disappear, hidden under the mattress or deposited in accounts outside the 'independent' Catalonia.
- Consequence V: To continue to operate in Catalonia, banks resident outside Catalonia would have to create subsidiaries.
- Consequence VI: To counter the run on banks and the flight of investment, the government of an 'independent' Catalonia would have to impose restrictive measures, freeze bank deposits and prevent the withdrawal or transfer of money.
- Consequence VII: Independence would therefore generate a serious liquidity problem. The government of an 'independent' Catalonia would have to issue its own currency, let's call them *pujoletes* (in honour of the formerly right honourable president of the Generalitat, Jordi Pujol).
- Consequence VIII: Given the incapacity of the bankrupt new state to access external finance to support the larger public deficit (see the previous chapter), more and more *pujoletes* would have to be issued, generating hyperinflation in proportion.

- Consequence IX: Salaries, rents and assets denominated in the new currency would be seriously devalued.
- Consequence X: The hypothetical secession of Catalonia would cause a financial, economic, social and political crash. Recalling the separatist propaganda slogan, 'We are prepared for independence!' one has to ask: 'Are you prepared for the run on banks, and a bank freeze? Are you prepared for them to rob your euros? Are you prepared for them to convert your euros into *pujoletes*?' In this way, the new independent Catalan state would be a failed state, a pariah state, a hooligan state, and a vassal state.

IMPACT ON SPAIN OF A HYPOTHETICAL SECESSION OF CATALONIA

Spain without Catalonia ... from a material point of view, it would be a country between 16 and 20% smaller in territory, population, and total GDP. An amputated Spain would also be somewhat less rich insofar as Catalonia is somewhat richer than the Spanish average, and especially because the reduction in bilateral trade would impoverish both Catalonia and Spain.

The secession of Catalonia would naturally affect the rest of Spain, albeit to a lesser extent than it would affect Catalonia itself. Considering the medium-level scenario, a hypothetical separation would reduce the long-term permanent GDP of Catalonia by 16.1% and the GDP of the rest of Spain by 3.4%.

The remaining aspects of Spain's economy to be affected

- Negatively, the most important: employment, unemployment, per capita income.
- Positively, some: the balance of trade would improve slightly, foreign investment would increase, health and education would remain at similar levels. In various fields in which present-day Catalonia has a deficit, and where discontinued Spanish financing would send these deficits rocketing, (pensions, public deficit, debt), Spain's situation would be improved by being relieved of these responsibilities.

Summary

- Independence would mean the disappearance of the euro in Catalonia and the introduction of a bank freeze to avoid the flight of cash and deposits to the rest of Spain and the world.
- The issue of a sufficient quantity of Catalonia's own currency, necessary to replace the euro and pay the expenses of an 'independent' Catalonia, would create hyperinflation and devaluation of salaries, rents and properties.
- A financial, economic, social and political crash is the logical conclusion to a hypothetical independence of Catalonia.
- Spain without Catalonia would be something else. In terms of what is measurable, in absolute terms, the magnitudes of Spain would be reduced by between 16 and 20%. In relative terms, the loss for Spain without Catalonia would be in the order of 3%.
- There are some areas, however, in which a hypothetical separation of Catalonia would improve the situation in the rest of Spain. This is the case with the trade balance, foreign investment, social security and pensions and public debt.

CHAPTER 44

Brexit and Catexit

CATEXIT > BREXIT

The withdrawal of the United Kingdom of Great Britain and Northern Ireland (UK) from the European Union (EU) could be compared to a hypothetical separation of Catalonia from the rest of Spain. 'Catexit' would describe the departure of Catalonia from Spain and also, therefore, from the EU.

There are obviously very large differences between the UK and Catalonia and between Brexit and a hypothetical Catexit. Firstly, with regard to history, the UK is an independent country and was a Member State of the EU from 1973 until 2020; Catalonia is a region of a Member State of the EU. Since 1707 the United Kingdom has been a unitary state that today consists of four nations (Scotland, Wales, England, and Northern Ireland); Catalonia was never an independent state.

In terms of size, the differences between the UK and Catalonia are huge: 67 million people and 7.6 million. Their economic development has also been very different: the UK had one of the world's largest modern empires, comparable to Spain's, and in the nineteenth century, it was the workshop of the world; Catalonia was part of the Kingdom of Aragon, constitutive of Spain, played a key role in the Spanish history of the Iberian Peninsula, Europe and America and, in the nineteenth century, and for a

© The Author(s), under exclusive license to Springer Nature   265
Switzerland AG 2022
F. Brunet, *The Economics of Catalan Separatism*,
https://doi.org/10.1007/978-3-031-14451-6_44

large part of the twentieth century, Catalonia was the Manchester, or factory of Spain.

Leaving differences behind, the similarities between Brexit and Catexit lie in the fact that both processes are contemporary with each other, are based on lies, are sustained by populism and have led to chaos in British, Catalan and Spanish politics. With regard to the immediate, medium-term and permanent economic impact of Brexit, a reduction in Britain's GDP has been estimated to be between a broad range, from a fall of 1.25% to one of 10.5%.[1]

POLITICAL IMPLICATIONS OF BREXIT

A key element of Brexit, and also of a hypothetical Catexit, is the reduction in trade that each of these events can produce. It is here that we see a big difference between Brexit and a hypothetical Catexit: Catalonia is very specialised in selling to the rest of Spain while, relatively speaking, the UK is less specialised in selling to the rest of the EU. Catalonia is much more integrated in Spain than the UK is in the EU. Thus, taking the medium-level scenario as a guide, the impact of a hypothetical Catexit is five times greater on GDP than that of Brexit, ten times greater on trade, four times greater on unemployment and almost four times greater on personal income.

Forecasts about the economic impact of Brexit are, without doubt, of great interest. But it is worth saying that the political implications of Brexit were unsuspected and have been dramatic: political chaos in the most exemplary democracy and the probability of the breakup of the UK (it is said that Scotland wants to remain in the EU…).

---

[1] Bank of England (2018), *EU withdrawal scenarios and monetary and financial stability. A response to the House of Commons Treasury Committee*, London, BoE; McKinsey (2019), *Brexit: The bigger picture—Revitalizing UK exports in the new world of trade* <https://www.mckinsey.com/featured-insights/europe/brexit-the-bigger-picture-revitalizing-uk-exports-in-the-new-world-of-trade>.

SUMMARY

- The UK was less integrated with the EU than Catalonia is with Spain and the EU: the dimensions of Brexit and of a hypothetical Catexit are consequently quite different.
- An important similarity between Brexit and the separatist challenge to the rule of law in Spain is the political chaos and disintegration they have produced in both countries.

CHAPTER 45

Fantasising About the 'Viability' of an 'Independent' 'Catalonia'

FANTASIES

The magic financial viability of an independent Catalan economy is similarly based on two a priori falsehoods:

- Nothing bad would happen: trade with Spain and the rest of the world would not be affected, GDP would not plummet, investments would not disappear...[1] This is the denial of the reality of economic disaster that secession would entail.
- All good things would happen: the great fiscal dividend of independence (the former fiscal deficit which—precisely due to independence—would have disappeared and would no longer exist!), will enable us to pay... Oh, and to further distract people, another lie: the Catalan republic will continue to be a member of the European Union.

Fiction. The mantras about the economic viability of independence are science fiction, economic fiction: Not by a long way do they consider real aspects such as plummeting GDP, increased unemployment, the cost-benefits of independence, financial sufficiency, fiscal sustainability or

---

[1] These processes occur, and will occur, in all processes of disintegration and fragmentation of states. The only difference between them is the magnitude of the catastrophe: that is to say, if the GDP in case A fell by 30% and in case Z by 20%.

F. Brunet, *The Economics of Catalan Separatism*, https://doi.org/10.1007/978-3-031-14451-6_45

competitiveness. Furthermore, the effects of separation would not be a temporary 'walk in the wilderness', they would be permanent.

None of these aspects are dealt with by the separatist 'economists' because the very negative economic dynamics of an 'independent' Catalonia are obvious, and the impossibility of the economic viability of an 'independent' Catalonia is obvious, unless a miracle occurred, and an empire appeared to finance it. In such a case, the 'viable' Catalonia would be a poverty-stricken vassal state.

Separatists have vivid imaginations and the levels of fantasy reached by the authors of the 'reports' subsidised by the Generalitat are real. In the secessionists' imagination how could an independent Catalonia fail to be viable? Lubricated with a juicy grant, a senior position and a distinction, the sleep of reason and the absence of ethics have produced a powerful subsidised industry of economic fiction writing.

COMPLETE UNVIABILITY OF AN 'INDEPENDENT' CATALONIA

On the other hand, we should point out that the real unviability of the process was known and pooled amongst the coup plotters. Thus, for example, two 'government' documents make the following admissions:

- An independent Catalonia would have a 'war economy'.[2]
- According to the report: "Confidential. Economic implications of an independent Catalonia" by the so-called Contingency Group of the Generalitat de Catalunya (a report found by the Guardia Civil amongst the documents in the possession of the arrested member of the government, Santi Vila, a report he had received on 18 October 2017), Catalonia's GDP would fall by 20% and unemployment would rise to 34%. "The exit [from Spain and from the EU, which it recognises] would have very negative effects for exports (a drop of 45% to 50% of sales to the Spanish state and 18% of exports to the European Union). [...] It is thought that the boycott would cause a short-term reduction of Catalan sales to Spain of between 18 and

[2] Mayka Navarro and Carlota Guindal (2017), "Un manuscrito hallado en el despacho de Salvadó planteaba supuestos económicos en un "escenario de guerra"", *La Vanguardia*, 15 October   <https://www.lavanguardia.com/politica/20171015/432077657773/manuscrito-hallado-despacho-salvado-secretario-hisenda-plantea-supuestos-economicos-escenario-de-guerra.html>.

25%."[3] Well, the reader will have observed with fascination that these data (that is, 'confidential' data), are very similar to the data we have calculated in this investigation.

FINANCIAL FANTASY

Those who claim viability is possible make a case for financial engineering, in this case for financial fantasy, supposedly to counter the real unviability of the economy of an 'independent' Catalonia. The independence of Catalonia would bring about the establishment of a war economy financed by a foreign state. It would, of course, mean not having a fiscal deficit with the rest of Spain, but fabulously increasing its own fiscal deficit. It would mean reducing the trade surplus with the rest of Spain and increasing the trade deficit with third parties, in addition to losing the little foreign investment there is left after three decades of the *process*.

On the basis of the results of this investigation, especially this Part III on the economic consequences of independence, we have drawn up Fig. 45.1, which summarises the financial needs and possibilities of an 'independent' Catalonia. The final column of this figure indicates the contribution that 'someone' must make for Catalonia to be 'financially viable', that is to say, to compensate for the collapse of GDP and employment, the reduction of the trade surplus with Spain, the larger trade deficit with the rest of the world, the end of the bank funding gap, and the ending of Spanish state contributions through the Autonomous Liquidity Fund and Social Security. This amounts to €55,002 million per year. The financial 'viability' of an independent Catalonia depends on this hypothetical and exorbitant contribution.

An 'independent' Catalonia would consequently have to establish a war economy and receive €55,002 million every year from a foreign power. The only true 'viability' of an independent Catalonia would therefore be to become the colony of some state and the protectorate of some financiers. Is anybody interested in financing the 'independence' of Catalonia and in financing an 'independent' Catalonia? Well, yes:

---

[3] Ángeles Escrivá and Esteban Urreiztieta (2018), "El Govern ocultó datos sobre la inviabilidad de la secesión", *El Mundo*, 19 March <https://www.elmundo.es/espana/2018/0 3/19/5aaeb662468aeb57218b45e3.html>.

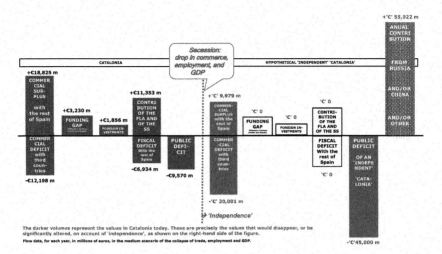

Fig. 45.1 'Independent' 'Catalonia': War economy and failed and vassal State. (Source: Author's calculations based on data from this research, especially that shown in Table 41.1)

- The enemies of freedom have shown their enthusiasm for the destruction of Catalonia, Spain and Europe.
- There is ample evidence of who has financed, is financing and can finance this undertaking. The viability of the independence of Catalonia therefore depends on geopolitics, that is, on handing Catalonia over to a foreign power.
- And so, this is the point we arrive at in the fantasy journey of the financial viability of an independent Catalonia. Russia and/or China and/or another emerging power could finance such an absurdity. An 'independent' Catalonia, a 'republic of Catalonia' would only be a poverty-stricken vassal state.

SUMMARY

- If North Korea can exist, and continue to exist, an independent Catalonia could exist and continue to exist.
- In order to exist and continue to exist, an 'independent' Catalonia would have to receive €55,002 million every year to cover the effects

of lower sales to Spain, a larger deficit with third countries, the ending of subsidies by Spain, the brutal collapse of fiscal income, and the massive increase in public spending.

- An 'independent' Catalonia would be 'viable' if there were a country willing to contribute €55,002 million a year to have a vassal state in Western Europe.
- 'Independence' means a war economy and a failed vassal state.
- To prattle on about the 'viability' of the independence of Catalonia at any price therefore shows: (a) complete contempt (1) for the truth; (2) for democracy; and (b) the profoundly ... (3) antisocial and (4) immoral character of the independence movement and of a hypothetical Catalan republic.

CHAPTER 46

From Tyrannical Mini-State to Dictatorial and Imperialist Vassal State

A HYPOTHETICAL 'INDEPENDENT' CATALONIA

The Catalonia of the separatist Generalitat is an authoritarian mini-state with a tendency towards totalitarianism. Fortunately, the separatist mini-state's empire is still not complete. The separatists still have to disconnect from the state of Spain completely and thereby consummate their work. They have already achieved a great deal and there is not much that remains to be done. Nevertheless, some limits still survive in Catalonia that derive from the rule of law and the European Union, and there is still some constitutionalist resistance.

In Catalonia, the regional government completely lacks neutrality; it engages in overwhelming propaganda; the hatred of separatist leaders, their media outlets, and that of numerous citizens felt towards constitutionalist Catalans, who constitute the majority, and Spaniards, is evident. There is a regional government with 17,000 armed police officers that intimidates the opposition, pursues dissidents, favours delinquents, especially if they support independence, and fails to uphold the law.

There is impunity for the separatists' own violence; the right to an education in one's mother tongue has been suspended, with serious implications for the social exclusion of the majority of young Catalans who are Spanish speakers; judges are put under pressure; court decisions that are not to the taste of the supporters of independence are not complied with; the separation of powers is disparaged, etc.

Present-day Catalonia is a foretaste of what a hypothetical independent Catalonia would be. Nationalism is a socio-political ideology that tends towards totalitarianism, given that violence is the necessary instrument to conquer and maintain power.[1]

Nationalism also tends towards imperialism, it seeks to extend its hinterland and lays claim to more territories, those, for example, where to some extent, the same, or a similar, language is spoken. Calm would not, therefore, follow on from the independence of Catalonia, but rather the conflict for the annexation of other territories in Spain and France where there are Catalan-speaking people. Figure 46.1 maps the territories claimed by the Catalan separatists (Països Catalans, or Catalan Countries) and the Basque separatists (Euskal Herria).

SUMMARY

- The separatist Generalitat is an extremely authoritarian administration that tends towards totalitarianism, it promotes and consents to abomination, hatred, segregation and violence against non-separatist Catalans and other Spaniards.
- Present-day Catalonia, where the separatist Generalitat does not recognise the rule of law, is a foretaste of what a hypothetical, independent, totalitarian and imperialist Catalonia would be like.
- The annexing agenda of an eventual independent Catalonia with regard to contiguous territories would keep the nationalist confrontation and the separatist challenge alive and would extend it geographically.
- The Generalitat de Catalunya would become the government of a pariah, failed, vassal, imperialist, hooligan state.

---

[1] Slavenka Drakulić (2017), "Entrevista con la gran cronista de los Balcanes: 'El virus del nacionalismo ha despertado en España'", *El Confidencial*, 8 October: "There is very little interest in reconciliation because reconciliation depends on truth, and that is very difficult to achieve." <https://www.elconfidencial.com/mundo/2017-10-08/independencia-catalana-nacionalismo-balcanes-espana_1457330/>.

Territories claimed by Catalan separatists and by Basque separatists

Fig. 46.1 Greater Catalonia and Greater Basque Country. (Source: The Wall Street Journal (2014), "Staking Claims. Some Basque and Catalan nationalists claim territories beyond the current borders", *The Wall Street Journal*, 23 April https://twitter.com/WSJGraphics/status/459084378971594752/photo/1)

CHAPTER 47

The 'Industry' of the Separatist Process: The 'Business' of Independence Is in the Separatist Challenge, Not in Independence Itself

THE SEPARATIST *PROCESS* IS AN INDUSTRY

Propaganda, rallies, outings, merchandising, people devoted body and soul to sowing discord and hatred. Some are elected or councillors of something or other and are paid. Others are civil servants and are paid. Most separatists, however, participate voluntarily in the *process*, and have no direct financial interest and, what is more, expend their affections, time and money on this vice.

How much money does the separatist defiance of Spain's democracy move? Subsidised propaganda moves money (€1000 million per year, €20,000 million since 1980), plus that part of the Generalitat's activities devoted to the separatist challenge (15% of the budget, that is, some €6300 million, in the form of salaries for senior post holders and civil servants), as well as individual donations and the expenses separatist citizens apply to the *process*. To this should be added the voluntary work of thousands of aspirants and supporters.

What do the separatists pay for their challenge? 4.6% of the Catalan GDP has failed to be produced on account of the *process*. But the separatists do not pay anything for it. They are immune. They are economically and criminally immune. On the contrary, they receive tasty subsidies for their hate-filled performances and side-shows.

© The Author(s), under exclusive license to Springer Nature Switzerland AG 2022
F. Brunet, *The Economics of Catalan Separatism*,
https://doi.org/10.1007/978-3-031-14451-6_47

What do the Catalans pay for the separatist challenge? They pay the 4.6% of GDP, the equivalent of €1384 per year, €115 per month or €4 per day. That is what the *process* currently costs and that is the magnitude of the decline in activity and drop in employment as a consequence of the separatist scheme. The budget of the Generalitat earmarks an annual €6300 million for the *process*. That is €833 per Catalan, per year, or €69 per month or €2.32 per day. That is what the government siphons off. But that is okay, in the end it's Madrid that pays!

Would the Catalans win or lose with independence? And the separatists? With independence the Catalans would lose between 9.3 and 24.4% of GDP and employment.

For their part, the separatists would immediately win everything! There would be no limit to what they could rake off. In the medium and long terms, however, due to the drop in GDP of between 9.3 and 24.4%, the size of their slice of cake would be substantially reduced.

Is independence possible? Is it probable? In an open society such as those in the west, and Spain, it would be possible. But improbable. In spite of the tremendous damage already done by the separatists, and tolerated by the Spanish governments, it is highly improbable that a process of separation would come to a head, including in Spain. To be precise, we have seen how, with the coup d'état of 2017, when the separatists had approached irreversible positions, the Spanish government had to act. It would seem that Spanish politics ignores the principle that prevention is better than cure: there was neither prudence, defence of democratic and constitutional values, nor the upholding of democracy and the rule of law in a part of the territory, nor support for the rights of Catalan citizens.

SUMMARY

- The business of separatism is in the *process*, not in independence itself. With all the foregoing in mind, it can be seen that the impetus and business of separatism lies in the *process*, not in independence itself, which is very unlikely to happen, and if it did, would be the ruination of Catalans, all Catalans; first the normal Catalans, and then the separatists.

CHAPTER 48

Who—What—When—Where—Why—How on Catalan Secessionism?

QUIS, QUID, QUANDO…

The 5 Ws + 1H, or as the Romans had it, *quis, quid, quando, ubi, cur, quem ad modum, quibus adminiculis*, will help us trace and outline the questions raised by Catalan separatism.

Who: The main agent of the separatist challenge is the regional government of the Autonomous Community of Catalonia. It exercises all public powers except for pensions, defence and foreign affairs. It levies 14.7% of taxes and is responsible for 49.2% of public expenditure in Catalonia, especially in the fields of health, education, police and infrastructure. The parties that are currently separatist started out with demands concerning grievances about the Catalan language, this transformed into a 'Spain robs us' campaign and has continued by undermining the rule of law in Spain and Spanish democracy.

What: Catalan secessionism is a socio-political movement that aims for the separation of Catalonia from the rest of Spain. Catalonia has never been independent. For a number of centuries, Barcelona, its metropolitan area, and Catalonia as a whole, constituted the most prosperous region in Spain.

When: Catalan secessionism has developed gradually and rapidly in Catalonia over the last 20 years. Its peak was in 2014 in the number of votes and with the number of people attending the 11 September rally that coincided with the end of the economic crisis that started in 2008.

© The Author(s), under exclusive license to Springer Nature Switzerland AG 2022
F. Brunet, *The Economics of Catalan Separatism*,
https://doi.org/10.1007/978-3-031-14451-6_48

Where: Inland, rural Catalonia, where separatists win large electoral and social majorities. Separatist control of the public space is complete in this part of Catalonia and the presence of the Spanish state and of its symbols is nil.

Why: In its origins, Catalanism had cultural and identity aspects, and the current separatism also has economic reasons, such as the crisis and deindustrialisation. For many years, the regional government has been the source of constant propaganda. The slogan 'Spain robs us' was a key detonator.

How: Due to the electoral law which over-represents the rural areas. With a minority of votes, the separatists regularly obtain simple majorities in the regional parliament and manage to form separatist regional governments. This puts into check the rule of law in a quality democracy such as Spain is, as well as the territorial integrity of one of the largest and oldest states in Europe. Successive Spanish governments have procrastinated in resolving the challenge of Catalan separatism with the result that in the autumn of 2017, there was a secessionist coup d'état. The cost of this separatist challenge in political terms is institutional chaos; in social terms, severe confrontation; and in economic terms, a drop in GDP of 4.6%, which is large, and rising.

SUCCESSES AND FAILURES OF THE SEPARATIST CHALLENGE

After this summary of the *process*, let us consider whether the *process* has been a success. It is glaringly obvious that, no, it has not been a success. It has been a failure. It has failed to achieve its ultimate aim of obtaining the independence of Catalonia. In this sense, the failure of the *process* was predictable, or more accurately, inevitable.

The *process* has not failed because its leaders and its two million followers did things wrong. In fact, they did things so well that they managed to pull things off. They 'repealed Spanish legality' on 6 September 2017, they carried out a 'referendum' on 1 October and declared independence and a Catalan republic on 27 October.

At last! Mission accomplished! At last application of article 155 of the Spanish Constitution! The Spanish state saw itself obliged to take effective action. The *process* failed… because of the success it had enjoyed. It was annulled by the Spanish state. It could not have been otherwise. The Spanish government and Senate, adhering to the Spanish Constitution, that is democracy and the rule of law and, of course, it meant that the coup d'état failed.

The *process* failed completely because of the success it had had, so its failure is a relative one. It is a failure in relation to the aim of separation, but, in itself, the *process* was a great success. It was a success with regard to the means it had at its disposal, it was a success with regard to the actions it took against the Spanish state, and it was a success with the number of souls it raised, and continues to raise, against Spain.

However, in addition to the foregoing, the separatist challenge has another major success—two, in fact. It managed to fragment Catalonia and finally it managed to fragment Spain. These are the two greatest successes of the *process*.

Undoubtedly, nothing similar has happened anywhere else in the world. And this in a region of a developed country that has never been a colony, that has never been independent, that has always been a region, and amongst the richest in the country, a region that owes its wealth to its success in that country's market, a region that administers a level of self-government greater than that of the most federal and decentralised countries in the world. Well, in such a region, a mass revolutionary movement developed which, in 2021 represented 26.8% of the census (from a minimum of 22.4% in 1980 and a maximum of 37.4% in 2017, as we saw in Chap. 19), a movement which organised publicly and delivered a coup d'état that was triumphant until... the last second.

The *process* has another impressive victory to its name: the de facto disconnection of Catalonia in relation to the Spanish state. The greater part of the territory of Catalonia, and official Catalonia, live in a kind of de facto 'independence'.

Failures and successes of the independence movement. After their coup, the question for the revolutionary, separatist, pro-sovereigntist movement is: it having been made abundantly clear that it was not, and will not, be possible to achieve the aim of independence, that separatists will never achieve their absolute aim, what is the point in continuing with the *process*? Why carry on?

PERMANENT CHALLENGE: WEARING CATALONIA AND SPAIN DOWN

Well, the process has to continue so that the independence parties can maintain their capture of the Generalitat de Catalunya, a very visible instrument of the conflict and, in the end, the source of employment and money for 200,000 'separatists'.

In light of the foregoing, and given the extraordinary current level of self-government, 'dialogue' and 'negotiation' are not what moves or interests the separatists. For separatists, dialogue and negotiation have no meaning. It would require them to recognise the legitimacy of the other side when the political energy of the independence movement is based, precisely, on denying the legitimacy of the Spanish state. Furthermore, how much could be achieved is merely a question of formality, it is symbolic, an appearance. The truth is, the Generalitat already has all the powers and all the money (except for the Social Security Reserve Fund, which they aren't that interested in, given the deficit of €3000 million per year that is covered by the rest of Spain), and exterior military defence, which the central government could never concede without ceasing to be a state.

The secessionist coup d'état of 2017 having been launched and having failed, was maintained in the subsequent autonomous elections to the Generalitat by the separatists. Also maintained were the lack of dialogue and the lack of understanding. All this said, the separatists need not exceed themselves by challenging the law (Spanish law of course) too much or too explicitly, in case the central government should find itself obliged to apply Article 155 of the Spanish Constitution once again.

The only thing left for the separatists now is to stay in the Generalitat, in an attitude of permanent agitation and legal and political guerrilla warfare against the government of Spain. The programme of the separatist Generalitat is now reduced to opposing whatever it is that the Spanish government does and hoping that the Spanish government itself proceeds towards the gradual demolition of Spanish democracy and the rule of law in Spain.

The Catalans, it is obvious, need empathy, harmony, and a good dose of the *seny*, or intelligence, common sense, and judgement, for which they are famed. Catalonia needs it too, but amongst the separatists, there are not many who are willing for this, and few are ready to calm themselves, get along with others and live in harmony. The neutrality of the institutions, respect for legality and the cessation of unilateralism are not part of the separatists' agenda.

SUMMARY

- How has the Barcelona elite succumbed to nationalism? What has made them take to the hills? How have they created a favourable atmosphere for the political, social and economic fragmentation of

Catalonia, and thence the destruction of the foundations of their own being? It is probably difficult to answer these questions, as it is difficult to answer similar questions about other cases of unsuspected political phenomena in the tormented history of Europe.

- The final result of the *process* was failure, to the extent that its annulment of Spanish legality, the declaration of independence and of the Catalan republic was thwarted by the Spanish state. It was an inevitable failure, due to its total success and full realisation.
- However, the *process* had two huge relative successes: the very wide popular mobilisation attained, and the tragic fragmentation of Catalonia and Spain.
- Given the impact of the separatist challenge (flight of people, companies, investment, activity, etc.), Catalonia's future is one of fragmentation and decline. Beyond this, if a hypothetical secession were ever to occur, Catalonia would collapse.

CHAPTER 49

Overcoming Catalan Separatism

SPECIFIC ASPECTS OF THE CATALAN CASE

Nationalism will be overcome in Catalonia as it has been in other places.[1] Specific aspects in the case of Catalonia are:

- Its gradualism (the parties themselves and their voters changed from being traditional conservatives to revolutionary separatists) and its radiance (ignited in 2006, it reached its zenith in 2014 and realised its maximalist programme in 2017).
- Behind it lies a regional administration, the origins of which are legal (majority of separatist and revolutionary seats in the regional parliament obtained, however, with a minority of votes), but whose behaviour is contrary to the law.
- The failure of the central government to correct the illegalities of the Catalan regional government, halt its attempt to substitute Spanish legality for a new separatist legality, and prevent the coup d'état.
- The executive power allowed the coup d'état to take place, and then it was the judicial power that had to take the measures for correction, annulment, detention, trial, sentencing and imprisonment.

---

[1] Dolça Catalunya (2019), *Dolça Catalunya. Tenemos un problema. Se llama nacionalismo. Lo vamos a superar,* Madrid, Libros Libres.

© The Author(s), under exclusive license to Springer Nature
Switzerland AG 2022
F. Brunet, *The Economics of Catalan Separatism,*
https://doi.org/10.1007/978-3-031-14451-6_49

287

- Who was obliged to guarantee, and could have guaranteed, the legality and rights of the Catalans did not do so. Who is obliged, and can, does not. Who will be obliged and will be able to, will they?
- Before the coup of 2017,[2] if at all, but even more clearly after the coup, nobody[3] thought that 'dialogue' between the government of Spain and the coup plotters would overcome the 'Catalan question', the 'political conflict' or the separatist challenge. The appeasement of the Catalan separatists is impossible.
- There is only one way to make the Catalan separatists happy: by handing them independence. This is contrary to the Constitution and the Statute. Furthermore, there is a by no means lesser question.

[2] For example, on the direction of the dialogue, see Soraya Sáenz de Santamaría (2016), "Comparecencia de la señora Vicepresidenta del Gobierno y Ministra de la Presidencia y para las Administraciones Territoriales para informar sobre las líneas generales de la política de su Departamento. A petición propia", *Diario de Sesiones del Congreso de los Diputados. XII Legislatura. Comisiones*, No. 65, 1 December <http://www.congreso.es/public_oficiales/L12/CONG/DS/CO/DSCD-12-CO-65.PDF>

[3] In spite of predominant bien-pensant political correctness, nobody in their heart of hearts, nobody in their right mind, nobody (if you permit me to say it) who has lived in Catalonia, nobody who has direct knowledge of Catalan separatism, believes in dialogue with the coup plotters. Of course not. Even though, of course, a democrat will never reject dialogue.

On the aspects of dialogue and agreement, see a list in Carlos Sánchez (2018), "Diez propuestas para encauzar (y resolver) la cuestión catalana", *El Confidencial*, 8 July <https://blogs.elconfidencial.com/espana/mientras-tanto/2018-07-08/propuestas-resolver-problema-cataluna_1588942/>.

With regard to dialogue, permanent destabilisation, the old and the new Catalanism, as well as the new normal deriving from the Covid-19 pandemic (and the failure of the coup d'état of autumn 2017), consider this: "The Covid-19 pandemic will not have brought an end to the dispute between Catalonia and the state, far from it, but it will have brought to an end the sovereigntist 'process' as we have understood it over these last years. [...] Those sectors of the independence movement who continue to maintain their intransigent, purist, and extreme positions, who aim to keep the conflict entrenched, who need continuous confrontation with the state to maintain their political capital, and who still speculate on the magical idea that from the collapse of Spain would emerge a free Catalonia, are repeating their mistake. [...] The country can not continue to be trapped in the logic of sterile, rhetorical confrontation that is wearing us down and that makes our collective progress impossible. [...] If Catalanism [...] does aspire to continue being the first political and cultural motor of the country, it must make the effort to build new ideas for this new era." (Carles Campuzano (2020), "El 'procés' del post-covid", *El Periódico*, 28 May <https://www.elperiodico.com/es/opinion/20200528/articulo-carles-campuzano-final-actual-proces-soberanista-postcovid-7978456>.)

Many more than half the Catalans and (to put it into constitutional, legal and political terms) Spaniards, do not want independence.

Ways of overcoming the challenge to the Spanish rule of law.

• There are two ways to overcome the challenge of Catalan separatism:

  – That there be a sufficient number of constitutionalist votes to produce a majority of seats in the regional parliament to form a constitutionalist Catalan government.
  – That the Spanish government urge the Senate to approve the application of Article 155 of the Spanish Constitution and the Generalitat de Catalunya be administered by the government of Spain.

The first way is very difficult if the regional separatist administration shows no neutrality and resorts to its habitual onslaught of propaganda. Throughout this investigation, we have drawn attention to how the distribution of votes in the territory and the electoral system that favours the rural areas explain the dynamics of the secessionist movement over the last decades.

Administration of the Generalitat by the Government of Spain

The second way, which is that the government of the nation administer the Generalitat, was implemented after the coup d'état of autumn 2017.[4] It was implemented without any collateral damage![5] But it was for a very short period and excluded TV3 and education! It also excluded significant changes to the regional police.

In the regional elections of 21 December 2017, the separatists and revolutionaries again won a majority of seats sufficient to form another separatist government on 29 May 2018. Direct administration was brief

[4] Mariano Rajoy Brey (2017), "Intervención del Presidente del Gobierno en el Pleno del Senado", 27 October <http://www.senado.es/legis12/publicaciones/pdf/senado/ds/ds_p_12_45.pdf>
[5] Enric Millo (2020), *El derecho a saber la verdad. El testimonio del Delegado del Gobierno en la Cataluña del 155*, Barcelona, Península.

(from 8.26 p.m. of 27 October 2017 until 12.41 p.m. of 2 June 2018). It should be said that if central administration lasted for five months after the autonomous elections it was because the separatist parties that had won a majority of seats could not agree on the formation of their government.

Application of Article 155 of the Spanish Constitution:

- It achieved its aim (stop the coup d'état, dismiss the separatist government of the Generalitat, administer this directly and call elections for the formation of a new government).
- It showed that nothing bad happens when the Spanish state takes the reigns of the Catalan political situation.
- But it could do little to contribute towards the reconstitution of Catalonia because of its brevity and because the government that succeeded it was equally separatist (although it did avoid the flagrant illegalities of the previous one that obliged the central government to intervene).

Basically, the normalisation of the rule of law in Catalonia will consist of reverting the present situation of severe confrontation, the result of many years of separatist Catalan governments. Three things are necessary to achieve this aim of overcoming separatism:

- Strong political will. Of the constitutionalist voters, given the first method, and of the Spanish government, given the second.
- Solid and attractive narrative. Separatism is based on emotion; reason alone is insufficient to revert the hegemony of the separatist narrative.
- A long time. What the separatists destroyed and built in three decades of fierce intervention will not be reverted in the short term. In the short term, the application of all the measures relating to the rule of law; in the medium-term, consolidation of reconciliation, understanding and stability; and in the long-term, full upholding of a narrative in the style of, "We are better off together!"

Constitutional Spain

Constitutional Spain rests on four pillars: (i) wide-ranging decentralisation to the Autonomous Communities; (ii) full democracy, rule of law, subjection to the law; (iii) extensive welfare state with social justice and interpersonal solidarity; and (iv) productive economy with juridical security and market competition.

Constitutionalism has a herculean task ahead of it for the reconstruction of Catalonia and the stabilisation of Spanish politics. After 40 years of the regional government and the Catalan separatists disconnecting from Spain, and in many ways effectively disconnected from Spain, reverting the situation will be more of a marathon than a sprint.

The Spanish constitutionalist narrative with regard to the secessionist defiance of democracy, the rule of law and the integrity of Spain has three sources:

- Understanding, harmony, peace, plurality and respect.
- Reason and interest, the place of the economy in reality and in the argument.
- Sentiment and emotion with respect to Spain and what is Spanish.

As we have seen in detail in this book, Catalonia is gripped by the consequences of the *process*, which has precipitated a profound decline. In this Part III, we have considered the various aspects of a hypothetical secession of Catalonia, and how the present decline springs from chaos. The sooner a stop is put to confrontation, the sooner the decline of Catalonia can be tackled, and the easier it will be to reconstitute its liberties and capacities and re-establish its progress and well-being.

Summary

- There are two ways to overcome Catalan separatism: (a) a constitutionalist government of the Generalitat; or (b) the administration of the Generalitat by the government of Spain.
- Whatever the case, overcoming Catalan separatism, reverting the destruction it has caused and healing the open confrontation between Catalans, will be an extraordinary task that will require political will, a narrative of understanding of Spanish democracy and a long time.

CHAPTER 50

As a Recap: Ten Questions and Answers About a Hypothetical Separation of Catalonia from the Rest of Spain

1.

Q—What would the impact of independence be on GDP?

A—The independence of Catalonia would substantially reduce its GDP. For two reasons: a drop in sales to the rest of Spain, and a drop in investment (and therefore, activity in Catalonia) in view of the greater risk of investing here. Employment would therefore also be reduced. It has been estimated that there would be a 9.3% reduction in permanent GDP in a low-level scenario, a 16.1% reduction in a medium-level scenario, and 24.4% reduction in a high-level scenario.

2.

Q—How would the independence of Catalonia affect trade with Spain and the European Union?

A—Very negatively, never positively, due to the so-called 'border effect'. When barriers are erected, trade is reduced. It is estimated that trade in industrial goods with the rest of Spain would fall by between 25% and 50%, and by between 35% and 60% in non-industrial goods. This would reduce Catalonia's GDP and level of employment by 9.3% in a low-level scenario, by 16.1% in a medium-level scenario, and by 24.4% in a high-level scenario. Since Catalonia would be outside the European Union, its

© The Author(s), under exclusive license to Springer Nature Switzerland AG 2022
F. Brunet, *The Economics of Catalan Separatism*,
https://doi.org/10.1007/978-3-031-14451-6_50

exports to the rest of Spain and the European Union would be subject to EU customs duties, the average rate of which is 4% of the value of the goods.

3.

Q—Would an independent Catalonia have more or less fiscal revenue?

A—Much less, without doubt, bearing in mind the reduction in activity, employment, sales to the rest of Spain and the lower GDP resulting from separation. To have the same fiscal revenue with a lower GDP, it would be necessary to raise taxes, principally VAT and income tax.

4.

Q—How would independence affect banks and financial institutions?

A—Being outside Spain, Catalonia would automatically be outside the European Union and out of the eurozone. Banks with their head offices in Catalonia would be outside the European System of Central Banks and of the European Central Bank. Given the need for currency, Catalonia could continue to use existing euros, but banks established in Catalonia would not have access to the credit, regulation and facilities of the ECB. Then, finally, a Catalonia outside Spain, the EU and the Eurosystem would have to issue its own currency. In light of Catalan risk, the new regional currency would be strongly devalued, it has been estimated by as much as 50%, and would continue to devalue as the Catalan financial system continued to collapse. This devaluation would in turn, and to the same degree, reduce the salaries paid to Catalans in the new currency. From a banking point of view, being out of the eurozone and having to use the new currency would cause a complete flight of the bank deposits in Catalonia to the rest of Spain, a flight the separatist authorities would attempt to stem by imposing restrictions. For banks domiciled in Catalonia, this would spell bankruptcy.

5.

Q—So bank restrictions would be probable in the event of independence?

A—They would be inescapable: it would be the only way to try and stop the flight of deposits from 'Catalan' banks to 'Spanish' and 'European' ones. Right now, those separatists who believe in the success of their enterprise will surely have their own money safely salted away in the rest of Spain, Europe or Switzerland.

6.

Q—Would there be a new currency, or would the euro continue to be used?

A—It being the case that Catalan banks would not have access to finance from the European Central Bank, it would be very difficult for an independent Catalonia to continue to use the euro. Thus, after having attempted to use the euro as currency, they would have to create their own currency, something that would entail the need for bank restrictions and a devaluation of no less than 50%. This would make imported products (from the rest of Spain and the world) more expensive, lead to high levels of price inflation and, therefore, much lower purchasing power for salaries. Other stocks, properties and rents, denominated in the new currency, would be devalued in a similar manner.

7.

Q—How would independence affect the pensions drawn by Catalans?

A—It must be borne in mind that since 2010 the Spanish Social Security system in Catalonia has an annual deficit with the rest of Spain of €3000 million. A rupture in the unity of the Social Security Reserve Fund would have a very negative effect on the amount of pension received by 1,738,000 Catalans. At present, the rest of Spain helps to pay the pensions, but in the event of independence, the annual €3000 million would no longer be received. Every Catalan pensioner would lose €1250 per year. Furthermore, instead of receiving their pensions in euros, they would receive them in the new currency, and the value of these smaller Catalan pensions would be further eroded in line with the reduction in salaries mentioned above.

8.

Q—How would it affect tourism?

A—In one way, very negatively. Whoever entered an independent Catalonia from Spain, the European Union or from the rest of the world, would have to have a passport and a visa! And a passport and visa is what

Catalans would have to have in order to leave, even if it were only to go and see their relations on the other side of the river Ebro. Visitors and tourists from the European Union—amongst them those from Spain—and the rest of the world, like Catalan tourists to the rest of the world, would think that, without doubt, they were in a different world! Free circulation would no longer exist. Furthermore, as mentioned before, since Catalonia would have its own currency, the impact of independence on tourism would be even more negative. It has been estimated that tourism destined for Catalonia would fall by some 45% and that the transit of tourists, through Barcelona airport, for example, would drop by 80%. At last, the Sagrada Familia would be free of tourists! The Passeig de Gràcia deserted! At last, Empuriabrava for the separatists!

9.

Q—How would it affect farmers?

A—It would be the end of the Common Agricultural Policy: that would be the end of European Union subsidies, some €500 million per year. For 50,000 active exploitations, this would come to €10,000 per year. On the other hand, the European Union, that is to say, Spain too, would levy tariffs on Catalan exports of tomatoes, meat, wine, and other Catalan produce. That would be the result of independence, the price of disintegration.

10.

Q—What would happen to public debt?

A—Upon secession, a part of the central administration's public debt would correspond to Catalonia. At the end of 2020, Spanish debt amounted to €1,345,570 million. The Catalan quota, 18%, would be €242,203 million. This would mean an annual payment (capital repayment and interest) of some €30,000 million. On the other hand, the Generalitat de Catalunya has accumulated €82,936 million of its own debt. With a BBB rating (junk status) the Generalitat does not have access to the financial markets, and it would have even less with hypothetical independence. Independence would mean, quite simply, the bankruptcy of Catalonia.

EPILOGUE

Mikel Buesa

Professor of Applied Economics, Universidad Complutense, Madrid, Spain
Former director, Institute for Industrial Analysis
Former president, Foro de Ermua
Constitutional Order of Merit

The question of secessionism is clearly a complex one—as the reader will have been able to see in this book—given the multiplicity of aspects that can be considered, from the strictly political and economic to the juridical, cultural, sociological and ideological. Secession is rupture; and all rupture brings with it changes, some of them desirable for nationalists, but most of them disturbing and painful for most of the population. Ferran Brunet has documented this profusely in these pages, bearing in mind the experiences in other countries that might serve as a guide for formulating the most reasonable hypotheses with which to approach an analysis of separatism in Catalonia. And the conclusion that can be drawn from all this can be stated quite simply: secession, at least in the abstract, is viable from the point of view of the economy—political and juridical questions are a different matter—but is enormously costly and promises to bring many long years of difficulties, of impoverishment and decline, and perhaps even violence.

This is the message we need to get across to people, not just those who aspire to independence, but also to those who would be damaged by it,

© The Author(s), under exclusive license to Springer Nature   297
Switzerland AG 2022
F. Brunet, *The Economics of Catalan Separatism*,
https://doi.org/10.1007/978-3-031-14451-6

being deprived of their present nationality, and those who, living more or less far away believe, mistakenly, that the question has nothing to do with them, that it is a political dispute and there is nothing to be done about it. Secession affects all of us, in Catalonia, Spain and in Europe. And many of those who advocate it know this. When the *lehendakari* Jesús María de Leizaola—who spent most of his presidency of the Basque government in exile between 1960 and 1978—was asked what the consequences would be of independence for *Euskadi*, he replied tersely, "A hundred years of poverty".

I found this quote when, in the early 2000s I started to become interested in the economics of secession as a result of the project for the Basque Country being announced by the *lehendakari*, Juan José Ibarretxe. It was a very difficult time; ETA had resumed its terrorist campaign with force after the truce it had established in 1998 failed. Furthermore, in my case specifically, I had been very seriously affected by the assassination of my brother Fernando, a socialist politician committed to the defence of everyone's rights through the use of the word. Ibarretxe had agreed to the rupture with Spain with this terrorist organisation in the *Pacto de Lizarra* and, in spite of the return of violence to the streets of the Basque Country, set about promoting it through the formulation of a constitutive rule of the new Basque state that was camouflaged as part of a statutory reform. In essence, the *Plan Ibarretxe* was nothing other than this, although its preparation was delayed for a number of years because it was essential, for nationalist interests, to carry out a propaganda campaign in the heart of Basque society to try and convince people of the benefits of independence. "What's bad about it?" Ibarretxe would repeat time and time again, while launching a barrage of propaganda that promised not only prosperity, but also peace.

The debate in the Basque Country was an intense one, mainly because those of us who did not identify with nationalism set about, not only countering separatist arguments, but also studying the mainly political, economic and juridical consequences that could derive from secession. My commitments here were focussed on economic aspects, although, given that at that time it had befallen me to preside the *Foro Ermua*, I also participated in other fields. I should mention that in our endeavours to have serious public discussion about, and research into, the multiple aspects of secession, we had the support, not only of civil society organisations—I have already mentioned *Foro Ermua*, but also in the forefront were *¡Basta ya!*, the *Fundación para la Libertad* and the *Colectivo Vasco de Víctimas del*

Terrorismo (COVITE)—but also of the Spanish Government, which thought it should help these movements, and other regional and local institutions, with their moral support and also with resources.

One day I will have to study all this with rigour in order to highlight the fact that, in the face of nationalism and its secessionist pretensions, it was possible to unfold a multifaceted policy, that did not yield to them. Amongst the actors involved were not only professional politicians, but also many anonymous people who, forming part of civic movements, felt the weight of the events taking place in the streets and the demonstrations, and of the work involved in establishing communication and an ideological debate. Some of them, it is true, were assassinated by ETA, and another 1300, according to the most reliable estimates, had the uncomfortable and very often irritating inconvenience, and I speak from experience, of living under permanent police protection. In my own particular case, I can say I witnessed the interest the prime minister, José María Aznar, took in this matter throughout his second term of office.

During those years, Aznar would invite a wide range of Basques, from different quarters and with different ideological orientations, to dinner at his residence in order to hear what we could say about the events at the time. My impression is that the prime minister was trying to absorb as much information as possible in order to understand that very strange situation in which some, those of the PNV, were attempting to satisfy the demands of others, those of ETA, without considering, as the polls showed then and continue to show now, that most Basques wanted nothing to do with independence.

It so happened that one day, when I arrived at the Moncloa, during the preliminaries to the dinner, Aznar took me aside to say, "The things you wrote in *Papeles de Ermua* and in the bulletin of *¡Basta ya!* are very important and we have to go more deeply into it". What these magazines had published was, quite simply, a very preliminary estimate of the costs that might be involved in Basque secession. So I said to the prime minister, "José María, to do this it would be necessary to bring together a wide range of academic economists who, with the necessary means, could devote themselves to disentangling and measuring the consequences of secession. Financial resources would be necessary, as well as all the information the government can provide on the subject". His reply was brief, "Speak to Javier". From there we passed through to the dining room for a relaxed discussion about Basque affairs.

Javier was no other than Javier Zarzalejos, at that time secretary general at the Prime Minister's Office. I had a meeting with him a few days later and I proposed an outline of the questions the work might cover, who the various academic economists might be to study the various subjects, and I gave him an indicative estimate of the costs it would be necessary to finance. He made no objections, even when I warned him that some of the colleagues I was suggesting were politically poles apart from the Partido Popular, and he gave me total liberty to act as I saw best, with the total support of the prime minister.

That is how the research project was sketched out in which academics from various universities and departments participated. The project gave rise to a book entitled, *Economía de la secesión. El proyecto nacionalista y el País Vasco,* published in 2004 by the Instituto de Estudios Fiscales. It was, almost certainly, the first work in Spain to deal with the question of independence from the economic point of view. But, besides its possible academic merits, perhaps the most important aspect was the political impact it had. The book's findings in the various fields covered were widely disseminated in the press before its publication and made a powerful contribution to the continuing debate in the Basque Country. It was a source of great satisfaction to me to know that, in the Basque parliament, the nationalists referred to us, given the lack of other arguments, as the 'statistics front'. Well, this statistics front contributed—of course, alongside other political and civic actions, some of them much more important—to discrediting the promises of limitless prosperity emanating from the *Plan Ibarretxe*, by putting the numbers on the table and discussing the question of secession seriously. I can therefore say, without presumption, that our intellectual work contributed something to the nationalists' failure, in spite of the fact that the 'Basque Parliament's Proposal for Coexistence in Euskadi, New Political Statute for Euskadi' was approved by the parliament in Vitoria on 30 December 2004 with 39 votes in favour and 35 votes against, 52%. An ephemeral achievement this, since barely 32 days later, on 1 February 2005, the proposal was rejected by the Congress of Deputies by an overwhelming majority of 313 votes, almost 90%. In the end, subjected to democratic procedures the nationalists' pretensions became diluted. Ibarretxe managed to keep in government for another term, rather precariously, thanks to a couple of votes lent to him by ETA, whose parliamentary agent at the time was the Partido Comunista de las Tierras Vascas (Communist Party of the Basque Lands). He then tried, without success, to call a self-determination referendum which was nipped in the bud by the Constitutional Court. His popularity plummeted and in 2009 the PNV lost power.

The foregoing shows that a policy that does not by any means yield to separatism can be effective. But let's not flatter ourselves, its undoubted merit had an important precedent in the Canadian experience in the late 1990s when the Québécois, Stéphane Dion, the then Minister for Intergovernmental Affairs, embarked on what he called a Clarity Act which, with that name, was passed by parliament in Ottawa in June 2000, and became law. It was a policy that consisted in nothing other than making the nationalists face up to democratic procedures, without ambiguity and with rigour. And it was possible because, as Dion expressed in his writings, it broke two golden rules that had previously governed the debate with the separatists: the first, that nationalists needed to be courted with kind words, and the second, that you should never admit in public that your adversary could win.

To stop talking to nationalists mildly, even at the cost of hurting their feelings, says Dion, is to deprive them of the advantage of accepting that in something, above all, their complaints, they are right, and it certainly shows that their reasons for independence, which would deprive their fellow citizens of their nationality, are not accepted. And admitting that they might win also implies that they might lose. He also wrote, "If I believe in the legitimacy of my cause and my convictions, I should never be afraid of being clear about what is at stake in all its dimensions. [...] Clarity and frankness are my allies, confusion, and ambiguity my enemies".

So, let us stop speaking mildly—as, most certainly, Ferran Brunet does in this book—and let us put the falsehoods that Catalan secessionism has been resting on into the political arena. In my modest contribution to the debate about the independence of Catalonia, I think that, apart from the calculations and estimates that replicate the ones I had already studied in case of the Basque Country, I think my main input is focussed on the discussion of the central nationalist idea that 'Spain robs us'. I will summarise it now.

This idea emerged, in a quantitative sense, in 1933, when the Menorcan, Jaume Alzina, associated with Francesc Cambó and the Lliga Regionalista, had his, *L'economia de la Catalunya autónoma* published by the Tipografía Emporium publishing company in Barcelona. From the conceptual and methodological point of view, it was a rather mediocre work, but it had the merit of having calculated the Catalan fiscal deficit for the first time, this being understood as the difference between the taxes paid in Catalonia and the state's expenditure in the region. Alzina calculated, for 1930, that the first of these variables was equivalent to 18.8% of the revenue of the national treasury, while the second of them was only 5.5% of public expenditure.

On this basis he concluded that "the injustice that the Monarchy commits in Catalonia could not be clearer", while complaining at the same time that the Republic had not changed this and that its government "favours Madrid once again". Alzina thus sowed the seed of the grievances that, many years later, would be cultivated and nurtured in many studies about Catalonia's trade balance—in which recognised economists participated, such as Eduardo Escarra, Carlos Pi-Sunyer, Ernest Lluch and Ramón Trias Fargas, amongst others—and which culminated with the extension of the analysis to include all the balances of payments together, by Jacinto Ros Hombravella and Antonio Montserrat.

This last contribution is crucial for the subject we are discussing since the question of the fiscal deficit thus came to form part of the wider field of accounting with respect to exterior economic relations as a whole. For non-professional readers it is important to point out that, as we teach our economics students, in a balance of payments, all the flows of income and expenditure balance so that, in the end, the sum of the balances is always the same, zero, and when, because of insufficient information this does not occur, an entry is made for errors and omissions to prevent that from happening. That means that if a country or a region presents a current account surplus with respect to the exterior, the result of its exporting potential, there will be a financial deficit balance to compensate for it. Both Ros and Montserrat knew this and showed that the trade surplus between Catalonia and Spain—of around 20,000 million pesetas in 1962—was balanced by other items analysed.

Then what do we find but one of the authors I mentioned before— Ramón Trias Fargas—manipulating the data of Ros and Montserrat's balances and performing an astonishing intellectual pirouette by denying the basic principle that the final balance must always be the same as zero. This he did in his, *Introducció a l'economia de Catalunya*, published in 1972, and not on account of ignorance—in this book he stated, "the balance of payments must balance by definition"—but on account of bad faith when, after confusing the issue with numbers culled from different sources, he says that the trade surplus, which "is not as important as might seem" was "more than compensated for by the deficit in other accounts" so that "in the end there is a general deficit in our balance of payments with the rest of Spain". Having laid the trap, it only remained to identify where this mysterious 'general deficit' lay. Trias had no doubt in attributing it to the 'public sector account deficit', which he estimated at 32,093 million pesetas—we do not know for which year, since the hodgepodge of numbers covers most of the 1960s—accountable to the fact that the state 'spent in Catalonia 52% of what it had received'. And it was in this way that the doctrine was established that 'Catalonia's exterior balance would be comfortably compensated if the public sector account deficit did not exist', as well as the idea that 'the quantity (of taxes) that does not return to the region of origin (Catalonia) and which remains in the hands of the central administration is excessive'.

Trias Fargas certainly never said, 'Spain robs us', surely because, even in its dying days, Franco's regime could have deprived him of several of his lucrative sources of income, but he did lay the foundations for others to claim so. By affirming that the balance of payments did not work in Catalonia in the same way as they work in the rest of the world, he made it possible for other, willingly ignorant economists to unlink the calculation of the fiscal deficit from the context of exterior relations so that, this having been done, it was enough to come up with some figures to demonstrate the state's economic oppression of Catalonia. Let me say, however, that I do not deny that there is a fiscal deficit, although it is certain, as Ferran Brunet shows in this book, there are estimates of it which are very exaggerated. Of course there is a fiscal deficit, as happens in other rich regions of Spain, with the notorious exception of the Basque Country and Navarre, where the state spends much more than it receives on account of a badly calculated quota that does, indeed, favour nationalist and *foral* (charter) interests which, in this sense, rigorously follow the doctrine that 'the Fuero (Charter) is not to pay', established by Pedro Egaña in his *Breves apuntes en defensa de las libertades vascongadas*, written in 1852. But his interpretation is very distant from the one disseminated in nationalist propaganda: it is not a question of Spain robbing the Catalans, it buys from them, and it buys a lot, it buys their manufactured goods, the fruits of its agriculture and the services of its tertiary sector.

Thus, all the economic foundations for secessionism are based on a lie, wrapped in deception, the fruit of falsification. That is all there is to it. Readers who have reached this point in this excellent book by Brunet will have seen how the suppositions, many of them very twisted, drawn from this entanglement of deception have met with an extraordinary popular response because they promise an untold wealth that would not be possible even in *La tierra de Jauja* that Lope de Rueda once imagined. Let me, therefore, conclude this epilogue with a poem by Jon Juaristi which, although referring to Basque nationalists, could just as well, at least at the end, apply to the Catalans:

> Do you wonder traveller why we have died so young
> and why we have killed so stupidly?
> Our parents lied: that is all.

References

References [from 272 footnotes]

Acemoglu, Daron (2017), "La Contra. Entrevista con Lluís Amiguet", *La Vanguardia*, 26 June <https://www.lavanguardia.com/lacontra/20170626/423699679648/la-corrupcion-es-la-ultima-herencia-del-franquismo.html>.

Acemoglu, D., & Robinson, J. A. (2012). *Why Nations Fail: The Origins of Power, Prosperity, and Poverty*. Profile Books.

Acemoglu, D., & Robinson, J. A. (2019). *The Narrow Corridor: States, Societies, and the Fate of Liberty*. Penguin.

Ajuntament de Barcelona. Departament d'Estadística (2022), *Estadística i difusió de dades* <https://www.bcn.cat/estadistica/castella/dades/inf/pobest/pobest20/part2/nt11.htm>.

Alandete, David (2017), "La maquinaria de injerencias rusa penetra la crisis catalana. La red global que actuó con Trump y el Brexit se dedica ahora a España", *El País*, 25 September.

Alandete, D. (2019). *Fake news: la nueva arma de destrucción masiva. Cómo se utilizan las noticias falsas y los hechos alternativos para desestabilizar la democracia*. Barcelona.

Albalat, J. G. (2017), "Una agenda detalla la hoja de ruta del separatism. La Guardia Civil intervino en el domicilio de Josep Maria Jové unas anotaciones claves sobre el plan soberanista", *El Periódico*, 11 December <https://www.elperiodico.com/es/politica/20171211/guardia-civil-halla-agenda-hoja-de-ruta-soberanismo-papel-de-los-principales-politicos-catalanes-6488665>).

Alcaide Inchausti, J. (2003). *Evolución económica de las regiones y provincias españolas en el siglo XX*. Bilbao.

F. Brunet, *The Economics of Catalan Separatism*,
https://doi.org/10.1007/978-3-031-14451-6

Alcaide, Carmen (2014), "El debate sobre las balanzas fiscales", *El País*, 16 February <https://elpais.com/economia/2014/02/14/actualidad/1392390790_505427.html>.

Alesina, A., & Spolaore, E. (1997). On the Number and Size of Nations. *The Quarterly Journal of Economics, 112*(4), 1027–1056.

Alesina, Alberto, and Enrico Spolaore (2003), *The size of nations*, Cambridge, MA, MIT University Press.

Alesina, Alberto, Enrico Spolaore, and Romain Wacziarg (2000), "Economic Integration and Political Disintegration", *American Economic Review*, Vol. 90, No. 5, pp. 1276–1296.

Alto Consejo Consultivo de la Comunidad Valenciana. Comisión de Economía (2013), Informe sobre la deuda, déficit y financiación de la Comunidad Valenciana. Propuesta de bases para un nuevo sistema de financiación autonómica <http://www.presidencia.gva.es/documents/80920710/80950149/Informe+Financiaci%C3%B3n+Final+12+11+13.pdf/1f966b00-0147-42d9-bcd7-2c966afd9bcb>.

Álvaro García, D. (2019). *Cataluña, la construcción de un relato: ¿Cómo se ha servido el independentismo del populismo identitario para convencer a la mitad de la población catalana de las virtudes de la independencia?* Barcelona.

Alzina, J. (1930). *L'economia de la Catalunya autónoma*. Barcelona.

Amat, J. (2018). *Largo proceso, amargo sueño. Cultura y política en la Cataluña contemporánea*. Barcelona.

Amat, O., & Guinjoan, M. (2014). *Economia de Catalunya—Preguntes i respostes sobre l'impacte econòmic de la independència*. Barcelona.

Anon. (1990), "La estrategia de la recatalanización ["Programa 2000"]", *El Periódico de Cataluña*, 28 October <http://www.tolerancia.org/updocs/ElPeriodico_Programa2000_CiU_1990.pdf>.

Anon. (2014a), "Jordi Pujol confiesa haber tenido dinero sin regularizar en el extranjero", *eldiario.es*, 25 July <https://www.eldiario.es/catalunya/Jordi-Pujol-confiesa-regularizar-extranjero_0_285222219.html#carta>.

Anon. (2014b), "Separatism in Europe (1)—Characteristics of separatist movements", *[Library of the Council of the European Union] Library Note*, 12 February <https://www.consilium.europa.eu/en/documents-publications/library/library-blog/posts/separatism-in-europe-1-characteristics-of-separatist-movements/>.

Anon. (2020), *Una cronologia del Procés. 40 anys d'impunitat de l'elit catalana*, <https://resd9.blogspot.com/2014/11/una-cronologia-dels-fets-35-anys.html>.

Anon. (2021), *Racialistas catalanes* <https://racialistascatalanes.home.blog/2019/12/28/razacatalana/>.

Anon. (n.d.), *Mitos and falsedades del separatismo catalán* <http://statics.ccma.cat/multimedia/pdf/6/2/1508933378226.pdf>.

Arendt, Hannah (1951), *The Origins of Totalitarianism*, London, Penguin, 2017.
Arruñada, Benito and Victor Lapuente Giné (2015), "Las peligrosas ilusiones de Cataluña", *Project Syndicate*, 23 September <https://www.project-syndicate. org/commentary/Cataluña-independence-election-by-benito-arrunada-and-victor-lapuente-gine-2015-09/spanish?barrier=accesspaylog>.
Arza Mondelo, Juan Francisco, and Joaquim Coll i Amargós (2014), *Cataluña. El mito de la secesión. Desmontando las falacias del soberanismo*, Córdoba, Almuzara.
Asociación Estatal de Directores y Gerentes en Servicios Sociales (2020), *Evolución de los presupuestos autonómicos en España* <https://www.directoressociales. com/images/Noticias/EvolgastoCCAA2018/GR%C3%81FICOS%20 Evol.%20presupuestos%20auton%C3%B3micos%20_1.pdf>.
Assemblea Nacional Catalana (2016), *Full de ruta 2016–2017* https://assemblea. cat/documentos/.
Assemblea Nacional Catalana (2019), *Servei d'assistència psicológica* <https:// twitter.com/assemblea/status/1186297179490734081>
Assemblea Nacional Catalana. Sectorial d'Economia (2015), *Impacte de la independència en l'empresa. La visió de l' ANC* <http://economistes.assemblea. cat/wp/wp-content/uploads/2015/05/5.1-doem.-complet-v1.00-dossier-impacte-de-la-independencia-en-lempresa-11052015.pdf>.
Audiencia Nacional. Juzgado Central de Instrucción Número 5 (2020), *Diligencias Previas 141/2012. Auto de Procedimiento Abreviado*, 16 de julio <http://www. poderjudicial.es/cgpj/es/Buscadores/?categoria=&actuales=&text=Diligenci as+Previas+141%2F2012.+Auto+De+Procedimiento+Abreviado%2C+16+de+j ulio+%3C%3E.+&paginacion=10>.
Autoritat Catalana de la Competència (2012), *Efectes del caràcter restrictiu de la normativa comercial sobre la competitivitat de l'economia catalana* <http:// acco.gencat.cat/web/.content/80_acco/documents/arxius/actuacions/ estudi_comerc_cat.pdf>.
Balmes, Jaime (1845), *El criterio* <http://www.ataun.eus/bibliotecagratuita/ Cl%C3%A1sicos%20en%20Espa%C3%B1ol/vJaume%20Balmes/El%20crite-rio.pdf>.
Banco de España (n.d.), *Boletín Estadístico* <https://www.bde.es/webbde/es/ estadis/infoest/bolest13.html>.
Bank of England (2018), *EU withdrawal scenarios and monetary and financial stability. A response to the House of Commons Treasury Committee*, London, BoE.
Baquero, Antonio, Kevin G. Hall, Alina Tsogoeva, Jesús G. Albalat, Christo Grozev, Lorenzo Bagnoli, IStories, and Stefano Vergine (2022), "Fueling Secession, Promising Bitcoins: How a Russian Operator Urged Catalonian Leaders to Break With Madrid", Organized Crime and Corruption Reporting Project <https://www.occrp.org/en/investigations/fueling-secession-promising-bitcoins-how-a-russian-operator-urged-catalonian-leaders-to-break-with-madrid>.

Barclays (2014), "Sovereign implications of Catalonian independence", *Economics Research Europe*, 24 October <http://www.empresarisdecatalunya.org/wp-content/uploads/2014/11/EC-Noticias-Barclays-24Oct14.pdf>.

Barraycoa, J. (2013). *Cataluña hispana*. Barcelona.

BBVA Research (2020), *Situación España*, First Semester <https://www.bbvaresearch.com/publicaciones/situacion-espana-primer-trimestre-2020/>.

Béjar, Helena (2008), *La dejación de España. Nacionalismo, desencanto y pertenencia*, Madrid, Katz.

Bloomberg (2017), "Catalans Think Twice About Risks of Rupture as Good Life Returns", 9 August <https://www.bloomberg.com/news/articles/2017-08-09/catalans-think-twice-about-risks-of-rupture-as-good-life-returns>.

Bloomberg (2019), *These Are the World's Healthiest Nations* <https://www.bloomberg.com/news/articles/2019-02-24/spain-tops-italy-as-world-s-healthiest-nation-while-u-s-slips>.

Boix Palop, Andrés (2017), "El conflicto catalán and la crisis constitucional española: una cronología", *El Cronista del Estado Social and Democrático de Derecho*, No. 71–72, pp. 172–181.

Bolea, Ignacio (2019), "Madrid capta 71.807 millones más de inversión que Cataluña desde 2012", *Expansión*, 19 January <https://www.expansion.com/economia/2019/01/18/5c4181d222601d834d8b4589.html>.

Borrell, J., & Llorach, J. (2015). *Las cuentas and los cuentos de la independencia*. Los Libros de la Catarata.

Borrell, Josep, and Joan Llorach (2014), "¿Dónde están los 16.000 millones?", *El País*, 20 January.

Bosch, Josep Ramon (2020), *Cataluña, la ruta falsa: El problema catalán: cómo solucionarlo y no sólo conllevarlo*, Barcelona, Deusto.

Brand Finance (2020), *España 100, 2020. Informe anual de las marcas más valiosas and más fuertes de España* <https://brandirectory.com/download-report/brand-finance-spain-100-2020-preview.pdf>.

Bricall, Josep Maria (2017), *Una certa distància. Assaig de memòries*, Barcelona, RBA La Magrana.

Bricall, Josep Maria (2022), "Una mirada llarga sobre el 'procés'", *Política & prosa*, No. 42 <https://politicaprosa.com/el-tipus-dinteres-compost/>.

Brualla, Alba and Mónica G. Moreno (2019), "El alquiler de oficinas despunta and se situará este año en niveles precrisis", *El Economista*, 26 September <https://www.eleconomista.es/empresas-finanzas/noticias/10106942/09/19/El-alquiler-de-oficinas-despunta-y-se-situara-este-ano-en-niveles-precrisis.html>.

Brunet i Solà, Manuel (1936), "¿L'oasi", *La Veu de Catalunya*, 4 March.

Brunet, F. (1994). *The Economics of Barcelona 1992 Olympic Games*. Lausanne.

Brunet, Ferran (2010), *Curso de Integración Europea*, Madrid, Alianza Editorial, 2ª ed.

Brunet, Ferran (2021), "Consecuencias económicas del separatismo catalán", *Revista de Libros*, 10 November <https://www.revistadelibros.com/consecuencias-economicas-del-separatismo-catalan/>.

Brunet, F. (2022). *Economía del separatismo catalán*. Barcelona.

Buchanan, A. (1997). Theories of Secession. *Philosophy and Public Affairs*, 26(1), 31–61.

Buchanan, J. M., & Faith, R. L. (1987). Secession and the limits of taxation. Toward a theory of internal exit. *American Economic Review*, 77(5), 1023–1031.

Cabrillo, Francisco (2021), *The Economic Cost of Catalonia's Hypothetical Independence and Departure from the EU*, Bruselas, European Policy Information Center <http://www.epicenternetwork.eu/publications/the-economic-cost-of-catalonias-hypothetical-independence/>.

Calero, Jorge, and Álvaro Choi (2019), *Efectos de la inmersión lingüística sobre el alumnado castellanoparlante en Cataluña*, Madrid, Fundación Europea Sociedad y Educación <https://www.sociedadyeducacion.org/site/wp-content/uploads/SE-Inmersion-Cataluna.pdf>.

Calleja, Mariano (2020), "Ocho de cada diez catalanes y vascos elogian al Ejército contra el coronavirus", *ABC*, 13 April <https://www.abc.es/espana/abci-ocho-cada-diez-catalanes-y-vascos-elogian-ejercito-contra-coronavirus-202004122035_noticia.html?utm_source=piano&utm_medium=email&utm_campaign=2257&pnespid=kLVmo_dHWwONvnfB_I4DRS1dAnTMYvttxKvB3X1x>.

Calvet, Agustí, a. Gaziel (n.d.), *Tot s'ha perdut. El catalanisme polític entre 1922 i 1934*, Barcelona, RBA, 2013.

Cámara de Comercio de Barcelona (2014), *El sector públic a Catalunya i Espanya: impacte econòmic de diferents escenaris polítics*, Barcelona, COCINB.

Cámara Oficial de Comercio, Industria and Navegación de Barcelona (2018), *Estudis Econòmics i d'Infraestructures* <https://www.cambrabcn.org/>.

Campos Cura, C. (2019). *La anomalía catalana ¿Y si el problema fuera Cataluña y España la solución?* Barcelona.

Campuzano, Carles (2020), "El 'procés' del post-covid", *El Periódico*, 28 May <https://www.elperiodico.com/es/opinion/20200528/articulo-carles-campuzano-final-actual-proces-soberanista-postcovid-7978456>.

Canal, J. (2015). *Historia mínima de Cataluña*. Turner.

Canals Vidal, F. (2006). *Catalanismo and Tradición catalana*. Barcelona.

Carbajosa, Ana (2018), "La inteligencia alemana afirma que Rusia apoyó al independentismo catalán. El jefe de la inteligencia afirma que ve "muy plausible" and "razonable" que Moscú se prestara a una campaña de desinformación en los días previos al referéndum", *El País*, 14 May <https://elpais.com/politica/2018/05/14/actualidad/1526297741_890840.html>.

Cardenal Nicolau, Juan Pablo. (2020). *La telaraña: La trama exterior del procés*. Barcelona.

Carreras, Albert, Leandro Prados de la Escosura, and Joan R. Rosés (2005), "Renta and riqueza", in Albert Carreras and Xavier Tafunell (coords.) (2005), *Estadísticas históricas de España. Vol. III*, Bilbao, Fundación BBVA, 2ª ed., pp. 1365–1367.

Casassas, L., & Clusa, J. (1981). *L'organització territorial de Catalunya*. Barcelona.

Castells, A., R. Barberán, N. Bosch, N., M. Espasa, F. Rodrigo, F., and J. Ruiz-Huerta (2000): *Las balanzas fiscales de las Comunidades Autónomas (1991–1996). Análisis de los flujos fiscales de las Comunidades Autónomas con la Administración Central*, Barcelona, Ariel.

Castells, Antoni (coord.), Enoch Albertí, Francesc Amat, Núria Bosch, Ignacio Lago, Guillem López i Casasnovas, Toni Rodon, Albert Solé-Ollé and Maite Vilalta (2021), *Conseqüències econòmiques i financeres dels diferents escenaris de la relació Catalunya-Espanya*, Barcelona, Generalitat de Catalunya, Institut d'Estudis de l'Autogovern <https://presidencia.gencat.cat/web/.content/ambits_actuacio/desenvolupament_autogovern/iea/publicacions/01_IEAg/IEAg_arxius-i-vincles/IEAg-12.pdf>.

Castro Sanz, Carles. (2020). *Cómo derrotar al independentismo en las urnas*. Barcelona.

Cátedra José María Martín Patino de la Cultura del Encuentro (2018), *Informe España 2018* <https://blogs.comillas.edu/informeespana/wp-content/uploads/sites/93/2019/05/IE2018Cap5-1.pdf>.

Cayuela, Ricard (2019), «L'únic objectiu dels instigadors del procés era escripturar la finca», El Triangle, 7 December <https://www.eltriangle.eu/ca/entrevistes/lunic-objectiu-instigadors-proces-escripturar-finca_104387_102.html>.

CEOE (2019), *La producción normativa en 2018* <https://contenidos.ceoe.es/CEOE/var/pool/pdf/publications_docs-file-601-la-produccion-normativa-en-2018.pdf>.

Cercle d'Economia (2017), *Tras el 1-O. Para evitar los peores escenarios*, Barcelona, 4 October <https://cercledeconomia.com/es/tras-el-1-o-para-evitar-los-peores-escenarios>.

Chislett, William (2013), *Spain. What everyone needs to know*, Oxford, OUP.

Christophe Guilluy. (2018). *No society. La fin de la classe moyenne occidentale*. Flammarion.

C-Intereg (2019), *Comercio interregional* <https://www.c-intereg.es/informe-trimestral-de-c-intereg-julio-2019/>.

Closa, C. (2020). A Critique of the theory of democratic secession. In C. Closa, C. Margiotta, & G. Martinico (Eds.), *Between democracy and law. The amorality of secession*.

Col.lectiu Treva i Pau (2020), "¿Referéndum? No, gracias", *La Vanguardia*, 20 March.

Col.lectiu Wilson (2022), *Llista d'adherits* <http://www.wilson.cat/ca/component/chronoforms?chronoform=list_data>.

Colegio de Registradores de la Propiedad, Mercantiles y Bienes Muebles de España (CORPME) (2021), *Estadísticas Mercantiles* <http://www.registradores.org/>.

Coll, J., & Fernández, D. (2010). *A favor d'Espanya i del catalanisme. Un assaig contra la regressió política.* Barcelona.

Collado-Ramírez, Marc (2016), *L'estructura del discurs independentista: una proposta d'anàlisi mitjançant la metodologia de xarxes,* end of degree project in Political Science and Public Administration, Facultat de Ciències Polítiques i Sociologia, Universitat Autònoma de Barcelona <https://ddd.uab.cat/pub/tfg/2016/163110/TFG_mcolladoramirez.pdf>.

Colldeforns, Montserrat and M. Antònia Monés (2022), "Apunts per a una reforma federal del sistema de finançament autonòmic", *Papers de la Fundació Rafael Campalans,* No. 172 <https://fcampalans.cat/uploads/publicacions/pdf/frc_papersdelafundacio172_web.pdf>.

Comerford, D., & Rodríguez Mora, J. V. (2019). The gains from economic integration. *Economic Policy, 34*(98), 201–266. https://doi.org/10.1093/epolic/eiz004

Commission of the European Communities (1977), *The MacDougall Report (Volume I. Study group on the role of public finance in European integration,* Brussels <https://www.cvce.eu/content/publication/2012/5/31/c475e949-ed28-490b-81ae-a33ce9860d09/publishable_en.pdf>.

Consejo General de Economistas de España. Registro de Economistas and Asesores Fiscales. (2020). *Panorama de la Fiscalidad Autonómica y Foral, 2020.* REAF.

Consejo General de Economistas de España. Registro de Economistas and Asesores Fiscales. (2019). *Panorama de la Fiscalidad Autonómica and Foral, 2019.* CGEE.

Consell de l'Audiovisual de Catalunya (2020), *Informe 71/2020. Observança del pluralisme polític a la televisió i a la ràdio. Maig-desembre 2019* <https://www.cac.cat/sites/default/files/2020-05/Acord_43_2020_ca.pdf.pdf>.

Constitute Project (2022), *The World's Constitutions* <https://www.constituteproject.org/>.

Convivencia Cívica Catalana (2013), *El maquillaje de la balanza fiscal de Cataluña* <https://s.libertaddigital.com/doc/el-maquillaje-de-la-balanza-fiscal-de-cataluna-41912941.pdf>.

Convivencia Cívica Catalana (2018), *Las inversiones en infraestructuras en Cataluña. Licitación de obra pública. Análisis de los años 2011 a 2016* <http://files.convivenciacivica.org/Las%20inversiones%20en%20infraestructuras%20en%20Catalu%C3%B1a.pdf>.

Convivencia Cívica Catalana (2019a), *Análisis de la PIRLS 2016 en Cataluña* <https://files.convivenciacivica.org/Analisis%20de%20losin%20resultados%20de%20in%20PIRLS%20in%202016.pdf> on data from *PIRLS 2016 International Database* <https://timssandpirls.bc.edu/pirls2016/international-database/index.html>.

Convivencia Cívica Catalana (2019b), *Análisis de los resultados de PIRLS 2016 en Cataluña* <http://convivenciacivicacatalana.blogspot.com/p/informes.html>.

Convivencia Cívica Catalana (2019c), *La aportación del resto de España a la economía catalana ¿Cuántos empleos, beneficios empresariales y riqueza genera el resto de España en Cataluña?* <https://files.convivenciacivica.org/La%20aportaci%C3%B3n%20del%20resto%20de%20Espa%C3%B1a%20a%20la%20econom%C3%ADa%20catalana.pdf>.

Convivencia Cívica Catalana (2019d), *Las inversiones en infraestructuras en Cataluña. Licitación de obra pública. Análisis por administración* <http://files.convivenciacivica.org/Las%20inversiones%20en%20infraestructuras%20en%20Catalu%C3%B1a%202016.pdf>.

Convivencia Cívica Catalana (2019e), *Las lenguas de los comercios en Cataluña* <http://files.convivenciacivica.org/Las%20lenguas%20en%20los%20comercios%20de%20Catalu%C3%B1a.pdf>; and Convivencia Cívica Catalana (2018), *Las lenguas en las señales de tráfico en Cataluña* <http://files.convivenciacivica.org/Campa%C3%B1a%20por%20una%20se%C3%B1alizaci%C3%B3n%20biling%C3%BCe.pdf>.

Convivencia Cívica Catalana (2020), *Análisis del comercio de Cataluña. Las ventas catalanas al resto de España y al extranjero* <https://files.convivenciacivica.org/Analisis%20del%20Comercio%20de%20Catalu%C3%B1a.pdf>.

Council of the European Union (2019), "Council Recommendation of 9 July 2019 on the 2019 National Reform Programme of Spain and delivering a Council opinion on the 2019 Stability Programme of Spain, 2019/C 301/09", *Official Journal of the European Union*, Vol. 62, No. C 301 <https://eur-lex.europa.eu/legal-content/EN/TXT/PDF/?uri=OJ:C:2019:301:FULL&from=EN>.

Countryeconomy.com (2022), *Sovereigns Ratings List* <https://countryeconomy.com/ratings/spain>.

Credit Suisse (2012), «Catalonia's Choice», *Economics Research*, 19 November, <http://www.credit-suisse.com/researchandanalytics>.

Cuenca, José (2022), Cataluña y Québec. *Las mentiras del separatismo*, Sevilla, Renacimiento.

Davies, L. (2015). *Le nouvel égoisme territorial. Le gran malaise des nations.* Seuil.

DBRS Morningstar (2017), "Spain: Political Noise Rises as Catalonia's Planned Vote Nears", *Global Sovereign Ratings*, 30 August <https://www.dbrs.com/research/315566>.

De Carreras, Francesc (2014), *Paciencia e independencia: La agenda oculta del nacionalismo*, Barcelona, Ariel.

de España, Ramón (2013), *El manicomio catalán*, Madrid, La esfera de los libros.

de la Fuente, Ángel (2014), "¿Maltrato fiscal?", in Ángel de la Fuente and Clemente Polo (2014), *La cuestión catalana II. Balanzas fiscales and tratamiento fiscal de Cataluña*, Madrid, Instituto de Estudios Fiscales, pp. 11–29.

de la Fuente, Ángel (2019), "La evolución de la financiación de las comunidades autónomas de régimen común, 2002–2017", *BBVA Research. Documento de trabajo*, No. 19/12.

de la Fuente, Ángel, and Sevi Rodríguez Mora (2012), "Las cuentas de la lechera", *El País*, 24 September.

de la Fuente, Ángel, Michael Thöne, and Christian Kastrop (2016), "Regional Financing in Germany and Spain: Comparative Reform Perspectives", *Fedea Policy Papers*, No. 2016/05.

de la Fuente, Ángel, Ramón Barberán and Ezequiel Uriel (2014), *Informe sobre la dimensión territorial de la actuación de las Administraciones Públicas* <https://www.fundacionsepi.es/investigacion/publicaciones/otrasPublicaciones/Dimensi%C3%B3n%20territorial%20Act.%20AAPP%20propuesta%20metodologica.pdf>.

de Ramón Jacob-Ernst, Juan Claudio (2018), *Diccionario de lugares comunes sobre Cataluña. Breviario de tópicos, recetas fallidas e ideas que no funcionan para resolver la crisis catalana*, Barcelona, Deusto.

Delgado-Téllez, Mar, Víctor D. Lledó, and Javier J. Pérez (2017), "On the Determinants of Fiscal Non-Compliance: An Empirical Analysis of Spain's Regions", *IMF Working Paper*, WP/17/5.

Derblauemond (2017), *La economía de guerra y el problema catalán*, 9 October <https://www.elblogsalmon.com/>.

Deutsche Bank Research (2015), "Better off on their own? Economic aspects of regional autonomy and independence movements in Europe", *EU Monitor. European Integration*, 6 February <https://www.dbresearch.com/prod/rps_en-prod/prod0000000000441775/better_off_on_their_own%3f_economic_aspects_of_regio.pdf>.

Dion, Stéphane (n.d.), *Straight Talk: Speeches and Writings on Canadian Unity*, Montreal, Quebec, McGill-Queen's University Press, 2000.

Dolça Catalunya (2018), "La Generalitat compra a 533 medios de comunicación con al menos 310.000.000 € al año", *Dolça Catalunya*, 14 January <https://www.dolcacatalunya.com/2018/01/la-generalitat-compra-533-medios-comunicacion-al-menos-310-000-000e-al-ano/>.

Dolça Catalunya (2019a), "Un vídeo i un gràfic que resumeixen la Marmotada 2019", *Dolça Catalunya*, 11 September <https://www.dolcacatalunya.com/2019/09/un-video-i-un-grafic-que-ensorren-la-marmotada–2019/>.

Dolça Catalunya. (2019b). *Dolça Catalunya. Tenemos un problema. Se llama nacionalismo. Lo vamos a superar.*

Dolça Catalunya (2020a), "A Tordera també resisteixen", *Dolça Catalunya*, 24 June <https://www.dolcacatalunya.com/2020/06/a-tordera-tambe-resisteixen/?fbclid=IwAR1dTzYbdu8hDmV5eU3LsOfZYhcUv41NVqlCeCAqVjkhZkXv41kIJgoirkY>.

314 REFERENCES

Dolça Catalunya (2020b), "Desplome apocalíptico de la Marmotada", *Dolça Catalunya*, 11 September <https://www.dolcacatalunya.com/2020/09/desplome-apocaliptico-de-la-marmotada/>.

Drakulić, Slavenka (2017), "Entrevista con la gran cronista de los Balcanes: 'El virus del nacionalismo ha despertado en España'", *El Confidencial*, 8 October: "Hay muy poco interés en la reconciliación porque la reconciliación depende de la verdad y esto es realmente difícil de conseguir." <https://www.elconfidencial.com/mundo/2017-10-08/independencia-catalana-nacionalismo-balcanes-espana_1457330/>.

Durán-Pich, Alfons, and Joaquim Torra i Pla (2012), *Catalunya, a la independència per la butxaca*, Barcelona, El fil d'Ariadna.

Economist Intelligence Unit, The (n.d.), *Democracy Index* <https://www.eiu.com/n/democracy-index-2021-less-than-half-the-world-lives-in-a-democracy/>.

Economist, The (2018), *The Strain in Spain. Special Report*, London, The Economist.

EFE (2019), "Casi 600 heridos, 200 detenciones, daños... Las cifras de una semana de disturbios", *La Vanguardia*, 20 October <https://www.lavanguardia.com/politica/20191020/471095242135/cataluna-disturbios-detenidos-policia-heridos-barcelona.html>.

EFE (2020), "Abren expediente sancionador a la Asamblea Catalana por su campaña de boicot a empresas no independentistas", *20 Minutos*, 21 December <https://amp.20minutos.es/noticia/4519473/0/abren-expediente-sancionador-a-la-asamblea-catalana-por-su-campana-de-boicot-a-empresas-no-independentistas>.

El Confidencial (2017), *Elecciones catalanas* <https://www.elconfidencial.com/espana/cataluna/elecciones-catalanas/2017-12-22/resultados-municipios-comarcas-independentistas-constitutionalists_1497168/>.

El Confidencial Digital (2018), "Las 22 veces que Europa ha dicho "no" a la independencia de Cataluña", 1 March <https://www.elconfidencialdigital.com/articulo/politica/veces-Europa-dicho-independencia-Cataluna/20180228190710088609.html>.

El Corredor Mediterráneo (2022), *Quiero Corredor* <https://elcorredormediterraneo.com/estado-de-las-obras>.

El Cronista del Estado Social and Democrático de Derecho (2017), *El Cronista del Estado Social and Democrático de Derecho*, No. 71-72, monográfico ¿Cataluña independiente? <https://dialnet.unirioja.es/ejemplar/470557>.

El País (2019), "Resumen del 11 de septiembre", *El País*, 11 September <https://elpais.com/tag/fecha/20190911>.

Elliot, J. H. (2020). *Scots and Catalans: Union and Disunion*. CT, Yale UP.

Elliott, J. H. (2006). *Imperios del mundo atlántico: España y Gran Bretaña en América (1492–1830)*. Taurus.

Elliott, J. H. (2009). *Spain, Europe and the Wider World, 1500–1800*. CT, Yale UP.

Enache, Cristina (2019), *Índice Autonómico de Competitividad Fiscal (IACF) 2019*, Madrid, Fundación para el Avance de la Libertad <http://www.fundalib.org/wp-content/uploads/2019/10/IACF-2019-final-baja-resoluci%C3%B3n.pdf>.

Escrivá, Ángeles, and Esteban Urreiztieta (2018), "El Govern ocultó datos sobre la inviabilidad de la secesión", *El Mundo*, 19 March <https://www.elmundo.es/espana/2018/03/19/5aaeb662468aeb57218b 45e3.html>.

Europa Press (2019), "Los jubilados evitan Catalunya: el 40%de plazas del Imserso, sin cubrir", *La Vanguardia*, 13 November <https://www.lavanguardia.com/economia/20191113/471579113342/cataluna-imserso-viajes-jubilados-proces-disturbios.html>.

Europa Press (2020), "La ocupación hotelera en Barcelona apenas llega al 10%este verano por la crisis del covid", *Catalunya*, 16 September <https://www.europapress.es/catalunya/noticia-ocupacion-hoteles-barcelona-apenas-llega-10-verano-crisis-covid-20200916120727.html>.

Europa Press (2021), "Resultados elecciones Cataluña 14 de febrero de 2021, en datos and gráficos", *epdata* <https://www.epdata.es/datos/resultados-elecciones-cataluna-14-febrero-2021-datos-graficos/576>.

European Commission (2014), *Eurobarometer*, No. 709.2.

European Commission (2019a), *European Quality of Government Index 2017* <https://ec.europa.eu/regional_policy/en/newsroom/news/2018/02/27-02-2018-european-quality-of-government-index-2017>.

European Commission (2019b), *European Regional Competitiveness Index* <https://ec.europa.eu/regional_policy/mapapps/regional_comp/rci2019.html>.

European Commission (2019c), *European Social Progress Index* <https://ec.europa.eu/regional_policy/en/information/maps/social_progress>

European Commission. Directorate-General for Regional and Urban Policy (2022), *Annual Regional Database* ARDECO <https://knowledge4policy.ec.europa.eu/territorial/ardeco-database_en>.

European Commission. Directorate-General for Regional and Urban Policy (2018), *Final report on updating the Regional Authority Index (RAI) for forty-five countries (2010–2016)* <https://op.europa.eu/en/publication-detail/-/publication/5562196f-3d3a-11e8-b5fe-01aa75ed71a1>.

European Parliament (2022a), *Report on foreign interference in all democratic processes in the European Union, including disinformation (2020/2268(INI))* <https://www.europarl.europa.eu/doceo/document/A-9-2022-0022_EN.html>.

European Parliament (2022b), *Debates on the Council and Commission statements. 18. The relations of the Russian government and diplomatic network with parties of extremist, populist, anti-European and certain other European political parties in the context of the war* <https://www.europarl.europa.eu/doceo/document/CRE-9-2022-07-06_EN.html#creitem30>.

European Patent Office (2022), *European Patent Applications* <https://www.epo.org/about-us/annual-reports-statistics/statistics.html>.

European Union (2022), *Treaty on the European Union* <https://eur-lex.europa.eu/resource.html?uri=cellar:2bf140bf-a3f8-4ab2-b506-fd71826e6da6.0023.02/DOC_1&format=PDF>

Eurostat (2022a), *Database* <https://ec.europa.eu/eurostat/web/main/data/database>.

Eurostat (2022b), *Estadísticas de migración y población migrante* <https://ec.europa.eu/eurostat/statistics-explained/index.php?title=Migration_and_migrant_population_statistics/es>

Eurostat (2022c), *Population on 1 January by sex, citizenship, and broad group of country of birth* <https://ec.europa.eu/eurostat/databrowser/view/MIGR_POP5CTZ__custom_647694/default/table?lang=e>.

Eurostat (2022d), *Statistics by theme* <https://ec.europa.eu/eurostat/data/browse-statistics-by-theme>.

Expansión (2022), *Datosmacro* <https://www.epdata.es/datos/listas-espera-sanidad-publica-datos-graficos-comunidad-autonoma/28/cataluna/297>.

F. Will, George (2020), "Catalan secessionists ladle a soup of fiction and paranoia", *The Washington Post*, 24 January <https://www.washingtonpost.com/opinions/catalan-secessionists-ladle-a-soup-of-fiction-and-paranoia/2020/01/23/b5e62280-3e0a-11ea-baca-eb7ace0a3455_story.html>.

Fàbregas, Laura, and Alberto Sierra (2022), "Junqueras y otros líderes de ERC se reunieron con una 'agente rusa' tras recibir los indultos", *The Objective*, 23 March <https://theobjective.com/espana/2022-03-23/junqueras-erc-agente-rusa-eurocamara/>.

Farrow, Ronan (2022), "How Democracies Spy on their Citizens", The New Yorker, Issue April 25 & May 2 <https://www.newyorker.com/magazine/2022/04/25/how-democracies-spy-on-their-citizens>.

Federal Republic of Germany (2022), *Basic Law for the Federal Republic of Germany* <https://www.gesetze-im-internet.de/englisch_gg/englisch_gg.html#p0184>

Feito Higueruela, José Luis (2014), *Razones y sinrazones económicas del independentismo catalán*, Madrid, Panel Cívico <http://panelcivico.es/images/archivos/razones_y_sinrazones_economicas_del_independentismo_catalan.pdf>.

Fernández Leiceaga, Xoaquín, and Santiago Lago Peñas (2016), "Balanzas fiscales vs cuentas públicas territorializadas: Análisis and valoración de las diferencias", *Revista de Estudios Regionales*, No. 105, pp. 225–262.

Fernández, Antonio (2021), "Separatismo de talonario: Cataluña destinó miles de euros en comprar 'amigos' fuera", *El Confidencial*, 4 de mayo

<https://www.elconfidencial.com/espana/cataluna/2021-05-04/cataluna-subvencion-onu-banco-mundial_3061675/>.

Fidrmuc, Jan, and Jarko Fidrmuc (2000), "Disintegration and Trade", *Review of International Economics*, Vol.11, No. 5, pp. 811–829.

Fitch Ratings (2014), "Fitch Places Autonomous Community of Catalonia and Institut Catala de Finances on RWN", *Ratings Endorsement Policy*, 29 September <https://www.fitchratings.com/site/pr/884815>.

Fitch Ratings (2019), Interactive Sovereign Rating Model <https://www.fitchratings.com/research/sovereigns/interactive-sovereign-rating-model-05-05-2020>.

Foment del Treball Nacional (2017), *La movilidad empresarial derivada del contexto político en Cataluña*, 28 October <https://www.foment.com/wp-content/uploads/2017/11/Presentaci%C3%B3n-Nota-de-Econom%C3%ADa.pdf>.

Foment del Treball Nacional (2022), *El dèficit d'inversió en infraestructures a Catalunya 2009–2020* <https://www.foment.com/wp-content/uploads/2022/01/El-deficit-dinversio-en-infraestructures-a-Catalunya-2009-2020.pdf>.

Foment del Treball Nacional. Comissió d'Infraestructures i Equipaments (2020), *Catàleg d'infraestructures bàsiques pendents d'executar a Catalunya. CAT-100*, June <https://www.foment.com/wp-content/uploads/2020/07/Cataleg-infraestructures-basiques_-Actualitzacio_2020.pdf>.

Forbes (2022), *Forbes Lists* <https://www.forbes.com/lists/list-directory/#85e8b69b274d> and Global Entrepreneurship Monitor (2019), *Informe GEM España 2018–2019* <http://www.gem-spain.com/wp-content/uploads/2019/05/GEM2018-2019.pdf>.

Freedom House (2019), *Freedom in the World 2019* <https://freedomhouse.org/sites/default/files/Feb2019_FH_FITW_2019_Report_ForWeb-compressed.pdf>

Freixes Sanjuan, Teresa, and Juan Carlos Gavara de Cara (coords.) (2018), *Repensar la Constitución. Ideas para una reforma de la Constitución de 1978: reforma y comunicación dialógica*, Madrid, CEPC-BOE, 2 vols.

Fukuyama, F. (2018). *Identity: Contemporary Identity Politics and the Struggle for Recognition*. Profile Books.

GAD3 (2017), *Encuesta sobre la imagen de Catalunya* <https://societatcivilcatalana.cat/sites/default/files/encuesta-gad3-2017>.

GAD3 (2021), *Investigación sociopolítica en Cataluña*, Madrid, GAD3.

Delgado, G., Luis, J., Alonso, J. A., & Jiménez, J. C. (2012). *Valor económico del español*. Barcelona.

Generalitat de Catalunya (2020), *Eleccions al Parlament de Catalunya* <http://gencat.cat/economia/resultats-parlament2017/09AU/DAU09999>.

Generalitat de Catalunya (2022a), *Normativa electoral* <http://www.gencat.cat/governacio/parlament2015/es/normativa-electoral/index.html>.

Generalitat de Catalunya. Centre d'Estudis d'Opinió (2017), *Baròmetre d'Opinió Política. 1a onada 2017* <https://ceo.gencat.cat/ca/barometre/detall/index. html?id=6168>

Generalitat de Catalunya. Centre d'Estudis d'Opinió (2022b), *Baròmetre d'Opinió Política. 1a onada 2022* <https://ceo.gencat.cat/ca/barometre/detall/index. html?id=8308>.

Generalitat de Catalunya. Centre d'Estudis d'Opinió (2019), *Barómetro de Opinión Política. 2ª ola 2019* <http://upceo.ceo.gencat.cat/wsceop/7188/ Dossier%20de%20premsa%20-942.pdf>. The Spanish version of this report is full of spelling and grammatical mistakes, from the title to the last page. That it be published like this is an

Generalitat de Catalunya. Centre d'Estudis d'Opinió (2021), *Baròmetre d'Opinió Política. 3a onada 2020* <https://ceo.gencat.cat/es/barometre/detall/index. html?id=7808>.

Generalitat de Catalunya. Consell Assessor per a la Transició Nacional (2014), *La viabilitat fiscal i financera d'una Catalunya independent* <http://dades.grup-naciodigital.com/redaccio/publicitat/18.pdf>.

Generalitat de Catalunya. Consell Assessor per a la Transició Nacional (2014a), *Les relacions comercials entre Catalunya i Espanya* <https://presidencia.gencat. cat/web/.content/ambits_actuacio/consells_assessors/catn/informes/ inf_11_relacions_comercials.pdf>.

Generalitat de Catalunya. Consell Assessor per a la Transició Nacional (2014b), *Llibre blanc de la Transició Nacional de Catalunya* <https:// presidencia.gencat.cat/ca/ambits_d_actuacio/desenvolupament_autogov-ern/comissionat-de-la-presidencia-per-al-desplegament-de-lautogovern/ llibre-blanc-de-la-transicio-nacional-de-catalunya/>.

Generalitat de Catalunya. Departament de la Vicepresidència i d'Economia i Hisenda (2020), *Els pressupostos de la Generalitat de Catalunya per al 2020* <http://economia.gencat.cat/ca/ambits-actuacio/pressupostos/2020/>.

German Federal Constitutional Court (2016), Verfassungsbeschwerde gegen die Nichtzulassung einer Volksabstimmung über den Austritt Bayerns aus der BRD erfolglos <https://www.bundesverfassungsgericht.de/SharedDocs/ Entscheidungen/DE/2016/12/rk20161216_2bvr034916.html>.

GESOP (2014), *Barómetro Político de Cataluña, marzo 2014* <https://cronica-global.elespanol.com/politica/ni-son-chonis-ni-son-independentistas_ 6506_102.html>.

GESOP (2017), *Encuesta del GESOP para Societat Civil Catalana. Informe de resultados 2017* <https://www.societatcivilcatalana.cat/sites/default/files/ docs/1034_GESOP_Informe_para_SCC_febrero_2017_castella.pdf>

Global Power City Index (2022), *Barcelona in the Rankings* <https://www.barce-lonaglobal.org/es/know-how/barcelona-en-los-rankings/>

Globalization and World Cities Research Network (2022), *The World According to GaWC 2021* <https://www.lboro.ac.uk/gawc/index.html>.

Government of Spain (2022), *Institutions of Spain* <https://www.lamoncloa.gob.es/lang/en/espana/spanishinstitutions/Paginas/index.aspx>.

Gozzer, Stefania (2017), "Lo que pierden España and Cataluña si se separan", *BBC Mundo*, 27 October <https://www.bbc.com/mundo/noticias-internacional-41513571>.

Grijelmo, Àlex (2017), "Nunca hubo un millón", *El País*, 3 October <https://elpais.com/elpais/2017/09/29/opinion/1506674781_614116.html>.

Guix, Pau (2017), *El hijo de la africana: Reflexiones de un catalán libre de nacionalismo*, Barcelona, Hildy.

Guixà, José, and Manuel Trallero (2019), *Pujol: todo era mentira (1930–1962). Desvelando el relato fundacional independentista*, Córdoba, Almuzara.

Helliwell, J. F. (1998). *How Much do National Borders Matter?* Washington.

Hermi Zaa, Miriam, and Manuel Blas García Ávila. (2019). El intento secesionista en Cataluña (España) y la movilidad del capital. *Atelié Geográfico*, *13*(1), 6–34.

His Majesty King Felipe VI (2017), *Mensaje*, 3 October <https://www.rtve.es/alacarta/videos/telediario/mensaje-integro-del-rey-tras-referendum-cataluna/4247341/>.

Ibarz, M. (2019). *La corrupción en España: Un pozo sin fondo*. Barcelona.

Informa DB (2019), *Comparativa de Madrid y Cataluña* <https://cdn.informa.es/sites/5c1a2fd74c7cb3612da076ea/content_entry5c5021510fa1c000c25b51f0/5d81ee0e0d773500b2d55a88/files/Comp_Madrid_Cataluna_2019.pdf?1568796174>.

INSEAD (2021), *2021 Global Talent Competitiveness Index* <https://gtcistudy.com/the-gtci-index/#gtci-country-comparison-view/Switzerland/CH>.

Institut d'Estadística de Catalunya (2021), *Anuari estadístic de Catalunya* <https://www.idescat.cat/pub/?id=aec&n=246&lang=es>.

Institut d'Estadística de Catalunya (2022a), *Anuari estadístic de Catalunya* <https://www.idescat.cat/pub/?id=aec&n=198&lang=es>.

Institut d'Estadística de Catalunya (2022b), *GDP i GDP per habitant* <https://www.idescat.cat/pub/?id=aec&n=358&lang=es>.

Institut d'Estadística de Catalunya (2022c), *Generalitat de Catalunya. Pressupostos* <https://www.idescat.cat/pub/?id=aec&n=535&lang=es>.

Institut d'Estadística de Catalunya (2022d), *Indicadores anuales* <https://www.idescat.cat/indicadors/?id=conj&n=10246&lang=es>.

Institut d'Estadística de Catalunya (2022e), *Indicadors de natalitat* <https://www.idescat.cat/pub/?id=aec&n=287&lang=es&t=2002>.

Institut d'Estadística de Catalunya (2022f), *Marco Input-Output de Cataluña 2014* <https://www.idescat.cat/pub/?id=mioc&lang=es>.

Institut d'Estadística de Catalunya (2022g), *Població* <https://www.idescat.cat/tema/xifpo>.

Institut d'Estadística de Catalunya (2022h), *Población extranjera por comarcas* <https://www.idescat.cat/poblacioestrangera/?b=4&lang=es>.

Institut d'Estadística de Catalunya (2022i), *Producte interior brut (Base 2010). Oferta. Avanç* <https://www.idescat.cat/indicadors/?id=conj&n=10233>.

Institut d'Estadística de Catalunya (2022j), *Sector público Generalitat. Presupuesto. Gastos. Por áreas políticas de gasto* <https://www.idescat.cat/pub/?id=aec&n=683&lang=es>.

Instituto de Estudios Económicos (2022), *Libro Blanco para la reforma fiscal en España. Una reflexión de 60 expertos para el diseño de un sistema fiscal competitivo y eficiente*, Madrid, IEE <https://www.ieemadrid.es/wp-content/uploads/IEE.-LIBRO-BLANCO-para-la-reforma-fiscal-en-Espana.pdf>.

Instituto Nacional de Estadística (2020a), "Contabilidad Regional de España", *Notas de Prensa*, 17 December <https://www.ine.es/prensa/cre_2019_2.pdf>.

Instituto Nacional de Estadística (2020b), *Contabilidad regional de España* <https://www.ine.es/dyngs/INEbase/es/operacion.htm?c=Estadistica_C&cid=1254736167628&menu=resultados&idp=1254735576581#!tabs-1254736158133>.

Instituto Nacional de Estadística (2020c), *PIB y PIB per cápita. Serie 2000–2019* <https://www.ine.es/dyngsINEbase/esoperacion.htm?c=Estadistica_C&cid=1254736167628&menu=resultados&idp=1254735576581#!tabs-1254736158133>.

Instituto Nacional de Estadística (2022a), *Cifras de población y Censos demográficos* <https://www.ine.es/dyngs/INEbase/es/categoria.htm?c=Estadistica_P&cid=1254735572981>.

Instituto Nacional de Estadística (2022b), *Datos por temas* <https://www.ine.es/>.

Instituto Nacional de Estadística (2022c), *Estadísticas territoriales* <https://www.ine.es/jaxiT3/###Table.htm?t=4247>.

Instituto Nacional de Estadística (2022d), *Inversión extranjera directa en España* <https://www.ine.es/dyngs/IOE/es/fichaProg.htm?cid=1259946010777>.

Instituto Nacional de Estadística (2022e), *Principales series de Población desde 1998* <https://www.ine.es/jaxi/Datos.htm?path=/t20/e245/p08/l0/&file=02001.px#!tabs-###Table>.

International Institute for Democracy and Electoral Assistance (2022), *Global State of Democracy* <https://www.idea.int/-publications/catalogue/global-state-of-democracy-2019?lang=en>.

Intervención General del Estado (2022), *Ejecución de inversiones reales del sector público empresarial por CCAA* <https://www.igae.pap.hacienda.gob.es/sitios/igae/es-ES/Contabilidad/ContabilidadPublica/CPE/EjecucionPresupuestaria/Paginas/isdistribucioninversion.aspx>.

Italian Republic (2022), The Constitution of the Italian Republic <http://www.prefettura.it/FILES/AllegatiPag/1187/Costituzione_ENG.pdf>.

Jaigu, Charles (2019), "Pourquoi la Catalogne est devenue folle", *Le Figaro*, 20 February <https://www.lefigaro.fr/vox/monde/2019/02/20/31002-20190220ARTFIG00238-pourquoi-la-catalogne-est-devenue-folle.php>.

Jaume, Francisco (1907), *El separatismo en Cataluña. Sociología aplicada. Crítica del catalanismo según el análisis de los hechos*, Barcelona, Imprenta de Francisco Altés y Alabart.

Jiménez Losantos, Federico (2019), *Barcelona. La ciudad que fue: La libertad y la cultura que el nacionalismo destruyó*, Madrid, La esfera de los libros, 2ª ed.

Johnson, Enrique, and Yeray Carretero (2017), "Informe sobre el impacto del desafío independentista", *Reputation Institute* <https://documentcloud.adobe.com/link/review?uri=urn:aaid:scds:US:1341c361-86e3-4afa-b594-2fc06bd4515d#pageNum=32>.

Jorrín, Javier G., and Jesús Escudero (2019), "Cataluña se queda atrás en la carrera con Madrid por liderar la economía española", *El Confidencial*, 28 de septiembre <https://www.elconfidencial.com/economia/2019-09-28/exodo-urbano-espana-cataluna-madrid-poblacion_2240171/>.

Jorrín, Javier G., María Zuil, and Jesús Escudero (2019), "La metropolización de Madrid vacía las provincias ricas de España", *El Confidencial*, 27 September <https://www.elconfidencial.com/economia/2019-09-27/exodo-urbano-espana-llegadas-madrid-ciudades_2240155>.

Kamen, Henry (2015), *España y Cataluña. Historia de una pasión*, Madrid, La Esfera.

Kearney (2019), *2019 Global Cities Report* <https://www.atkearney.com/global-cities/2019>.

Klein, Nicolas (2018). "Le séparatisme ruine la Catalogne", *Le Figaro*, 9 January <https://www.lefigaro.fr/vox/economie/2018/01/09/31007-20180109ARTFIG00122-nicolas-klein-le-separatisme-ruine-la-catalogne.php>.

Klemperer, Victor (1947), *Language of the Third Reich: LTI: Lingua Tertii Imperii*, London, Bloomsbury, 2013.

Laínz, Jesús (2010), *Negocio and traición: La burguesía catalana de Felipe V a Felipe VI*, Madrid, Encuentro.

Laínz, Jesús (2011), *Desde Santurce a Bizancio: El poder nacionalizador de las palabras*, Madrid, Encuentro.

Laínz, Jesús (2017), *El privilegio catalán. 300 años de negocio de la burguesía catalana*, Madrid, Encuentro.

Llaneras, Kiko (2021), "Así se relacionan en Cataluña la renta, el voto, el origen y la independencia", *El País*, 20 February <https://elpais.com/politica/2021/02/19/actualidad/1613741557_146092.amp.html>.

Llorca-Asensi, Elena, Alexander Sánchez Díaz, Maria-Elena Fabregat-Cabrera, and Raúl Ruiz-Callado (2021), ""Why Can't We?" Disinformation and Right to Self-Determination. The Catalan Conflict on Twitter", *Social Sciences*, No. 10: 383. <https://doi.org/10.3390/socsci10100383>.

Lluch, Ernest (1992), "¿Cataluña expoliada?", *La Vanguardia*, 13 August <http://hemeroteca.lavanguardia.com/preview/1992/08/13/pagina-12/33521851/pdf.html>.

López Alegre, Joan (2020), "La 'procesización' de la política española", *Economía Digital*, 13 June <https://ideas.economiadigital.es/joan-lopez-alegre/la-procesizacion-de-la-politica-espanola_20072130_102.html>.

Luján, Enrique (2019), "Una élite clandestina está a punto de lograr el control efectivo de todo un territorio, operando desde la oscuridad", *Despierta al futuro*, 17 October <http://despiertaalfuturo.blogspot.com/2019/10/una-elite-clandestina-esta-punto-de.html>.

Macià, M., & Martí, P. (2022). *Els que manen: Vida i miracles de les 50 famílies que mouen els fils de Catalunya*. Barcelona.

Madiès, Thierry, Grégoire Rota-Grasiozi, Jean-Pierre Tranchant, and Cyril Trépier (2018), "The economics of secession: A review of legal, theoretical, and empirical aspects", *Swiss Journal of Economics and Statistics*, Vol. 154, No.1, pp. 142–154 <https://doi.org/10.1186/s41937-017-0015-6>.

Madridejos Muñoz, Martín (2016), *El ciclo de protesta del independentismo catalán: Un análisis del periodo 2009–2016*, end of degree project in Political Science and Public Administration, Facultat de Ciències Polítiques i de Sociologia, Universitat Autònoma de Barcelona <https://ddd.uab.cat/pub/tfg/2016/163129/TFG_mmadridejosmunoz.pdf>.

Magallón, Eduardo (2019), "Sólo Madrid, Baleares, Canarias y Murcia cubren el pago de pensiones", *La Vanguardia*, 25 March <https://www.lavanguardia.com/economia/20190325/461210858274/pensiones-espana-comunidades-autonomas-deficit.html>

Magallón, Eduardo (2020), "Catalunya recibirá el 16,5% de la inversión estatal, menos que su peso en el PIB", *La Vanguardia*, 28 October <https://www.lavanguardia.com/economia/20201028/4959602249/inversiones-catalunya-PIB-regionalizable-presupuestos-estado-2021.html>.

Malet Perdigó, Jaime (2015), "¿Adónde vas, Catalunya?", *La Vanguardia*, 16 November.

Maluquer i Sostres, Joaquim (1963), *L'estructura econòmica de les terres catalanes*, Barcelona, Barcino.

Mangas Martin, Araceli (2014), "Cataluña: ¿No habrá independencia?", *El Cronista del Estado Social and Democrático de Derecho*, No. 42, pp. 54–65.

Many authors (2014a), *El coste de la no-España*, Madrid, Fundación Progreso and Democracia.

Many authors (2015), *Scenarios of Macro-economic Development for Catalonia on Horizon 2030. Economic effects of a potential secession of Catalonia from Spain and paths for integration with the EU. Final Report*, Barcelona, CIDOB <https://www.vilaweb.cat/media/continguts/000/104/312/312.pdf>.

Many authors (2019), "Conseqüències econòmiques del 'procés'", *Política i Prosa*, No. 7, May.

Many authors (2014b), *20 preguntas con respuesta sobre la secesión de Cataluña*, Madrid, FAES <https://fundacionfaes.org/file_upload/publication/pdf/2015062913291520_preguntas_con_respuesta_sobre_la_secesion_de_cataluna.pdf>.

Marginedas, Marc (2020): "Rússia, Catalunya i el 'procés', una història que es repeteix", *Política i Prosa*, 10 March <https://www.politicaprosa.com/russia-catalunya-i-el-proces-una-historia-que-es-repeteix/>.

Marín, Salvador, and Raúl Mínguez (dirs.), *45 años de evolución económica, social y empresarial de las Comunidades Autónomas en España, 1975–2020. Una visión por Comunidades*, Madrid, Consejo General de Cámaras de España <https://www.camara.es/sites/default/files/publicaciones/45-caa1502_1.pdf>.

Marks, Gary (2021), *Regional Authority Index* <https://garymarks.web.unc.edu/>.

Martí, Ernesto Wetzel (2020), *La demencia catalana. El hundimiento de un país en 62 entradas, 2011–2020* <https://www.amazon.es/demencia-catalana-hundimiento-entradas-2011-2019-ebook/dp/B07N6FQ27S>.

Mas i Gavarró, Artur (2012), "Debat sobre l'orientació política general del Govern", *Diari de Sessions del Parlament de Catalunya*, Serie P, No. 67, 25 September <https://www.parlament.cat/document/dspcp/57786.pdf>.

Mas-Colell, Andreu (2014), "El Estado obtendrá en el 2015 de Catalunya 3.228 millones más de los que gastará", *El Periódico*, 4 December <https://www.elperiodico.com/es/economia/20141204/el-estado-obtendra-en-el-2015-de-catalunya-3228-millones-mas-de-los-que-gastara-3744285>.

Maskin, Eric (2015), "Plantear una secesión da más beneficios que conseguirla", in "La Contra", *La Vanguardia*, 19 February.

McKinsey (2019), *Brexit: The bigger picture—Revitalizing UK exports in the new world of trade* <https://www.mckinsey.com/featured-insights/europe/brexit-the-bigger-picture-revitalizing-uk-exports-in-the-new-world-of-trade>.

Miguel Fernández-Dols, José (2018), "Fina lluvia de odio", *El asterisco. Notas y opiniones al margen*, 3 June <https://www.elasterisco.es/author/aut_079/#.Xdl9Uuj0nBQ>.

Millo, Enric (2020), *El derecho a saber la verdad. El testimonio del Delegado del Gobierno en la Cataluña del 155*, Barcelona, Península.

Ministerio de Asuntos Exteriores y Cooperación (2014a), *Cataluña en España. Por la convivencia democrática* <http://www.exteriores.gob.es/portal/es/saladeprensa/multimedia/publicaciones/documents/porlaconvivencia/por%20la%20convivencia%20democratica.pdf>.

Ministerio de Asuntos Exteriores y Cooperación (2014b), *Consecuencias económicas de una hipotética independencia de Cataluña* <http://www.exteriores.gob.es/Portal/es/SalaDePrensa/ElMinisterioInforma/Documents/Consecuencias%20econ%C3%B3micas%20de%20una%20hipot%C3%A9tica%20independencia%20de%20Catalu%C3%B1a.pdf>.

Ministerio de Educación y Formación Profesional (2022), *Resultados TIMSS de matemáticas y de ciencias, 2019* <https://www.educacionyfp.gob.es/inec/evaluaciones-internacionales/timss/timss-2019.html>.

Ministerio de Hacienda (2020), *Financiación Autonómica* <https://www.hacienda.gob.es/esES/Areas%20Tematicas/Financiacion%20Autonomica/Paginas/Financiacion%20Autonomica.aspx>.

Ministerio de Hacienda (2021), *Informe sobre el impacto del sector público autonómico en la actividad económico-financiera de las Comunidades Autónomas* <https://serviciostelematicosext.hacienda.gob.es/SGCIEF/ISPANET/index.aspx?ejercicio=2020&periodo=01>.

Ministerio de Hacienda y Administraciones Públicas (2016), *Sistema de Cuentas Públicas Territorializadas* <https://www.hacienda.gob.es/Documentacion/Publico/GabineteMinistro/Notas%20Prensa/2015/S.E.%20administraciones%20p%c3%9ablicas/21-07-15%20np%20cuentas%20territorializadas.pdf>.

Ministerio de Industria, Comercio y Turismo (2022), *Inversiones extranjeras* <https://comercio.gob.es/Inversionesexteriores/Paginas/Index.asp>.

Ministerio de Justicia (2021), *Reales Decretos 456/2021 a 464/2021, Boletín Oficial del Estado*, 23 June <https://www.boe.es/boe/dias/2021/06/23/>.

Ministerio del Interior (2022), *Resultados electorales* <http://www.infoelectoral.mir.es/infoelectoral/min>.

Miró, Manuel (2022), "Auge y caída del Tribunal de Cuentas", *elliberal.cat*, 20 July <https://www.elliberal.cat/2022/07/20/opinion-auge-y-caida-del-tribunal-de-cuentas/>.

Mitchell, Daniel J. (2016), "Secession, Federalism, and National Comity", *International Liberty*, 17 November <https://danieljmitchell.wordpress.com/2016/11/17/secession-federalism-and-national-comity-plus-more-intentional-and-unintentional-election-related-humor/>.

Moody's Investors Service (2014), "Catalunya independence debate likely to shift to greater devolution within Spain", *Issuer Comment*, 20 October <https://ep00.epimg.net/descargables/2014/10/21/ada5e956ede78972eda734da-b37e80b4.pdf>.

Morel, S. (2018). *En el huracán catalán. Una mirada privilegiada al laberinto del procés*. Barcelona.

Morgan Stanley (2014), "Spain: Catalonia Independence: 'What If' Scenarios", *Morgan Stanley Research*, 8 October.

Moss, George L. (1975), *The Nationalization of the Masses: Political Symbolism and Mass Movements in Germany, from the Napoleonic Wars Through the Third Reich*, New York, NY, Howard Fertig.

Mouzo Quintáns, Jessica (2019), "Las listas de espera se disparan desde que Torra está en el Govern", *El País*, 26 March <https://elpais.com/ccaa/2019/03/25/catalunya/1553541446_950963.html>.

Muñoz Machado, Santiago (2012), *Informe sobre España: Repensar el Estado o destruirlo*, Barcelona, Crítica.

Muñoz Machado, Santiago (2014), *Cataluña y las demás Españas*, Barcelona, Crítica.

Muñoz, J., & Tormos, R. (2015). Economic expectations and support for secession in Catalonia: between causality and rationalization. *European Political Science Review*, 7(2), 315–341. https://doi.org/10.1017/S1755773914000174

Nadal, Jordi (1984), *El fracaso de la revolución industrial en España, 1814–1913*, Barcelona, Ariel.

Natixis (2017), "Catalonia: The Separatists' Last Throw of the The Dice", *Natixis Special Report*, 1 September.

Navarro, Mayka, and Carlota Guindal (2017), "Un manuscrito hallado en el despacho de Salvadó planteaba supuestos económicos en un "escenario de guerra"", *La Vanguardia*, 15 October <https://www.lavanguardia.com/politica/20171015/432077657773/manuscrito-hallado-despacho-salvado-secretario-hisenda-plantea-supuestos-economicos-escenario-de-guerra.html>.

Nicolau, Roser (2005), "Población, salud y actividad", in Albert Carreras and Xavier Tafunell (coords.) (2005), *Estadísticas históricas de España*, Vol. I, 2n ed., Bilbao, Fundación BBVA, p. 153.

Nieto, Alejandro (2014), *La rebelión militar de la Generalidad de Cataluña contra la República. Los sucesos de octubre de 1934 en Barcelona*, Madrid, Marcial Pons.

Noguer, Miquel, and Camilo S. Baquero (2021), "Diada de división ante la mesa de diálogo", *El País*, 11 September <https://elpais.com/espana/catalunya/2021-09-11/el-independentismo-se-manifiesta-dividido-antes-de-la-mesa-de-dialogo.html>.

Observatori Econòmic de Catalunya (ed.) (2021), *Consecuencias económicas del separatismo. 50 + 1 artículos*, Barcelona, OEC.

Observatori Electoral de Catalunya (2020), *Investigación sociolingüística en Cataluña. Encuesta realizada por GAD3*, 11 December <https://www.gad3.com/solo-uno-de-cada-10-catalanes-defiende-que-el-catalan-sea-la-unica-lengua-vehicular-en-la-ensenanza/>.

Observatorio Cívico de la Violencia Política en Cataluña—Impulso Ciudadano (2019), *Informe sobre violencia política en Cataluña. Primer semestre de 2019* <https://www.impulsociudadano.org/wp-content/uploads/2019/08/Informe-sobre-violencia-pol%C3%ADtica-en-Catalu%C3%B1a_Primer-semestre-de-2019_Difusi%C3%B3n-online.pdf>.

OECD (2022), *Regional Wellbeing* <https://www.oecdregionalwellbeing.org/ES51.html>.

OECD (2020), *Subnational Governments in OECD Countries: Key Data 2020 edition* <http://www.oecd.org/regional/regional-policy/Subnational-governments-in-OECD-Countries-Key-Data-2020.pdf>.

Oliva, Salvador (2017), "Corrupció del llenguatge", *El País*, 8 December <https://cat.elpais.com/cat/2017/12/08/cultura/1512735074_256284.html>.

Olivas Osuna, José Javier (2022), "CatalanGate: escándalo útil, investigación teledirigida", *El Mundo*, 29 April <https://www.almendron.com/tribuna/catalangate-escandalo-util-investigacion-teledirigida>.

Oller, José Luis (2019), "Cataluña hace tiempo que no tiene clase dirigente", *Crónica Global*, 15 December <https://cronicaglobal.elespanol.com/pensamiento/conversaciones-sobre-cataluna/oller-arino-cataluna-no-clase-dirigente_300833_102.html>.

Oller, Josep Maria, Albert Satorra, and Adolf Tobeña (2019a), "Evolución and legados de la aventura secesionista en Cataluña: fronteras lingüísticas, influencia de los "media" and estratos económicos en una sociedad dividida", *Policy Network*, 14 October, <https://docplayer.es/168238376-Evolucion-y-legados-de-la-aventura-secesionista-en-cataluna.html>.

Oller, Josep Maria, Albert Satorra, and Adolf Tobeña (2019b), "Secessionists vs. Unionists in Catalonia: Mood, Emotional Profiles and Beliefs about Secession. Perspectives in Two Confronted Communities", *Psychology*, Vol. 10, No. 3, pp. 336–357 <https://doi.org/10.4236/psych.2019.103024>.

Oller, Josep Maria, Albert Satorra, and Adolf Tobeña (2020), "Privileged Rebels: A Longitudinal Analysis of Distinctive Economic Traits of Catalonian Secessionism", *Genealogy*, Vol. 4, No. 1 <https://doi.org/10.3390/genealogy4010019>.

Oller, J. M., & Satorra, A. (2017). "Toward an Index of Political Toxicity", *Boletín de Estadística e Investigación Operativa. No., 33*, 163–182. http://www.seio.es/bbeio/beiovol33num2/index.html#86

Organized Crime and Corruption Reporting Project (2021), "Fueling Secession, Promising Bitcoins: How a Russian Operator Urged Catalonian Leaders to Break with Madrid" <https://www.occrp.org/en/investigations/fueling-secession-promising-bitcoins-how-a-russian-operator-urged-catalonian-leaders-to-break-with-madrid>.

Orwell, George (1938), *Homage to Catalonia*, London, Penguin, 2000.

Orwell, George (1949), *1984*, London, Collins, 2021.

Ghemawat, P., Llano, C., & Requena, F. (2010). Competitiveness and interregional as well as international trade: The case of Catalonia. *International Journal of Industrial Organization, 28*, 415–422.

Parlament de Catalunya (2021), *Parlament 2021* <https://www.parlament2021.cat/es/inici/index.html>.

Parlament de Catalunya. Comissió d'Investigació sobre el Frau i l'Evasió Fiscals i les Pràctiques de Corrupció Política (2015), "Dictamen Tram. 261-00004/10", *Butlletí Oficial del Parlament de Catalunya*, X legislatura, N. 642, Sexto período, 16 July, pp. 1–128.

Parlament de Catalunya. Departament de Comunicació (2022), *Eleccions al Parlament 1980–2017* <https://www.parlament.cat/document/composicio/150360.pdf>.

Payne, Stanley G. (2011), *Spain: a unique history*, Madison, WI, University of Wisconsin Press.

Payne, Stanley G. (2021), "Antifascism without Fascism", *First Things*, 22 January <https://www.firstthings.com/issue/2021/01/january>.

Pérez, Manuel (2022), *La burguesía catalana. Retrato de la élite que perdió la partida*, Barcelona, Ediciones Península.

Pericay, Xavier (2007), *¿Libertad o coacción? Políticas lingüísticas and nacionalismos en España*, Madrid, FAES.

Pi Sunyer, Carles (1927), *L'aptitud económica de Catalunya*, Barcelona, Barcino.

Pi Sunyer, Carles (1959), *El comerç de Catalunya amb Espanya*, México, DF, Club del Llibre Català.

Pich, Valentín (2021), "Panorama sobre la fiscalidad autonómica en los tributos cedidos", in Instituto de Estudios Económicos (2021), *La competitividad fiscal de las comunidades autónomas. Condición necesaria para el desarrollo económico* <https://www.ieemadrid.es/wp-content/uploads/IEE-Opinion.-La-competitividad-fiscal-de-las-comunidades-autonomas.pdf>.

Piketty, Thomas (2017), "Le syndrome catalan", *Le Monde*, 14 November <https://www.lemonde.fr/blog/piketty/2017/11/14/le-syndrome-catalan/>.

Piketty, Thomas (2019), *Capital and Ideology*, Cambridge, MA, Harvard UP, and <http://piketty.pse.ens.fr/files/ideologie/pdf/G16.5.pdf> <http://piketty.pse.ens.fr/files/ideologie/pdf/G16.6.pdf>.

Polo, Clemente (2014), "Panorámica del argumentario economicista a favor de la independencia de Cataluña: mitos y realidad" in Ángel de la Fuente y Clemente Polo (2014), *La cuestión catalana II. Balanzas fiscales y tratamiento fiscal de Cataluña*, Madrid, Instituto de Estudios Económicos, pp. 31–85.

Porras, Victor, and Santiago López (2015), *El proceso hacia la independencia según el CATN: una lectura crítica, I, II and III*, <http://finestradoportunitat.com/catnlecturacriticaparteuno/>.

Porta Perales, Miquel (2019), "Teoría, práctica and función de la desobediencia civil durante el proceso secesionista de Cataluña", *Cuadernos de Pensamiento Político*, N. 61, January-March, pp. 17–27.

Preston, P. (1986). *The Triumph of Spanish Democracy*. Routledge.

Preston, P. (2020). *A People Betrayed: A History of Corruption, Political Incompetence and Social Division in Modern Spain, 1874–2018*. William Collins.

PricewaterhouseCoopers (2014), *Temas candentes de la economía catalana. Visión de los empresarios* <https://www.pwc.es/es/publicaciones/economia/temas-candentes-economia-catalana.html>.

Rajoy Brey, Mariano (2017), "Intervención del Presidente del Gobierno en el Pleno del Senado", 27 October <http://www.senado.es/legis12/publicaciones/pdf/senado/ds/ds_p_12_45.pdf>

Ramon Bosch, J. (2020). *Cataluña, la ruta falsa*. In *El problema catalán: cómo solucionarlo y no sólo conllevarlo*. Deusto.

Real Instituto Elcano (2019), *The independence conflict in Catalonia* <https://www.realinstitutoelcano.org/en/work-document/the-independence-conflict-in-catalonia/>.

Real Instituto Elcano (2021), *Elcano Global Presence Index* <https://www.globalpresence.realinstitutoelcano.org/en/home>.

Redacción (2022), "'Catalangate', un montaje propagandístico preparado hasta el mínimo detalle desde hace meses", *El Triangle*, 22 April <https://www.eltriangle.eu/es/2022/04/22/catalangate-un-montaje-propagandistico-preparado-hasta-el-minimo-detalle-desde-hace-meses>.

Registro de Economistas Asesores Fiscales and Instituto de Economía de Barcelona (2022), *Declaración de Sociedades, 2021*, Madrid, Consejo General de Economistas de España <https://reaf.economistas.es/estudios-e-informes/>.

Reign of Spain (2022), *The Spanish Constitution* <https://www.boe.es/legislacion/documentos/ConstitucionINGLES.pdf>.

Reino de España (2022), *Constitución Española* <https://app.congreso.es/consti/constitucion/indice/sinopsis/sinopsis.jsp?art=155&tipo=2>

Reixach, Jaume (2019), "El porqué de todo", *El Triangle*, 15 October <https://www.eltriangle.eu/es/opinion/el-porque-de-todo_103864_102.html>.

Reixach, Jaume (2020), "Fills de Pujol", *El Triangle.*, 1 September <https://www.eltriangle.eu/ca/opinio/fills-de-pujol_39457_102.html>.

Reporters Without Borders (2017), *Respect for media in Catalonia* <https://rsf.org/en/news/rsf-publishes-report-respect-media-catalonia>.

Reporters Without Borders (2022), *World Press Freedom Index* <https://rsf.org/en/index-methodologie-2022?year=2022&data_type=general>,

Reputation Institute (2017), *Informe sobre la reputación de marca España en el contexto europeo* <http://www.crones.es/pdf/Reputation_Institute_Marca_Espana2017.pdf>.

Reynaerts, Jo, and Jakob Vanschoonbeek (2016): "The Economics of State Fragmentation: Assessing the Economic Impact of Secession" <https://mpra.ub.uni-muenchen.de/72379/>.

Riera, José Ramón (2022), "Cataluña sigue drenando la recuperación del turismo. España tiene un grave problema con la pérdida de ingresos en esta región", *El Debate*, 15 september <https://www.eldebate.com/economia/20220915/cataluna-sigue-drenando-recuperacion-turismo_60188.html>.

Rius, Xavier (2020), "Toni Soler ve la luz", *enoticies.com* <https://www.youtube.com/watch?v=XLGPTLmV6HY>.

Rivero, Ángel (2020), "The new Catalan nationalism", *Przegląd Narodowościowy/ Review of Nationalities*, No. 10/2020, special on "A new wave of separatism in the world", <http://reviewofnationalities.com/index.php/RON/article/view/189/207>.

Robles, A. (2013a). *Historia de la resistencia al nacionalismo en Cataluña*. Barcelona.

Robles, A. (2013b). *Historia de la resistencia al nacionalismo en Cataluña*. Barcelona.

Roca Barea, María Elvira (2019), *Fracasología: España y sus élites: de los afrancesados a nuestros días*. Premio Espasa 2019, Madrid, Espasa.

Rodríguez-Pose, A., and M. Stermšek (2015), "The Economics of Secession: Analysing the Economic Impact of the Collapse of the Former Yugoslavia", *Territory, Politics, Governance*, Vol. 3, No. 1, pp. 73–96.

Rodríguez-Pose, Andrés and Daniel Hardy (2020), "Reversal of economic fortunes: Institutions and the changing ascendancy of Barcelona and Madrid as economic hubs", *Growth and Change*, Special Issue, pp. 1–23 <https://doi.org/10.1111/grow.12421>.

Ros Hombravella, Jacint (1991), *Catalunya: una economia decadent?*, Barcelona, Barcanova.

Ros Hombravella, Jacint, and Antoni Montserrat Soley (1967), *L'aptitud financera de Catalunya: la balança catalana de pagaments*, Barcelona, Edicions 62.

Ros Hombravella, Jacint, Joan Clavera, Joan Esteban, Maria Antònia Monés, and Antoni Montserrat. (1978). *Capitalismo español: De la autarquía a la estabilización, 1939–1959*. Edicusa.

Roser Nicolau (2005), "Población, salud and actividad", in Albert Carreras and Xavier Tafunell (coords.) (2005), *Estadísticas históricas de España*, Vol. I, 2ª ed., Bilbao, Fundación BBVA.

Rosiñol, José (2022), "Las tres Españas", *The Objective*, 16 August <https://theobjective.com/elsubjetivo/opinion/2022-08-16/tres-espanas/>.

Rul Gargallo, J. (2019). *Nacionalismo catalán and adoctrinamiento escolar. Estrategia y práctica de control social and modelaje conductual*. Salamanca.

Ruta, M. (2005). Economic theories of political (dis)integration. *Journal of Economic Surveys, 19*(1), 1–21.

Sáenz de Santamaría, Soraya (2016), "Comparecencia de la señora Vicepresidenta del Gobierno and Ministra de la Presidencia and para las Administraciones Territoriales para informar sobre las líneas generales de la política de su Departamento. A petición propia", *Diario de Sesiones del Congreso de los Diputados. XII Legislatura. Comisiones*, n. 65, 1 December <http://www.congreso.es/public_oficiales/L12/CONG/DS/CO/DSCD-12-CO-65.PDF>.

Sánchez Cartas, Juan Manuel (2015), *Herramientas económicas y secesión. Un enfoque heurístico para el caso catalán*. end of master project in Applied Economic Analysis, Universidad de Alcalá de Henares, 1 July <https://www.researchgate.net/publication/312811462_Herramientas_Economicas_y_Secesion_Un_enfoque_heuristico_al_caso_catalan>.

Sánchez, Carlos (2018), "Diez propuestas para encauzar (y resolver) la cuestión catalana", *El Confidencial*, 8 July <https://blogs.elconfidencial.

com/espana/mientras-tanto/2018-07-08/propuestas-resolver-problema-cataluna_1588942/>.

Sánchez-Costa, Fernando (2014), "El coste de la no-España", *Claves de razón práctica*, No. 238, pp. 54–63.

Santacruz, Javier (2017), "El sistema financiero catalán ante el riesgo secesionista", *El Economista*, 6 October.

Sardà Dexeus, Joan (1983), "Prólogo", in Many authors (1983), *La economía de Cataluña hoy y mañana*, Barcelona, Banco de Bilbao.

Savater, F. (2017). *Contra el separatismo*. Barcelona.

Scott-Railton, John, Elies Campo, Bill Marczak, Bahr Abdul Razzak, Siena Anstis, Gözde Böcü, Salvatore Solimano, and Ron Deibert (2022), "CatalanGate. Extensive Mercenary Spyware Operation against Catalans Using Pegasus and Candiru", *CitizenLab Report*, 18 April <https://citizenlab.ca/2022/04/catalangate-extensive-mercenary-spyware-operation-against-catalans-using-pegasus-candiru>.

Segura Just, Juan Carlos (2015a), "La usucapión de Cataluña", *Crónica Global,* 28 November <https://cronicaglobal.elespanol.com/pensamiento/la-usucapion-de-cataluna_28829_102.html>.

Segura Just, Juan Carlos. (2015b). *El libro negro de la independencia*. Barcelona.

Semur Correa, Almudena (2012), "La perversidad de las balanzas fiscales", in Many authors (2012), *La cuestión catalana hoy*, Madrid, Instituto de Estudios Fiscales, pp. 93–100.

Seopan (2022), *Licitación pública* <https://seopan.es/licitacion/>.

Servimedia (2020), "El 'procés' hizo perder a Barcelona 100.000 visitantes y 230 millones al quedarse sin la Agencia Europea del Medicamento" <https://www.servimedia.es/noticias/1334923>.

Societat Civil Catalana (2016), *La inversión en obra pública en Cataluña* <https://societatcivilcatalana.cat/assets/documents/InversionObraPublica.pdf>.

Societat Civil Catalana (2017), *Déficits de calidad democrática en Cataluña: La vulneración de los derechos fundamentales (2015–2017)* <https://societatcivilcatalana.cat/sites/default/files/docs/Informe-Deficits-2017.pdf>.

Societat Civil Catalana (2020), "Informe sobre el recuento de individuos presentes en la gigafoto de la Vía Catalana", <https://societatcivilcatalana.cat/assets/documents/informe-gigafoto-via-catalana-scc.pdf>.

Societat Civil Catalana. (2022). *Las inversiones del Estado en Cataluña*. Barcelona.

Societat Civil Catalana. Comissió d'Economia i Empresa (2014), *Consecuencias económicas de una hipotética secesión de Cataluña* <https://societatcivilcatalana.cat/assets/documents/informe-economia-hipotetica-secesion.pdf>.

Societat Civil Catalana. Observatori Electoral de Catalunya (2017), *La Cataluña inmune al "procés". El referéndum: una falsa salida* <https://www.societatcivilcatalana.cat/sites/default/files/docs/La-Cataluna-inmune-vf.pdf>.

Sorens, J. (2005), "The Cross-Sectional Determinants of Secessionism in Advanced Democracies", *Comparative Political* Studies, No. 38, pp. 304–326 <https://doi.org/10.1177/0010414004272538>.

Statista (2022), *Database* <https://www.statista.com/markets/>.

Storm, Eric (2016), *La construcción de identidades regionales en España, Francia and Alemania, 1890–1939*, Madrid, Ediciones Complutense, 2019.

Tamames, Ramón (2022), *¿A dónde vas, Cataluña? Cómo salir del laberinto independentista*, Barcelona, Ediciones Península, 5th ed.

Tarradellas, Josep (1981), "Carta a Horacio Sáenz Guerrero, Director", *La Vanguardia*, 16 abril <http://hemeroteca.lavanguardia.com/preview/1981/04/16/pagina-10/32926422/pdf.html>.

Tey, M., Fidalgo, S., Cardenal, J. P., & Planas, P. (2021). *El libro negro del nacionalismo. La ideología totalitaria que ha conducido Cataluña al desastre.* Barcelona.

Tax Foundation (2022), *International Tax Competitiveness Index 2021*<https://taxfoundation.org/publications/international-tax-competitiveness-index/>.

TD (2022), Independence Day <http://td-architects.eu/projects/show/independence-day/img-2577>.

Tinsa (2021), *Índice Tinsa IMIE Mercados Locales* <https://www.tinsa.es/precio-vivienda/catalunya/barcelona/barcelona/>.

Tobeña, A. (2021). *Fragmented Catalonia. Divisive legacies of a push for secession.* Policy Network.

Torra, Quim (2012), "La llengua i les bèsties", *Catalunya Digital*, 19 December <https://tarragonadigital.com/opinio/5052/la-llengua-i-les-besties>.)

Tortella Casares, Gabriel (2014), "Cataluña and España: el coste de la separación", in Mnay authors (2014), *Cataluña en claro. Economía. Derecho. Historia. Cultura*, Madrid, FAES.

Tortella, Gabriel, José Luis García Ruiz, Clara Eugenia Núñez and Gloria Quiroga (2016), *Cataluña en España. Historia y mito*, Madrid, Gadir.

Townson, N. (Ed.). (2015). *Is Spain Different? A Comparative Look at the 19th & 20th Centuries.* Sussex Academic Press.

Trallero, M. (2012). *Música celestial: Del mal llamado caso Millet o caso Palau.* Barcelona.

Trías Fargas, Ramon (n. d. [1962?]), *Balance of payment studies for the region of Catalonia*, [S.l.: s.n.].

Trías Fargas, Ramon (1960), *La Balanza de pagos interior: estudio relativo a la provincia de Barcelona*, Madrid, Sociedad de Estudios y Publicaciones.

Trías Fargas, Ramon (1972), *Introducció a l'economia de Catalunya: una anàlisi regional*, Barcelona, Edicions 62.

Tribunal Superior de Justícia de Catalunya. Sala Contenciosa Administrativa. Secció Cinquena (2020), *Sentència Núm. 5201/2020* <https://www.poder-judicial.es/cgpj/es/Poder-Judicial/Tribunales-Superiores-de-Justicia/TSJ-Cataluna/Noticias-Judiciales-TSJ-Cataluna/El-TSJC-obliga-a-un-

minimo-del-25%2D%2Dde-ensenanza-en-castellano-dentro-del-sistema-educativo-de-Catalunya>.

Tribunal Supremo. Sala de lo Contencioso Administrativo. Sección Primera Providencia (2021), *R. Casación 1676/2021* <https://www.poderjudicial.es/cgpj/es/Poder-Judicial/Tribunales-Superiores-de-Justicia/TSJ-Cataluna/Noticias-Judiciales-TSJ-Cataluna/El-Tribunal-Supremo-inadmite-el-recurso-de-la-Generalitat-sobre-el-25%2D%2Dde-castellano-en-las-escuelas-de-Cataluna>.

Tribunal Supremo. Sala de lo Penal (2018), *Causa especial núm.: 20907/2017. Auto de procesamiento* <http://www.poderjudicial.es/stfls/tribunal%20supremo/documentos%20de%20inter%c3%89s/auto%20procesamiento.pdf>.

Tribunal Supremo. Sala de lo Penal (2019), *Sentencia núm. 459/2019 de la causa especial núm. 3/20907/2017, seguida por los delitos de rebelión, sedición, malversación, desobediencia and pertenencia a organización criminal* <http://www.poderjudicial.es/cgpj/es/poder-judicial/noticias-judiciales/el-tribunal-supremo-condena-a-nueve-de-los-procesados-en-la-causa-especial-20907-2017-por-delito-de-sedicion>.

Trillas, F., Vegara, J. M., Antoni, Z., Antònia Monés, M., & Colldeforns, M. (2014). *Economía de una España federal: razones para una Europa sin fronteras*. Barcelona.

Ucelay-Da Cal, Enric (2003), *El imperialismo catalán. Prat de la Riba, Cambó, D'Ors and la conquista moral de España*, Barcelona, Edhasa.

UK Government. The Secretary of State for Scotland (n.d.), Collection Scotland Analysis <https://assets.publishing.service.gov.uk/government/uploads/system/uploads/attachment_data/file/321369/2902216_ScotlandAnalysis_Summary_acc2.pdf>.

UNESCO (2022). *Atlas of the World's Languages in Danger* <http://www.unesco.org/languages-atlas/index.php>.

United Nations (2022a), *Human Development Index* <http://hdr.undp.org/en/content/human-development-index-hdi>.

United Nations (2022b), *Insights From the First Global Survey of Balance and Harmony* <https://worldhappiness.report/ed/2019/>.

University of Notre Dame. Kellogg Institute for International Studies. Varieties of Democracy Institute (2022), *Varieties of Democracy Project* <https://kellogg.nd.edu/research/major-research-initiatives/varieties-democracy-project>.

University of Southern California. Center on Public Diplomacy (2019), *The Soft Power 30. A Global Ranking of Soft Power 2019* <https://softpower30.com/wp-content/uploads/2019/10/The-Soft-Power-30-Report-2019-1.pdf>.

US Central Intelligence Agency (2022), *The World Factbook* <https://www.cia.gov/library/publications/the-world-factbook/geos/xx.html>.

US Council for Economic Education (2020), *The South's Decision to Secede: A Violation of Self Interest?* <https://www.econedlink.org/resources/the-souths-decision-to-secede-a-violation-of-self-interest/>.

Vandellós, J. A. (1935). *Catalunya, poble decadent*. Barcelona.

Vanschoonbeek, J. (2020). Regional (in)stability in Europe a quantitative model of state fragmentation. *Journal of Comparative Studies, 48*, 605–641.

Vaubel, Roland (2013), "Secession in the European Union", *Economic Affairs*, Vol. 33, No. 3 <https://doi.org/10.1111/ecaf.12028>

Velarde Fuertes, Juan (2019a), "Promotores del suicidio económico catalán", *El Economista*, 4 noviembre.

Velarde Fuertes, Juan (2019b), "Raíces del disparatado separatismo catalán", *El Economista*, 10 diciembre.

Verificat (2021), "D'on surt la xifra dels 16.000 milions d'euros de dèficit fiscal a Catalunya?"<https://www.verificat.cat/fact-check/don-ve-la-xifra-dels-16.000-milions-deuros-de-deficit-fiscal-a-catalunya>.

Vicens Vives, Jaume (1965), *Historia económica de España*, Barcelona, Editorial Vicens-Vives, 1987.

Vidal-Folch, Ignacio (2015), "Cómo escribir un artículo", *El País*, 18 July.

Vidal-Folch, Xavier, and José Ignacio Torreblanca (2017), "Mitos y falsedades del independentismo", *El País*, 24 September <https://elpais.com/politica/2017/09/24/actualidad/1506244170_596874.html>.

Vila-Sanjuán, Sergio (2018), *Otra Cataluña: Seis siglos de cultura catalana en castellano*, Barcelona, Destino.

Villa, José Luis (2022), *El mátrix catalán*, Barcelona, José Luis Villa de la Torre.

Villanueva, D. (2021). *Morderse la lengua: Corrección política and posverdad*. Espasa.

Wind, M. (2020). *The Tribalization of Europe: A Defence of our Liberal Values*. Polity Press.

World Bank (2018), *Doing Business in Spain* 2015 <https://subnational.doingbusiness.org/en/reports/subnational-reports/spain>.

World Bank (2020), *Doing Business 2020* <https://openknowledge.worldbank.org/bitstream/handle/10986/32436/9781464814402.pdf>

World Bank (2022), *Governance Indicators* <https://databank.bancomundial.org/Governance-Indicators/id/2abb48da>.

World Economic Forum (2022), *The Global Competitiveness Report 2022* <https://www3.weforum.org/docs/WEF_The_Global_Risks_Report_2022.pdf>.

World Justice Project (2022), *WJP Rule of Law Index 2021*<https://worldjusticeproject.org/our-work/research-and-data/wjp-rule-law-index-2021>.

Young, R. A. (1994). The political economy of secession: The case of Quebec. *Constitutional Political Economy, 5*(2), 221–245.

Zabalza, Antoni (2014), "Measuring the Regional Incidence of Taxes and Public Expenditure: The Available Methodology and its Limitations", *Hacienda Pública Española*, No. 209, pp. 11–54.

Index[1]

A
Abandonment of Catalonia by the Spanish governments, 90
Attractiveness of Barcelona, 167–170, 234
Autonomous Communities, 8, 9, 15, 16, 35–41, 49, 83, 94–96, 104, 114, 124, 152, 154, 168, 171–175, 184, 193, 195, 196, 198, 200, 202, 203, 209, 214, 216, 217, 219, 222, 223n6, 226, 256, 290

B
Barcelona, v–xv, 1, 15, 16, 21, 22, 26, 30, 30n10, 31, 44, 59, 59n8, 63, 65, 72n9, 73n12, 75, 75n23, 84, 104n2, 112n8, 128, 129, 131, 138–140, 145, 159, 164, 167–170, 179–184, 192n3, 202, 205, 207, 211, 234, 281, 284, 296, 301

Barcelona *vs.* Madrid, 31, 179–181, 189
Boycott of Catalan products and services, 16, 210
Brexit *vs.* Catexit, 265–267

C
Chaos of Catalan politics, 9
Chronology, 20
Competitiveness of Catalonia, 163–165, 234
Constitutionalist movement, 120, 125
Corruption, 16, 19, 72n11, 89, 103–108, 120, 151, 174, 225
Cost
of the abandonment of Catalonia by the Spanish government, 90
of not Spain, 229–232
of political instability, 152

---

[1] Note: Page numbers followed by 'n' refer to notes.

© The Author(s), under exclusive license to Springer Nature Switzerland AG 2022
F. Brunet, *The Economics of Catalan Separatism*,
https://doi.org/10.1007/978-3-031-14451-6

Separatism, ix, xi, xiv, xv, 1, 2, 29n8,
  33, 41, 45, 49–50, 57, 58n4,
  60–65, 67, 70, 72n9, 78, 79, 93,
  96, 100, 106, 109–115,
  117–120, 127, 130, 131, 140,
  149–152, 164, 165, 198,
  280–282, 287–291, 297, 301
Separatist regime, 66–67, 69–79, 107,
  136, 141, 143–144, 150
Separatist violence, 135–142, 197
Social security and pensions,
  199–200, 264

T
Taxation
  regional taxes, 173, 281
  tax hell, 15, 174
Tourism, 16, 167, 169, 209,
  211–212, 234, 241, 247,
  295, 296
Trade with the rest of Spain
  drop because of hypothetical
    secession, 1, 26, 50, 200, 244,
    247, 251
  drop over recent decades, 1, 2

Printed by Printforce, United Kingdom